ISBN 978-1-331-16206-3
PIBN 10152428

English
Français
Deutsche
Italiano
Español
Português

www.forgottenbooks.com

Mythology Photography **Fiction**
Fishing Christianity **Art** Cooking
Essays Buddhism Freemasonry
Medicine **Biology** Music **Ancient
Egypt** Evolution Carpentry Physics
Dance Geology **Mathematics** Fitness
Shakespeare **Folklore** Yoga Marketing
Confidence Immortality Biographies
Poetry **Psychology** Witchcraft
Electronics Chemistry History **Law**
Accounting **Philosophy** Anthropology
Alchemy Drama Quantum Mechanics
Atheism Sexual Health **Ancient History**
Entrepreneurship Languages Sport
Paleontology Needlework Islam
Metaphysics Investment Archaeology
Parenting Statistics Criminology
Motivational

War Diary

OF

Luman Harris Tenney

1861 – 1865

Printed for Private Circulation
by
FRANCES ANDREWS TENNEY
Oberlin, Ohio

Evangelical Publishing House
CLEVELAND, O.
1914

Copyright, 1914, by Frances Andrews Tenney

To my Husband

in

Loving Memory

III

Preface

MY thanks are here tendered to those who have helped me in getting together the contents of this book: to General A. B. Nettleton who so shortly before his death showed his interest by writing the Introductory notes and making various explanations; to Captain Henry Chester who kindly allowed the use of the map he had drawn and who spent time in verifying the names of places and in elucidating certain doubtful points; to Miss Helen E. Keep who compiled the Genealogical Chart; to Mr. W. R. Austin who gave the use of the Custer Badge; to others who were always ready to answer questions and to Mrs. Theodore E. Tenney who aided in deciphering the fine script of the five well worn little diary books, and in putting them into typewritten form.
—F. D. T.

Oberlin, August, 1914.

Illustrations

INTRODUCTORY NOTES

By A. B. Nettleton, June 10, 1911.

When the Civil War began, early in April, 1861, by the Secessionists firing upon and capturing Fort Sumter in Charleston Harbor, S. C., the general though transient belief at the North was that in about sixty days the United States Government, with an army of about a hundred thousand men, could certainly crush the rebellion and restore order. Acting upon this popular assumption, President Lincoln on April 15th, 1861, called for Seventy-five Thousand ninety-day Volunteers, which force added to the then existing though badly scattered regular army of about Twenty-five Thousand men, made up the desired force of One Hundred Thousand. Preliminary skirmishes and unimportant engagements took place during the next few weeks, and on July 21, 1861, occurred the first serious battle of the war—that of Bull Run, or Manassas, in Virginia, near Washington, in which the Union Army was badly defeated. The whole country was aroused and alarmed. Realizing the desperate nature of the conflict thus entered upon, President Lincoln, under an act of Congress, then promptly called for three hundred thousand volunteers, for three years or "during the war."

At that time Hon. Benjamin F. Wade was one of the two Ohio Senators in Congress, and Hon. John Hutchins, of Warren, Ohio, was the Representative in Congress from the District embracing Northeastern Ohio. Immediately following the battle of Bull Run these two men asked and received from the President authority to recruit and organize a regiment of cavalry from the counties of the Western Reserve, with headquarters at Cleveland. Under this authority the Second Ohio Volunteer Cavalry enlisted and organized, and their camp of rendezvous was named Camp Wade. No better material ever formed the rank and file of a volunteer regiment. Governor Denison appointed Charles W. Doubleday to be the first Colonel of the Regiment, as he had acquired some military experience while serving as a member of a filibustering expedition against Nicaraugua, and possessed energy and dignity. Lorain County furnished one company for the Second Cavalry, one hundred men. Most of these came from the southern part of the county, and mainly from the village of Wellington and vicinity. Between August 25th and September 9th, nine young men from Oberlin, mostly college students, enlisted in this so-called Wellington Company, designated as Company "H", and joined the regiment at Camp Wade as privates, none anticipating official position of any sort. This Oberlin contingent consisted of the following besides the writer: Luman Harris Tenney, Charles Grandison

Fairchild, Henry W. Chester, W. Tully Norton, John Devlin, (afterward killed in battle), Delos R. Haynes, William P. Bushnell and Hamlin S. Bigelow. This group was afterward increased to ten by the enlistment in the winter of 1862-3 of Theodore A. Tenney, who was killed in the last great battle of the War, at Five Forks, Va., April 1, 1865, nine days before Lee surrendered at Appomattox, as recorded in the following diary of Major Tenney. No better or braver soldier ever yielded up his life on the battle field. In the course of Major Tenney's diary entries he refers frequently to various members of this Oberlin party by initials, thus: To Wm. Robinson, (L. H. Tenney's assistant) as "Bob"; to Nettleton as A. B. or A. B. N.; to Delos Haynes as D. R.; to Fairchild as Charles, C. G. or C. G. F.; to Bushnell as Will; to Chester as Chet; to Theodore, his brother, as Thede.

The regiment was uniformed, mustered into the United States service, armed with carbines, sabres and revolvers, and drilled at Camp Wade, and then, in November, 1861, removed to Camp Denison, near Cincinnati, to be nearer the scene of action, and then in December and January transported to Fort Leavenworth, Kansas, and Platte City, Mo., on the following errand:

In December, 1861, the President, at the urgent solicitation of several influential but unwise western politicians, authorized the eccentric but forceful United States Senator James H. Lane of Kansas, commonly then called "Jim Lane", to organize and dispatch a force of about 20,000 Federal troops, Infantry, Cavalry and Artillery, intending to march southward through Kansas, Indian Territory, (now part of Oklahoma), and into Texas, in order as Lane expressed it, "to attack the Southern Confederacy through its back door." The Second Ohio Cavalry by military chance formed a part of this expeditionary force. Our Colonel Doubleday was its ranking officer, and from this fact and because of his undoubted competency was entitled to command the army, but Lane's favoritism preferred one Colonel Wier, of the tenth Kansas, and Colonel Doubleday, in June, 1862, resigned his position in rage and disgust, and never re-entered the army. Wier quickly proved to be a drunken good-for-naught, was placed in arrest by his subordinate officers and replaced by Colonel Salomon of the Ninth Wisconsin. This expeditionary army was increased by the addition of about 2,500 wild Indians, mainly Osages, Cherokees and Creeks. These were opposed to about an equal number of disloyal or Confederate Indians on the other side. Thus the Second Ohio boys had the novel experience of fighting with and against real red Indians, in their war-paint, and using their native war-whoop with a vengeance in every engagement.

Our expedition encountered almost torrid heat in the Indian Territory, lost great numbers of men and animals from this cause and other needless hardships, and in July turned east and north into Missouri and Arkansas where there was plenty of legitimate campaigning and fighting under competent commanders. At the close of 1862 the regiment was transferred to Camp Chase, Ohio, to be recruited, remounted, rearmed, and sent, under General Burnside through Kentucky into East Tennessee, as recorded in detail in this diary.

ORGANIZATION OF A CAVALRY REGIMENT

It may render clearer some entries in this diary if the organization of a Regiment of Cavalry, under the laws and regulations of that period, is explained here:

Each regiment contained twelve companies, of one hundred men each, exclusive of Commissioned Officers. These twelve companies were divided into three Battalions of four companies each, a Major being in immediate command of each Battalion.

Commissioned Officers: All commissioned officers serving in a volunteer regiment were commissioned by the Governor of the State, and mustered into the Army of the United States. In a Cavalry Regiment they were as follows:

FIELD OFFICERS

One Colonel, commanding the Regiment.
One Lieutenant Colonel, commanding in absence of Colonel.
Three Majors, one for each of the three Battalions.

LINE OFFICERS

12 Captains, one commanding each Company.
12 First Lieutenants, one for each Company.
12 Second Lieutenants, one for each Company.

STAFF OFFICERS

One Surgeon, with rank and pay of Major.
One Assistant Surgeon, with rank and pay of 1st Lieut.
One Chaplain, with rank and pay of Captain.
One Regimental Quartermaster, (First Lieutenant).
One Regimental Commissary, (First Lieutenant).
One Regimental Adjutant, (First Lieutenant).
Three Battalion Adjutants, (First Lieutenant).
Three Battalion Quartermasters, (First Lieutenant).
Three Battalion Commissaries, (First Lieutenant).

Non-commissioned Officers: All appointed by the Colonel of the regiment.

STAFF

One Regimental Sergeant-major.
Three Battalion Sergeant-majors.
One Regimental Quartermaster Sergeant.
Three Battalion Quartermaster Sergeants.
One Regimental Commissary Sergeant.
Three Battalion Commissary Sergeants.

Line:

Eight Sergeants to each Company.
Eight Corporals to each Company.
(These Company, or Line, noncommissioned officers were num-
    bered from one to eight, respectively, and bore rank and
    authority accordingly.)
During 1861 and 1862 Luman Harris Tenney served as (staff)
    Commissary Sergeant of Major Purington's Battalion.
    After being promoted to Second and then First Lieuten-
    ant he served mainly with Companies E and C; and when
    promoted to Captain he was assigned to command Com-
    pany "C." Because of his marked efficiency in and inti-
    mate knowledge of the Quartermaster's and Commis-
    sary's duties he was often detailed to perform these du-
    ties, when he would have much preferred duty "in the
    Line," that is, in the command of his Company or of a de-
    tachment of troops. When on the details referred to he
    almost always managed to get permission to go into bat-
    tles and on scouts where danger was greatest, although
    his duty did not call for such exposure.

CERTAIN CAVALRY BUGLE CALLS

In the Cavalry Service the following Bugle Calls were sounded
from Regimental or Company headquarters each day, except when
in action, or so near the Enemy that all sounds of this nature were
prohibited for prudential reasons:

"Reveille!" At daybreak, or sunrise usually and at such
earlier hour as the commanding officer may previously have directed when actively campaigning. Upon this signal the First
Sergeant, commonly called the Orderly Sergeant, of each Company
sees to it that every man of his Company falls promptly into line
for the morning Roll-call. Every soldier who fails to respond to
his name is marked "absent without leave" and he has a reckoning
to make afterward.

"Breakfast Call." Usually an hour or half hour after
"Reveille," to secure prompt and uniform breakfasting.

"Sick Call." At nine o'clock A. M. each morning when in
camp. The Orderly Sergeant of each Company brings to Regimental headquarters those men of his Company who claim or appear to be sick. There they are looked over or questioned by the
Surgeon or his assistant who either prescribes and furnishes medicine and excuses from duty for the day, or sends to the Hospital
or frankly tells the soldier that he is not sick.

"Retreat.' This sounded at sunset, when evening roll-call occurs by companies. Thereafter the soldiers who are not on night
duty proceed to amuse themselves as best they may in or about
their tents, singing songs, playing cards and other games, etc.,
but never boisterously. Under proper circumstances passes are

given to a certain number from each company to go outside camp lines, to the neighboring town for example.

"Boots and Saddles." This stirring call is given whenever a sudden emergency requires the command to be instantly in readiness to march and fight.

"Taps." At nine or ten o'clock P. M. according to previous general orders, when all lights must be out in camp, all soldiers unless on night duty must be in bed, and general quiet must prevail.

THE SECOND OHIO CAVALRY IN THE EAST

It will be noticed under date March 25th, 1864, in the diary, that the Second Ohio Cavalry had been ordered to return to duty in Tennessee after the "veteran furlough" given as partial reward for re-enlisting for three years more, and that upon reaching Cincinnati a telegram from the Secretary of War changed the destination of the Regiment to Annapolis, Maryland, to which place the command at once proceeded. This change meant that we were to serve the remainder of our time with the Armies of the East, and the boys were jubilant over the prospect, mainly for the opportunity given for variety and observation. The change was due to the special request made by General A. E. Burnside of Gen. Grant that our Regiment might be sent east and again attached to his Ninth (Infantry) Corps. We had been under his command throughout our service in Kentucky and Tennessee, and he had taken a great liking to our ways of doing things.

When Grant and Meade started the Army of the Potomac May 1, 1864, upon its great and sanguinary campaign against Lee, the Second Cavalry formed a part of the great army by being attached to Burnside's Ninth Corps. In this capacity we passed through a part of the Campaign of the Wilderness, as described in the diary. In May, '64, it became apparent that the cavalry must be massed, and the Second was accordingly merged in Sheridan's Cavalry Corps of the Army of the Potomac, in which connection it served to the end of the War. The Cavalry Corps was organized into three Divisions, the First, Second and Third. The Third Division was commanded by Gen's James H. Wilson and George A. Custer, and the Second Ohio Cavalry was made one of the five regiments constituting the First Brigade of that Division. At first the Cavalry Corps was commanded directly by General Sheridan, but when he was made Commander of the Army of the Shenandoah, which included the Cavalry Corps, the latter came under command of, first, General Wilson, and then General Torbert. Generals Sheridan and Custer probably have had no superiors in history as commanders of Cavalry.

The esteem in which the Second Ohio was held by the great generals under which it served is sufficiently indicated by, (1) the request by General Burnside, (already mentioned), to have the regiment sent from west to east so as to have it part of his command; (2) the comment by General Sheridan, quoted in this diary, that the second was without superior in the Army; (3) the fact that both Burnside and Custer with rare exceptions sent for the Second Ohio whenever any particularly difficult and dangerous task was to be performed; (4) in a letter to Governor Brough of Ohio, dated November, 1864, General Custer says: "Among all the twelve regiments of my Division none excels the Second Ohio. I have often seen it hold positions in battle when almost any other command would have felt compelled to retreat."

A PERSONAL WORD

It may not be out of place if I add this as a foot-note to the accompanying interesting record of personal Civil War experience:

As his companion-in-arms throughout the Great Conflict, and his regimental commander during the months and years when he rendered his most arduous and perilous military service, I can say, without one reservation, that a braver soldier, a more gallant, intelligent and effective regimental officer I did not know or meet in the Union Army than was Major Luman H. Tenney. In spite of the delicate physical constitution and resulting handicap with which he entered the army, he never spared himself, but was always ready and eager to share in the hardest enterprises. His clean and noble character never for a moment wavered in the presence of the often demoralizing environment and the moral strain of four years of life in the field. On the contrary, his example, bearing and conversation, always manly, soldierly, cheerful and friendly, exerted unpretentiously a robust influence for good. The whole atmosphere of his diary, which largely records his inmost thoughts and aspirations, written down often amid scenes of peril, anguish and slaughter, sufficiently reveals the high order of Christian faith and principle which actuated his conduct from start to finish.

In penning this memorandum I am not conscious that I am at all influenced toward unmerited commendation by the fact that Major Tenney during the War became my brother, and until his early death continued to be a brother in deed.

MEMORANDUM

Commanding Generals under whom the Second Ohio Served:

The Second Ohio Cavalry, during its four years of service in the Civil War, served under the following Commanding Generals:

From December, 1861, to December, 1862, under Major-General James G. Blunt, commanding The Army of the Frontier, in Missouri, Kansas, Arkansas and Indian Territory.

From March, 1863, until December 31, 1863, under Major-General Ambrose E. Burnside, commanding the Ninth Corps and The Army of the Ohio, in Kentucky, Tennessee, West Virginia, Ohio and Indiana.

From April 20th, 1864, to May 20th, 1864, under Major-General Ambrose E. Burnside, commanding The Ninth Army Corps of the Army Corps of the Army of the Potomac, in General Grant's campaign of the Wilderness, in Virginia.

From May 20, to Sept. 30, 1864, under Gen. James H. Wilson.

From Oct. 1, 1864, to the surrender of Lee's army at Appomattox, Virginia, April 9, 1865, under Bvt. Major-General George A. Custer, commanding the Third Division of the Cavalry Corps of the Army of the Potomac, the Corps being commanded by Major-General Philip H. Sheridan.

During this period Sheridan's Cavalry Corps, including Wilson's Third Division of Twelve Regiments, was joined with the Sixth and Nineteenth Corps of the Infantry with their complement of Artillery, to constitute the Army of the Shenandoah, and Middle Military Division, under the command of General Sheridan, for operation in the Shenadoah Valley of Virginia.

During the time from April 20th, 1864, to the close of the War, while the Second Ohio Cavalry was part of the Army of the Potomac proper it was under the general command of Major-General George G. Meade, commanding the Army of the Potomac, and under the general command all of the time of General Ulysses S. Grant commanding all the Armies of the United States and making his headquarters with General Meade and the Army of the Potomac.

States and Territories in which the Regiment rendered Active Service:

During its Four Years of Service it was the lot of the Second Ohio Cavalry to serve actively against the enemy in more States and Territories than any of the nearly three thousand Regiments of the Great Union Army, thus:

Missouri,	Kentucky,	Indiana,
Kansas,	Tennessee,	Maryland,
Arkansas,	West Virginia,	Virginia,
Indian Territory,	Ohio,	North Carolina,
	District of Columbia.	

Character of Service:

The function and duty of Cavalry in active campaigning require it to be ever on the alert, by means of scouting, raiding the enemy's lines, reconnoitering, protecting wagon trains and artillery, foraging, defending the rear of the army on retreat, furnishing advance guards and flanking parties on the march through the enemy's country, etc. All this service involves at times almost constant conflict with the enemy, with necessary danger, frequent casualties and captures on both sides, but this sort of work, although perilous enough, and productive of the utmost fatigue, exposure and hardship, cannot be classed under the head of "Battles" and seldom gets into press dispatches, or official reports which are preserved.

BATTLES AND IMPORTANT ENGAGEMENTS IN WHICH THE SECOND OHIO CAVALRY SHARED.

On January 2nd, 1865, the Commanding Officer of the Second Ohio Cavalry requested the War Department to authorize him to place on the Colors of the Regiment the names of the well-recognized and historic Battles and Important Engagements in which the Regiment had participated honorably prior to May 20, 1864. Pursuant to said request, and upon the recommendation of the respective Commanding Generals under whom the battle service referred to was rendered, the War Department duly authorized the names of the following battles to be thus inscribed:

"Headquarters, District of South Kansas,
Paola, Jan. 19th, 1865.

I respectfully recommend that the within request be granted. The 2nd O. V. C. participated in the engagements named under my command.

(Signed) JAS. G. BLUNT, *Major General.*"

Newtonia, Missouri, Oct. 4, 1862.
Cane Hill, Arkansas, Nov. 4, 1862.
Prairie Grove, Arkansas, Dec. 7, 1862.

"Providence, R. I., Jan. 10, 1865.

Respectfully forwarded with the recommendation that the within request be granted, as this Regiment while under my command always fought with conspicuous daring and efficiency.

(Signed) A. E. BURNSIDE,
Major General."

Steubenville, Kentucky, 1863.
Buffington Island, Ohio, July 19, 1863.
Richmond, Kentucky, July 28, 1863.
Cumberland Gap, Kentucky, Sept. 9, 1863.
Blue Springs, Tennessee, Oct. 10, 1863.
Knoxville, Tennessee, Nov. 17 to Dec. 4, 1863.
Russellville, Tennessee, 1863.
Bean Station, Tennessee, Dec. 14, 1863.

On the same date the Commanding Officer of the Second Ohio Cavalry made the following request of the War Department:

"I have the honor to ask permission to inscribe 'The Wilderness' upon the colors of my Regiment, in recognition of the part the 2nd Ohio Cavalry bore in the Wilderness Campaign, from the 5th to the 20th of May, 1864, while forming part of the Ninth Army Corps, under the command of Major-General Burnside."

The Wilderness, Virginia, 1864.

In his endorsement, dated Jan. 10, 1865, recommending the desired inscription, Gen. Burnside wrote as follows:

"I most cheerfully endorse my approval of your request, and shall be glad to know that your regimental colors bear upon their folds the names of those fields where its members have proved themselves faithful and efficient defenders of their Country."

From the Battles of the Wilderness campaign, in May, 1864, to the close of the War the service of the Second Cavalry, in common with its associate Regiments in Custer's Third Division, was nearly one continuous series of battles, engagements, skirmishes, raids and marches.

The principal Battles and Important Engagements in which the Second participated under Custer during the period now referred to are as follows:

The Wilderness, Virginia, (that part of Grant's Campaign of the Wilderness following the 20th of May, 1864, when we ceased to be under the command of Gen. Burnside and to form part of the Ninth Corps), 1864.

Hanover Court House, Virginia, 1864.

Ashland Station, Virginia, 1864.

The Wilson Cavalry Raid around the right of Lee's Army in June, 1864.

Siege of Richmond and Petersburg (including picket duty on the left of Grant and Meade's besieging army; and in the reserve force on the occasion of the mine explosion at Petersburg in July and early August), 1864.

Sheridan's Campaigns and Battles of the Shenandoah, Aug. '64 to Feb. '65, including the following battles:

Abraham's Creek, Virginia, 1864.

Winchester, Virginia, (or the Opequon), 1864.

Fisher's Hill, Virginia, 1864.

Tom's Brook, Virginia, 1864.

Cedar Creek, Virginia, 1864.

Waynesboro, Virginia, February, 1865.

Sheridan's Cavalry Raid, from Winchester, Va., to White House Landing, on the Pamunkey River, tide water, Feb. and March, 1865.

Grant's Appomattox Campaign, Va., which ended in the surrender of Lee and his army of Northern Virginia on April 9, 1865.

Five Forks, Dinwiddie, Sailor's Creek and Appomattox Station, Virginia, 1865.

Copy of Entries in the Diaries

Kept by

Major Luman Harris Tenney

During his Service in the

U. S. Army in the War of the Rebellion

From the date

Sept. 9, 1861, to the date of his Muster-Out, July 11, 1865

War Diary

Sept. 9th. Enlisted. At home till Sept. 14th. Splendid time.

Monday, 16th. Bid all the dear friends at home good-bye, and left Oberlin for the camp. (Camp Wade, Cleveland, Ohio.) Accompanied Lizzie Cobb home, and called on Helen Cobb. Took tea at Lizzie's with Charlie Fairchild. Commenced camp life.

Tuesday, 17th. Went through with the regular routine of camp life until five. Went over to Uncle's and took tea. Wrote home and to Fannie Andrews.

Wednesday, 18th. Arose at the firing of the cannon. After the morning drill started for town and met Uncle. (Albert Harris.) Returned and was introduced to Colonel (Chas. W. Doubleday), Major Miner and the Quartermaster. (Lt. Abbey.)

Thursday, 19th. Drilled during the day. Received bundle from home through Delos (Haynes), also a line.

Friday, 20th. Received appointment of Com.-Sergt.

21st. Commenced to learn my duties. Drilled with the non-commissioned officers by the Adjutant.

22nd. In the morning Lt. Nettleton and I went over to the Cathedral. In the afternoon visited at Uncle's. Returned to camp and found thousands of visitors. Such a Sunday. Prayer meeting in the evening.

23rd. Stayed in camp during the day, went out with non-commissioned officers. Stayed over night in camp. Had quite a visit with Sergeant Townsend—good fellow.

24th. Thede came. He went to the circus. I watched for horses. In the evening went in and saw them play billiards. Stayed at Uncle's.

25th. In the morning went over to camp. Commenced work. Thede went over to Uncle's after dinner. Went to tea. Called on Lizzie Cobb. Had a fine time.

26th. Fast day. In the morning Thede and I had our pictures taken for Aunt Rhodilla and one of Thede alone for Lizzie Cobb. Went to camp. Worked in the Quartermaster's barracks. Services at two. Aunt and Uncle were over.

28th. Went down and tried some horses. Took one that John Devlin chose for me. I stayed in camp. Thede at Uncle's.

29th. Went over to see Thede. Attended Mr. White's church —Thede the Cathedral. Took tea at Byron's. Heard Mr. Van Meter again in the evening.

30th. Thede returned in the morning. I felt rather ill from a hard cold.

OCTOBER, 1861.

1st. My birthday (twenty)—what a contrast between this one and that of the year before. Spent the day about as usual.

9th. My mother's birthday. The Wellington Three Hundred came to camp. Somewhat indisposed. Had a good time though.

10th. Played chess with Miss Hamlin, and visited with the other girls. Wrote to Fannie.

11th. Rainy and unpleasant in the morning. Cleared up rather cold in the afternoon. Fannie, Libbie, and Fannie Hudson came to camp. So surprised, but glad.

12th. The girls (Minnie and Lissa) came out. Met them at Uncle's. Found Fannie and the other girls at the camp. Attended a picnic, Company I, in the afternoon. Went to Aunt Jones', Fannie too. Spent the evening, good time. Col. Ratliffe.

Sunday. Took Fannie over to Helen's. Returned to camp to hear the Chaplain. Fannie and Mrs. Cobb came over too late for the preaching.

14th. Went to town with Will. (Bushnell.) Saw Fannie in the evening.

15th. Called to see Fannie in the morning. Saw her to Oberlin cars in the afternoon.

16th. A letter by the kindness of Mrs. Haynes. Stood guard for Delos a little while.

17th. Phoebe Haynes was in camp. Sang.

20th. Boys prepared Camp Taylor for our reception.

21st. Moved after a picked up breakfast to the fair grounds.

23rd. Changed my quarters for noncommissioned staff—was sorry.

24th. Rather strange life—smoking and such talk!

From Oct. 25th to Nov. 3rd stayed in camp; got our horses; duties occupied most of my time—rode some—horse almost sick.

NOVEMBER, 1861.

Nov. 4th. Rainy and unpleasant. Stayed in camp, rather dull, wrote home.

Nov. 5th. Rode to Uncle Jones' with Roxena and Watson.

6th. Attended concert at Academy of Music by invitation from Nell. She sang well. Nettleton there.

LUMAN HARRIS TENNEY
BEFORE ENLISTING AT THE AGE OF NINETEEN

7th. Went home with Nettie Chidgey and Lizzie Cobb. Went to hear the Minstrels—disgusted.

8th. At Charlie Abbey's candy-pull in the evening.

10th. Sunday. Remained in camp. Chaplain preached a good sermon on morals. Read the *Atlantic Monthly* and *Harper's*.

13th. By permission of the Colonel went to Uncle Jones', took my fatigue coat. Supper at Uncle Albert's—a pleasant visit.

14th. Returned from Uncle's. Letter from Fannie. Mrs. Helen Cobb, her mother-in-law and sister, Cousin Byron Harris and Miss Chidgey were in camp. Good visit.

15th. A cold rainy day. Some snow towards night. Spent the evening at the tent. Played checkers and read. Boys played euchre.

16th. Theodore surprised me in the morning. Took a ride to Woodland Cemetery. Lizzie and Nettie came to camp. Heard Slade, Riddle and several others in the evening.

17th. Sunday. Stayed at Uncle's in the morning. Theodore rode my horse to Uncle Jones'. Stayed over night.

18th. Monday. Theodore, Roxena and mother came to camp in the afternoon.

21st. Visited Uncle Washington's boat "The Rawson." Heard Gough lecture.

23rd. Brownell and Brooks left on furlough, so I had double duties.

24th. Sunday. Stayed in camp. D. R. H. and C. G. F. went up town. Read some and wrote home.

25th. Was kept very busy all day with wood.

26th. Made arrangements to go home but couldn't.

27th. Went home on the freight. Surprised the folks. In the evening attended a party at Delos'. Had a grand time—all the young people there.

28th. C. G. and D. R. returned to camp. Visited, called at Fannie's. Splendid time. Attended a small charade party at Mrs. Holtslander's. Thanksgiving meetings.

29th. At Prof. Morgan's to a tea party—a nice visit. Made several calls. Called at Fannie's.

30th. Made several calls with Fannie—enjoyed them so much. Returned to Cleveland with Ma and Theodore.

DECEMBER, 1861.

Dec. 1st. Sunday. Spent in camp and at Uncle's. Was paid off.

2nd. Wrote and sent a package to Fannie. Bid the friends good-bye and left for Camp Denison. A noisy time—boys drunk—slept in caboose.

3rd. Reached Camp Denison where were encamped 8,000 troops.

4th. Was obliged to work hard in the commissary.

Through the remainder of the month nothing of special interest occurred. The same daily routine of business. Through order of Quartermaster Thayer, the quartermaster and commissary sergeants formed a mess by themselves. Christmas lost my pocketbook containing upwards of five dollars.

JANUARY, 1862.

Jan. 1st. Wrote, rode and read some. In the morning went over to Company I's quarters. Wrote to Ella Clark. Made some resolutions for the future.

2nd. Wrote some and read in "Shirley."

3rd. Received a letter from Fannie. Was busy with wood until dark.

4th. Answered Fannie's letter. Received a package from home—letter, pocketbook, etc.

5th. A blustering, cold day. Delivered wood in the morning, then kept in the house quite closely.

6th. Word came that we should go under Jim Lane. (Senator Lane of Kansas.)

7th. Paymaster telegraphed to, and preparations for leaving Camp Denison.

8th. Men sent to Columbus to help in making out pay-rolls.

9th. Mr. Haynes came to camp, brought a letter to me. Went over and ate some doughnuts. Gay time in the evening.

10th. Visited some with Mr. Haynes. He and Delos went to Cincinnati.

12th. Sunday. No services. Read and wrote.

13th. Principal Fairchild came down. Letters from home and Fannie. Also a book from her—"Sermons on the New Life."

14th. Prin. Fairchild returned home. Stayed with John Devlin over night. Cooked rations and packed up.

Jan. 15th. Arrangements to move at 9 A. M. for Cincinnati—marched mounted by country road. Went on ahead with Robinson, overtook Abbey and Wood. Rode on my horse about the city. P. M. took cars for St. Louis—1,300 strong.

16th. Enjoyed the trip much, especially the prairies, saw one on fire. Left over one train.

17th. Reached the eastern bank of the Mississippi, unable to cross on account of ice.

18th. Rode out into the country with Delos and John. Got some milk.

19th. Moved over the river in afternoon, found our barracks (Benton) occupied and unfit. Camped out in the fair grounds. Men occupied the amphitheatre.

20th. Moved into tents. Found missing equipment. Severe cold and rash.

21st. First Battalion moved on horseback for St. Charles at nine A. M. Wrote to Uncle Albert.

22nd. Second Battalion moved, the distance nineteen miles, over the most lovely country I have yet seen—rolling and beautiful. Took care of Sergeant Dutton and our colonel during the night. First Battalion got to St. Charles. Lost my revolver.

23rd. Rode a little while about town. The boys better.

24th. Had quite a cold, so kept close to quarters.

25th. Arose at 3 A. M., fed, watered and prepared to move. Second Battalion moved at ten A. M. Some rolling country and some level prairie. Passed burnt bridge where guards were stationed.

26th. Arrived at Hudson, Mo., midnight. Next morning, Sunday, reshipped men and horses and left in the freight cars at nine P. M.

27th. Rode over prairies and rough road to St. Joseph, Mo. Moved toward Weston.

28th. After forty hours reached Weston at two P. M. Fed, watered and marched for Platte City at six P. M. Five letters. Major was fired at.

31st. Letter from Will Hudson. Wrote to Sarah Felton. Secesh arrested. Whiskey emptied out on the streets. Third Battalion arrived. Found new quarters in a house out by the seminary.

FEBRUARY, 1862.

1st. Mr. Hutchinson, our nearest neighbor, called and gave us some potatoes and biscuit. Had a good visit with him.

Feb. 2nd. Sunday. Read during the day in "Female Life Among the Indians." In the evening attended Disciples Church with Brownell.

3rd. Went down town and drew rations. Neighbors sent in some nuts and pickled beets.

4th. In the evening called at Mr. Courtell's. Treated us with cream and peaches, pie and nuts—seemed very hospitable.

5th. Went to town and commenced duty again. Seemed dull staying about town all day having little to do. Got clothes. Wrote Will Hudson.

6th. On duty again. Played chess with Adams. He beat me four games to my two.

7th. Friday. Went and saw Delos and Charlie. Wrote to Fannie.

8th. One day behind hand. Hardly realize that time passes so swiftly. Up town nearly all day on duty.

9th. Sunday. Went out and heard Chaplain Hawkins upon "Following Christ." Went to Mr. Campbell's to dinner—a good one. Stayed for some time, had hickory nuts.

10th. On duty up town again. Played chess with Bugler Adams. Called at Mr. Crockett's. Not at home. Played a game of pool.

11th. Commenced to make my quarters at Quartermaster Thayer's. Wrote a line home and sent it in Charlie's to sister.

12th. Read some in "Lessons in Life." Spent the evening at Mr. Campbell's.

13th. Wrote to Fannie and received a letter from her—dear girl!

14th. Very busy making out requisitions and settling the wood account.

15th. Squared up with Farmer and Thayer. First Battalion of our regiment moved for Fort Leavenworth at ten A. M. Roads very slippery. Passed through Leavenworth City after crossing on the ice.

17th. Sunday. At Fort Leavenworth. Read the papers and wrote home. Saw the regulars on parade. Very exact and nicely dressed. Very strict officers—too exact and overbearing. Major Prince made Reeve Spencer stand on the porch and me take off my cap.

18th. Drew requisitions for wood and attended to delivery. Had quite a cold.

19th. Commenced letter to Fannie. Cold better.

20th. Received letter from Fannie and finished letter to her. Wrote requisitions to balance wood drawn. Were mounted and started from Fort Leavenworth at ten A. M. Traveled about twenty miles over the rolling prairies, and encamped in a piece of woods on an Indian farm. Country finely settled. Indians upon the woodland. Saw a prairie wolf.

Feb. 21st. Continued our journey and reached Kansas City a little after noon. Arrested two men pretending to be secessionists—drunk. Encamped out on snow and ice a little distance from town. Major heard of a gang of jay-hawkers and secessionists at Independence under Parker and Quantrell. He detailed 150 men to go after them under Lieutenant Nettleton. Brownell and I got leave to go too. Was up nearly all night issuing cartridges and preparing to go.

Feb. 22nd. Started at 2 A. M. Went to and surrounded Independence. After search found none, so started to return at seven A. M. Stopped a little distance out of town, down a hill, and got feed for our horses. Ordered to be ready to go on at ten A. M. All ready at the time. Three or four fellows up town, fired upon, bring the report that rebel troops are in town. Forthwith all the companies, all ready, start at full gallop, Company L leading. The enemy after one volley, wheel and run down into the gully east, our troops following closely, and firing as they go. At the forks in the road they scatter, some going straight forward and some getting into lots behind buildings and stumps and then firing. The boys charged upon them, killing two and taking five prisoners. Brownell was shot. After passing him to see if there was a chance to shoot and finding none, I returned to him. Helped him up hill to barber shop. Citizens assisted zealously. Three wounded. Stayed by them until ready to return. In the meantime Nettleton and the command went up the road in search of the rebels. Found none. One of our men killed. Co. L. Saw two rebels dead—awful sight—all over dirt and such an expression upon their countenances. Reached camp at Kansas City at 4 P. M. All pleased with the expedition. Issued rations.

23rd. Sunday. Felt half sick all day, sore throat, hard cough. Lay still and did nothing all day.

25th. On duty around in the wet.

26th. Went down and saw Brownell and the other wounded boys. All getting along well. Guarded against Quantrell. The boys, about two hundred, saddled and went out to meet the wagons. Met them and escorted them in. Quantrell captured two horses. Another night alarm.

28th. Moved to Independence. Quartered in the Academy, a very pretty building. Met several acquaintances formed at the fight the other day—a good time—a beautiful town.

MARCH, 1862.

1st. Up town all day. Issued rations. Body guard went out on expedition for Quantrell. Failed. Orders to return to Kansas City. "General" (Colonel Doubleday) and Co. L returned. Co. H came with orders.

2nd. Returned to Kansas City.

3rd. Commenced a letter to Theodore but did not finish. Bathed all over and changed my clothes. Got my washing done and some baking.

Monday, March 4th. Procured rations for seven days preparatory to our trip to Fort Scott. First Battalion and "General" moved. Got some chickens baked by a woman who was a messenger in the Lexington fight, and who was a prisoner one week. Heard some little girls sing. Had a turkey baked by some Union ladies who were afraid we might be poisoned by the secesh. God bless these friends! Gave a lady some coffee and sugar.

5th. Packed and struck tents. Received a letter from home. Ready to march at 9 A. M. Called for the turkey and received the blessing of the good ladies. Had a very pleasant ride of fifteen miles toward Fort Scott, until we overtook the First Battalion. Trip delightful and novel. The scenes were truly grand as we crossed the rolling prairies and looked over them from some elevated spot—here and there oases, wood-covered and watered by pure clear streams. It made the trip restful and refreshing. I enjoyed it and walked some, leading my horse.

Wednesday, 6th. The three battalions of the Second Cavalry marched thirty miles to Harrisonville, the county seat of Cass County, once a thrifty town, almost entirely deserted. Day blustering and chilly. A march makes pretty busy times distributing rations, getting forage for so many horses. Letter from Fannie. Encamped by the side of a little stream.

7th.   Passed through the village and again struck the prairie. Pleasant day, enjoyed the ride very much indeed.   Rode by the side of Lieutenant Nettleton, enjoyed visiting with him much.

8th.   Struck tents and were ready to march at 7 A. M.   Enjoyed a ride of thirty miles to Butler, the burnt and deserted county seat of Butler County, once a thriving town, now but a few poor houses remaining.

9th.   Left Butler at 8 A. M.   Major Wilson of our regiment marched the rest of the distance to Fort Scott, under arrest by order of the General for drunkenness.   Rode by the side of Nettleton.   Crossed one of the branches of the Osage, Marais des Cygnes, very swift.   Great time crossing with the mules led by ropes—one team rolled down the bank.   Encamped by a little stream on the prairie.   Found considerable muddy road during the day along the river bottom.

10th.   Finished our march to Fort Scott.   Strong wind in our faces—great dust to trouble us.   Had colic most all way.   Thunderstorm during the night.   Encamped near the Ninth Wisconsin a little beyond the village.

Sunday, 11th.   Issued rations.   Wrote a letter to Theodore and read some.   Commenced a letter to Fannie.   Helped bring wood.

12th.   Finished letter to Fannie after work done.   Then took mail to post-office and helped get supper.   Mail leaves Mondays, Wednesdays, and Fridays.

13th.   Saw the boys jay-hawking from countryman who had apples, chickens, eggs, etc.   They stole half he had.   Read a chapter in Beecher's "Letters to Young Men."

14th.   Mail came.   Letters from Fannie and home for me. Numerous papers came, *Independent* and *Lorain News*.   Girls at Amherst.

March 15th.   Wrote to Sarah Felton and was on duty at the commissary.

16th.   Sunday.   Helped clean up in and about the quarters of Co. "H."   Heard the Chaplain preach from "Whatsoever a man soweth that shall he reap."   Used strong language against the drunkenness and profanity of officers especially, and of the men. Spoke of the increase of immorality—sad, but true.

17th.   Wrote home.   Helped weigh out beef.

18th.   Ruled the blank abstract provision return book—nineteen pages.   Wrote to Ella Clark.

19th.   Detailed to take charge of twenty men to chop and draw wood for Second Battalion.   Went out about two miles west by the creek.   Sawed, chopped and helped load eleven or twelve loads. Had a good detail and first-rate time.

20th.   Found the books in use, so busied myself in writing to Fannie Henderson.

21st.   Went out with a detail of twenty privates and two sergeants to cut wood for the regiment.   Had twelve mule teams. Drew twenty-two loads.   Saw a long overland train bound for

Humboldt with crackers. Another train coming loaded with nine yoke of oxen. One wagon had 17 yokes stuck fast in the mire of the creek. California Overland Route.

22nd. A report circulated that we are to be among the regiments disbanded. Hope not true—prefer to see the thing through without re-enlisting. After all would like a short furlough. Dealt out the bacon. Got a good piece of beef for myself. Heard the wolves howl during the night.

23rd. Read the papers received in the morning and wrote home. No preaching.

24th. New recruits came, so I moved over to the Major's quarters. Played chess with Nettleton.

25th. Commenced reading Scott's "Ivanhoe." Delighted with its principal characters, Rowena and Ivanhoe.

26th. Played several games of chess and read. Helped in the Q. M. department.

27th. News came that the staff would be paid off. All went to the Fort to sign pay-rolls. Returned to dinner. Rode the Major's horse. Saw a tame buffalo. Quite a curiosity. Sergeants receive only $17 per month—a joke on their extra stripes.

28th. No letters for poor me. Read the latest papers. Rode over with Nettleton for the mail. The boys set the prairie on fire in several places, making one of the grandest sights I ever saw. Slept last night out of doors on the ground with Nettleton.

March 29th. Had a good bath in the creek, and washed my clothes—new experience. Very warm and sultry.

30th. Sunday. Brigade review, Second Ohio Cavalry. Ninth Wisconsin Infantry and Rabb's Battery practiced with guns. Helped foot up officers account with Q. M. Received and answered a good letter from Fannie.

31st. In the morning read in "Ivanhoe." Learned to play whist, pleasant game, but unprofitable as all cards are—will not allow myself to play. Rainy and cool.

APRIL, 1862.

1st. The "Long Roll" was sounded at the Ninth Wisconsin headquarters for an April Fool. Another dark rainy day. Read "Ivanhoe" and issued rations.

2nd. Messenger came in and reported Indians coming north. A scouting party was sent out.

3rd. Camp moved to better ground for defense.

4th. Moved camp again. Nothing of importance occurred. Many rumors afloat. Scouting parties still being sent out.

6th. Sunday. Heard the minister make a few remarks from "Be ye not overcome of evil." Letters from home and Fannie Andrews both.

7th. After work was done went to the river and washed. Had a good visit with Ed June.

9th. Went out with a detail of woodchoppers. Had a good time. Boys caught a rabbit and cooked it—all ate a morsel. Went and saw squad of Indians—savage looking enough.

10th. Thursday. The First Battalion of the Second Cavalry (four companies) left at ten A. M. for Carthage, Mo. Issued to them ten days' rations. Reported that we shall leave in a few days for some point forty or fifty miles east.

11th. Day chilly with slow rain falling. In the evening Oakie McDowell and I kept a light in the commissary. Commenced a letter to Fannie. Came near being reported for having light. Captain Seward is under arrest!

13th. Sunday. In the morning cleared up to my disgust. In the afternoon had my horse shod and visited hospital, very neat and clean. There seems to be so much need of female nurses. Went down and saw Indians (Delawares and Osages) in their savage state—had heavy beads and rings in their ears—wore buckskin leggings and red blankets, faces all painted and marked. Good visit with A. B. N.

14th. Issued one day's rations in the morning and again in the afternoon three days' rations. Orders countermanded before taps in the evening.

15th. Morning passed as usual at work. Major's horse sick. Evening new orders to march with ten days' rations. Played chess with A. B. Regiment paid off for two months.

16th. Morning rainy. Issued ten days' rations. Major said that the boys of the non-commissioned staff could not go on expedition for lack of transportation. We were already packed up, tent down for the march. Finally to our joy another team came and we loaded, saddled and started. The sky cleared and the ground was nice for marching. After marching 6 or 7 miles we halted for the horses to graze. The grass has started considerably. Encamped on the Drywood Creek, east branch, at sundown. Baggage train being mired on the road, the men bivouacked without tents, without suppers, the distant thunder threatening rain. Our team came, no rain.

April 17th. Train came up about nine. Commenced to rain. Pitched tents and remained there during the day. Played chess some.

18th. Marched to Lamar, Mo. Met Major Miner's command from Carthage. Creek at Lamar was high, so we left the baggage and a detail to guard it, and went up the creek to a bridge. Found the town, county seat of Barton County, almost deserted. Only a few dwellings.

19th. Went down to the creek and practiced a while with our revolvers. Played chess in the evening.

20th. Sunday. Moved the camp over the creek. Heard the stories, pitiful indeed, of Union refugees driven from home by the jayhawkers. Wrote home.

21st. A rainy day. Felt most sick, feverish, took a blue pill. Did not do much during the day.

22nd. General Doubleday and bodyguard and a few officers came. In the evening a man came in saying Union man was shot by jayhawkers. Thirty men of Co. "D", Major, Adjutant, Assistant Surgeon and I, with three or four others started at noon for Horse Creek, twenty miles away. Took a backwoods road. Found no enemy. Orders from the General to burn the house. Major gave the wife and two daughters at home time to take out their valuables. Wife was sick. Declared her husband's innocence. Finally concluded for the women's sake not to burn the house. The scene of the women crying and the desolation the boys were spreading about the premises was painful. Two men from Price's rebel army came up and were taken prisoners. Their horses and arms were taken and they were told to leave. When not more than three rods off, the boys, instigated by Major Purington, commenced shooting at them. They ran. Boys mounted and gave chase, shooting. Lieutenant Pike probably fired the fatal shot. One of the fellows not killed, was brought into the house. Two daughters—one married. Feared her husband was killed. At 8 P. M. we started back. Arrived in camp at 3:30 A. M. Wednesday morning.

23rd. Slept until ten o'clock. Commenced letter to Fannie. Brooks went out and got a load of hams and bacon.

24th. In the morning early, Companies "A" and "G" came in with Major Burnett and staff. At noon fifty men from each of the four companies of Burnett's battalion left camp, marched twenty miles. Our ride was through a rich country, over Gen. Siegel's first battle field. Many pretty flowers. Passed a little deserted village. Encamped by a clear stream and occupied some vacant houses. After supper made our bed out of doors and had a good night's rest.

25th. Started south for Diamond Grove. Detachments kept leaving when we approached the grove, so as to surround and enter it from different directions. Nettleton and we of the non-commissioned staff took one course and scouted through the woods. None found any rebels. Went to the farm of a Mr. Holsell, a notorious rebel. Boys took everything takable from the house and premises. Abundance of apples and some ammunition. Encamped here for the night. One girl, good secesh, has brother in the rebel army.

26th. Sunday. In the morning separated and went by companies. Nettleton and staff went with Co. "G" to "Turkey Creek," stopped at nearly every house. Took what arms, horses and cattle we could find. The guides deceived several families making them think we were secesh to capture Carthage. All people here are rebels, loud in their praises of the rebel soldiery and in their imprecations against the Union boys. The girls sang the "Army Wagon." Was much amused. Had a good visit with them—"Challes" by name, said I was the only gentleman in the lot—asked my name and said possibly they could some time do me some good. Our men brought into camp cattle and horses. Eight prisoners were brought in, including John Dale, State Senator from Jasper County. Lots of interesting incidents.

27th. At 7 A. M. marched to Carthage leaving Co. "G" to guard cattle. Arrested some men in town. Our boys occupied Court House. We (of the staff) set up in a boot and shoe store and boarded at Mr. Hueston's a little out of town—pleasant people. Issued rations to the boys.

28th. People began to come into town for their property. Six prisoners were released. Somebody shot at them. I am tired of this barbarous way of soldiering. Doubleday returned to Fort Scott with body guard.

29th. Baggage train and remainder of companies came in. Letter from Lucy Randall and several papers—rich treat. Wrote to Will Hudson.

30th. Received letters from Fannie and Uncle Albert. Answered Fannie's. Beautiful day. Arrested a suspicious looking fellow, acted like a spy. Told of the fight at Neosho and the Indian band on Cowskin Prairie.

MAY, 1862.

1st. Wrote to Sarah Felton. Nothing of interest occurred.

2nd. Orders from Curtiss to go somewhere, of course we know not where, probably to Cowskin Prairie in extreme southwest corner of Missouri, near the border of Indian Territory. Went out to a grist mill, two miles, and got some flour. Enjoyed the ride very much. Letters from Uncle and L. Randall.

3rd. Saturday. Ninth Wisconsin, two companies, came in. Lieutenant-Colonel Orff. Major Purington under arrest for saying that he should obey the order of Curtiss. He went to Lamar. Sent returns for six days' rations. Played chess with Lt. Nettleton.

4th. Sunday. In the morning went with Archie to the river, saw some very pretty scenery, high bluffs, a cave, and fine foliage. Wrote home.

5th. Went out with Lt. McGowan after bacon. Went 14 miles. Saw the Challes-Louise. Enjoyed seeing the family again— talkative as ever. Took some hams from Mr. Robertson's and some others. Went to Mr. Webb's. Got some apples. Had a good time all around. Got back to camp at ten P. M. Major cross.

May 6th. Issued five days' rations, sugar and coffee. Started on the march southwest at one o'clock. Companies "L", "M", "G", "D" and "A" under Major Purington, and two Dutch companies under Lt. Col. Orff. Marched eighteen miles to Redding Mills. Secesh galvanized. Found plenty of corn and sheaf oats. Occupied a house deserted a few minutes before. A store near by. Nothing of importance left. News of rebels within twelve miles.

7th. Wednesday. At 2 A. M. prepared for another day's march. At 3 were on the way. Reached Sparlan's, a noted secesh, at nine A. M. Fed and ate breakfast. Jayhawked his store. They said the boys destroyed a great deal of property ruthlessly. Continued the march. During the day Orff and Purington had a fuss. Orff took his men and our wagons and turned east to Neosho. After going a few miles we got trace of a band of jayhawkers. Charged after three on horses. Quite a spirited time we had, but the men had a long start, getting on a high hill and in the woods. Scoured the woods, finding some suspicious characters but without arms. Kept eight prisoners. Encamped near by in the valley. They stole a horse during the night.

8th. Thursday. Marched on towards Cowskin Prairie. A little skirmish on the road. Our course lay mostly among the Ozark Hills. A rich country and beautiful scenery. Reminded me of Vermont scenes. Enjoyed the ride much. As we struck Cowskin Prairie, a little beyond Elk Mill, we saw a band of thirty armed and mounted men. When we learned they were rebels, we followed, Co. "G" pursuing on their track, and Co. "A" going around a piece of timber. They had too much of a start and escaped. Exciting time. Scouts and spies of the enemy out in every direction. The Major said after we had rallied, that our squad, who had gone three miles farther than most of them, had been within a mile of a camp of 400 men. We were fourteen miles from Marysville where Coffee with 1,000 men was reported. We were in the Cherokee nation. Fine country. Enjoyed it well.

9th. Friday. During the night we expected an attack every hour. Pickets fired two or three times. Companies were called out into line for a fight early in the morning—at four. Mounted at eight and went six or eight miles and fed oats and corn. Traveled through a fine valley, hills on both sides. Reached Neosho at dusk. Went for corn to a widow's a mile from town. Slept on the porch at a hotel. Ate there. Good joke on Lt. Nettleton. The next morning when he presented the lady a five dollar bill, she quietly doubled it up and gave no change. Hear cannonading east.

10th. Saturday. Boys broke into P. O. and a store. Major was very angry and arrested Lt. Lockwood there and made three boys walk to Carthage. Boys were mad. This morning I was sick of service or rather longed to get into some other department. Spencer, Archie and I went ahead and got a good dinner at Mr. Hammond's—old secesh. Found an old gun, which we carried through. Reached Carthage before dusk. Letter and papers from home. Learned that the day before, Co. "I" while out foraging met a squad of rebel soldiers. One was killed, two wounded and three taken prisoners. Next day Sergt. Smith was released on parole to get an exchange of three of Jockman's men for them.

11th. Sunday. Issued rations, slept and read *Independent*. Wrote to Fannie Andrews.

May 12th. Monday. Major Miner arrived at three A. M. Major Purington left early to report under arrest at Fort Scott. Miner commenced a rigid discipline and introduced a new system. Quite an alarm from shooting at an ox. Companies turned out.

13th. Issued four days' rations. Most all the horses were condemned for sore backs. Sent to mill for one day's ration of flour. Companies fell out several times from false alarms. I accidentally fired a gun while drilling with Reeve and Archie.

14th. Wednesday. Left Carthage at 8. Most of the boys footed it. My horse was well enough but I thought I would fare as the rest did. Stopped to graze our horses at ten miles. I was very tired. Got my haversack and gave my horse into Tom's care. I went to a little bush and ate a lunch in sight of my horse. Soon fell asleep and when I awoke, could not find my horse. Baggage wagons were going on. One of the boys said he saw the horse go ahead. Hurried on to see. Tom rode all about the field and prairie vainly. I got a horse and another man and went back and searched thoroughly and vainly. Reached Lamar in the evening.

15th. Thursday. Archie and I cooked a respectable meal. Took our ease until five P. M. Then we marched again. Reached East Drywood at midnight. Capt. Stanhope and Lt. Rush were ahead and were chased by thirty jayhawkers. Column halted. I went on with the advance two or three miles, no sign of any men.

16th. Rain obliged us to arise at five. Stayed under the wagon a while. Then went to the creek to wash. Reveille blew just before I got back. Lt. Hubbard arrested Brooks and me because somebody had wanted us and could not find us. Released us as soon as we came into camp. Rode partly on the wagons and walked some. Seemed good to get back to Fort Scott again. Found two letters from home.

17th. Saturday. Went up town and saw George Ashman. Went to the hotel and got breakfast. Cooked our own meals. Letter from Fannie Andrews.

18th. Sunday. Wrote to Fannie. Attended preaching by Mr. Hawkins, from Isaiah 1st, 3rd verse, "My people doth not consider."

19th. Made arrangements for another horse. Had the one lost examined and got an order from the General for another. Very pretty bay, well satisfied.

20th. Tuesday. Nettleton and Stewart went to Leavenworth. Rained.

21st. Wednesday. Archie and I went out and grazed our horses. Good time. Saw George Ashman. Bathed.

22nd. Drew rations. Archie grazed both horses. We washed our clothes.

23rd. Started at 8 A. M. for Iola. Marched fifteen miles. Saw George. Shaved by Charlie Fairbanks. Encamped out in the open air by Turkey Creek. A. B. and I cooked our suppers. Happy time. A grand ridge of mounds surrounds us.

24th. Saturday. Reveille at 4 A. M. Breakfasted, loaded wagon and horsed at six A. M. Grazed about five miles. Splendid prairie view. But one little bunch of woods in sight. Reached Iola about three o'clock. Good visit with the boys.

May 25th. Sunday. Wrote home, grazed my horse and rested.

26th. Helped unload seven loads of provisions. Played ball a little while. Reminded me of old times.

27th. Woods and I issued five days' rations. We boys carried ours to the woman where we board.

28th. Wednesday. Wrote to Fannie in time for the mail. Read Will's old journal.

29th. Thursday. Went to Neosho Falls, nine miles, to see the Indians play ball. Gay time and gay dinner. Visited them in their camp and home. Saw some slaves among them. Was disgusted with their primeval customs. Saw Seminoles and Delawares. About 7,000 encamped along the river.

30th. Friday. I wrote a letter to Ella Clark, in answer to one received weeks before. I am ashamed of my negligence or inability to write more. Showed the letter to the Oberlin boys.

31st. Saturday. Wrote a short letter to Uncle. Issued seven days' rations. The Major bought a mess box, $18, a splendid one. Received a letter from home.

JUNE, 1862.

1st. Wrote a line home. Marched south at 7. Went forward with Colonel Salomon and Adj. Ninth Wisconsin to find camping ground. Indian trading post. Several Indian graves. Cold day, drizzly rain. Enjoyed the trip well. 25 miles, Humboldt.

2nd. Passed a Catholic Mission for Indians. Very good conveniences. Many children. Three or four buildings. Stopped often to graze. Passed through a good country. Good oak and hickory timber. Passed an Indian village—Osages. Encamped upon a good plat of grass along the Neosho. After supper went to the river and bathed. Received invoice of provisions from "Buckshot."

3rd. Arose at 4 A. M. First Battalion off at 5 to join Doubleday, 35 miles. Loaded provisions from citizens to mule teams. Infantry, as usual got the start, artillery next. Had a pleasant march. Long time crossing the Lightning Creek. Narrow roads for the wagons through the woods. Grazed often. Encamped with Ninth Wisconsin on the banks of Cherry Creek. Artillery crossed and camped. Issued beef. Rained in the afternoon. Slept out in the open air. Several officers and men tight. McMurray.

4th. Wednesday. Reveille at 3:30 A. M. Breakfast and under way at 6 A. M. After riding ten miles, troops rested. Lieutenant Lisering of Doubleday's staff met us with the news that Col. Salomon had been made brigadier and Col. Weir of the Tenth Kansas had the command of the expedition. All seemed astonished. Lt.

Colonel said, "the news rather surprised him." Considerable sensation. Crossed the Neosho and encamped near the rest of the troops. A very pretty situation for a camp. A range of hills, overlooking large valley and woods.

June 5th. Learned and ordered the number of pounds of beef needed, also issued it. Issued rations for the five days' expedition under Doubleday. Took us till "taps." Orders came from Col. Wier, Tenth Kansas, to delay further movements. The Colonel (Doubleday) resolves to resign immediately, so enraged at the intrigue and rascality of Kansas officers and politicians in making Wier rank him. Officers sent a paper to him begging him not to do it. Seemed to regret the idea very much. Concluded to go on with the expedition anyway.

6th. Eight companies of the Second Ohio, Majors Miner and Burnett, four Ninth Wisconsin Infantry, three Tenth Infantry Kansas, one Sixth Kansas Cavalry were on the march at 8 A. M. Major P. was going independently. He had refused me several times, but after all the troops were gone, he consented. Left in a hurry with little provisions. Crossed Spring River and the Neosho. After marching fast 35 miles, came upon the camps of Standwaite and Coffee. Major P. conversed with pickets. Shelled the position of Standwaite, but probably too late, having escaped with Coffee south to Col. Rains. The shelling was splendid. The shells would bound from tree to tree and burst with a thundering noise. First Battalion took position between the two camps, if possible to prevent a junction of forces. Also went out as skirmishers. Third Battalion deployed along the woods to prevent escape and watch the movements of the enemy. The Battery took a position on the hill favorable for shelling the enemy. Was supported by the Kansas Infantry. Ninth Wisconsin deployed as skirmishers and entered the woods. Scouts went near Coffee's camp and represented them leaving. "General" (Col. Doubleday) immediately marched to the south of the camp and ceased operations for the night. It was now 1 o'clock A. M. Bivouacked with few blankets in the open air. Slept soundly till 3 A. M. I enjoyed all the doings very much, acted as carrier for the "General." Accompanied Major Purington. Saw large herds of horses and cattle. Took many prisoners. Some Coffee's men and some not.

7th. In saddle at 4 A. M. Went into the timber for breakfast. Ate with Co. "E." Good appetite, having eaten nothing of consequence since the morning before. Reconnoitering party was sent south to learn the position and force of the enemy supposed to be encamped 15 miles south. The command encamped in favorable positions in and near Round Grove, the former camp of Col. Coffee. The women in the grove reported that he moved at sundown. One sick man of Coffee's left behind, reported that he had 600 and Standwaite 1,000. Raines' unknown. Variously estimated from 500 to 2000. At night the First Battalion went out on picket. Some Co. H men fired on our patrol. Slept with Delos in No. 3.

8th. Sunday. Started on our return at 8 o'clock, with drove of cattle and horses. Major and Purps went ahead, and a few miles from the road, to a deserted camp and got a secesh wagon, old style, hitched in four horses and had a gay time. Lead horses whirled after a time and broke the tongue, fixed it and with two horses drove through the camp. Horses balked several times, once in the river. Hadley and I undressed and helped across. Command stopped at Hudson's. Jayhawked the people badly. ("Purps"— nickname for noncommissioned staff.)

9th. Monday. Did very little save rest and graze my horse. Letters from Fannie, home and Sarah.

June 10th. Tuesday. Great false alarm in camp. Major with Co. "I" went out seven miles. We saw nothing.

11th. Moved camp nearer the river on the edge of the woods on account of water. Issued rations to eight companies. Rather tired at night. Went fishing after supper with Major and Brownell. Caught no fish, pleasant time.

12th. Another false alarm. Whole brigade in arms. Scouted about some. Nothing unusual. Grazed my horse.

13th. Issued rations in the morning. Moved camp over the river west. Pitched our tent in a splendid grove in a secesh corn field. Found some mulberries.

14th. Wrote a letter home. Mail came bringing home letters and *Independent*. Issued rations to four companies, to go the next morning on expedition five days. Moved the Second Battalion again half a mile. After work had a gay time finding our tent. Wandered all through the woods.

15th. Sunday. A beautiful Sabbath morning. Would love to be at home or somewhere to enjoy peaceful rest. Read the *Independent*. Wrote to Emma McWade.

16th. Monday. Issued rations to several companies. Stayed at the Commissary most of the day.

17th. Wrote to Brockway. Part of the Missouri expedition returned with a load of bacon. Tired horses and men. Issued some.

18th. Wednesday. Grazed my horse. Did little more. Read some. Paymaster came from Leavenworth.

19th. Thursday. Went to the Commissary as usual at 9 A. M. Archie got thrown from his horse. Wrote to Fannie. Went bathing with Nettleton and Brownell. Talked Minnie and Professor. Two letters. Home and Fannie.

20th. Friday. Attended to my usual duties. Read papers.

21st. Saturday. Wrote home. Major Purington and Adjutant acted ridiculously in the evening. Out almost all night on a spree.

22nd. Sunday. Major Purington started at 5 for Ohio on 30 days furlough. Carried lots of money for the boys. We boys sent to Wilson Dodge, former Q. M., to get the Major a ring worth $10. Got our pay. Commissary and Q. M. received alike this time.

Issued some rations and drew enough from Brigade Com'y for ten days.

23rd. Monday. According to orders started for Neosho at 6 A. M. Up early and flew around to get chores done. Our road lay mostly through the woods. After 8 miles ride, mail came. A letter from good Fannie. Met Co. "A" and "D" from Sherwood, three miles north of Neosho. Met some Kansas Sixth who had fallen in with a band of 400 rebels on the road to Granby. Council of War—Burnett wanting to go on with 200 men—Ratcliff not thinking it best. Bivouacked for the night in open air.

24th. Tuesday. Arose before sunrise 3:45 A. M. Took the horses out to graze. Archie and I went with horses to an oat field up on a hill beyond the pickets. Good feed for the horses. Detachment went ahead to Neosho at 7 A. M. Entered N. and encamped a little after noon on the ground where the militia was surprised. An alarm in the night. False.

June 25th. Issued the remainder of the ten days' rations taken along. Received a letter from home.

26th. Turned over some commissary stores to the 4th and 9th Wisconsin, who came in that evening. Wrote to Fannie. Another false alarm. Citizens expected an attack.

27th. Friday. Was busy as usual. Battery came. Issued rations to them.

28th. Saturday. Got my horse shod. A good many ladies in camp. Straightened the provision returns and wrote letter to Fannie, and sent them by Corp. I., Co. M. Didn't get to bed till 12 P. M.

29th. Sunday. Started from camp at 5 A. M. Marched by long road from Neosho towards Cowskin. Encamped on a high piece of ground, over an excellent spring of water.

30th. Monday. Arose at 2:30. Marched at 4 A. M. Reached Cowskin at noon, and Rains' camp at 3 P. M., which he had deserted the day before. Found the Indians before us encamped near by. Four companies, Ninth Rabb's Battery and Second and Third Battalion came from Neosho. Nothing particular by the way. Noticed some places well remembered when Major Purington was down. Mustered for pay. Pitched tent loosely for the Major and Adjutant and made our beds outside. Thunderstorm camp up, tent blew over and such a time I never had before. Soaking wet all of us, but nearly the whole force fared the same way.

JULY, 1862.

1st. Reveille at three A. M. Started at 4 A. M. Moved 8 miles to where the command from the other way was, at Round Grove, where Coffee had camped. Indians in their natural state encamped there too. Laughable sight. Pleasant day. Cooler and grass good. Saw the Oberlin boys. Letter from Fannie. Rested. Wrote in the evening.

2nd. Wednesday. In our saddles at 5 A. M. Marched 8 miles west, near where the Major and we boys captured the wagon. Nothing special occurred.

3rd. Thursday. In saddles at three A. M. Rode 18 miles. Encamped on Grand River.

4th. Great day. So many drunk. Officers gave the freest license to the men. Both caroused. I was most disgusted. Bill and L. fought.

5th. Issued rations to two battalions. The reaction of the 4th was visible among the boys. Slept on the prairie by my horse.

6th. Sunday. Overslept and wakened at "forward." Hurried along. Rode a little obstinate pony. Passed the other brigade and encamped at two miles distant. Saw some Confederate papers, very neat. Warmest day of the season. Bathed in Grand River. Wrote a little, read two or three chapters in Philippians. I wish it were easier to be good, or rather I wish I were a better boy and doing some good.

July 7th. On the march at 4 A. M. We boys did not know we were to march, so awakened merely in time to hurry off without breakfast. Marched 8 miles and encamped on the prairie near the woods. Archie and I took our horses to a corn field. Read a chapter in Bushnell's "Respectable Sin," very applicable to myself. Veal noodle soup for supper. Hot day, no covering at night.

8th. Reveille a little before two. Got coffee and meat for breakfast. Started on the march, in the rear, at daybreak. Like Capt. Smith some better but I long for Major Purington to come back again. Second Brigade in the rear of the first ones. Issued rations.

9th. Marched all the forenoon, and went only five miles forward. So many blunders. Encamped on Grand River near it on the edge of the woods, good place.

10th. Grazed our horses and rested. Wrote some.

In a letter dated Camp Flat Rock, Ind. Ter., July 11, 1862, he says:

"The Fourth of July was duly celebrated at Cabin Creek Camp.

We did no marching, and perfect license was given to all to drink and carouse as much as they chose.

One officer even told his men that the one who wasn't drunk that night should be ducked in Grand river. . . .

When the 1st Brigade had their fight near here, Col. Weir, our commander, was so intoxicated that he could neither receive the report of the battle or give any orders.

One reason everybody liked Col. Doubleday so well was, that he never drank. . . . .

It seems good to get settled down again. While marching, the middle of the day was so very hot, that we commenced marching at three o'clock in the morning, so we had to get up very early to have breakfast out of the way and get ready.

The greatest trouble so far has been the scarcity of water.

Had we come down the other side of the river—people say—there would have been an abundance of water. But water has been very scarce—and mostly stale creek water for which we would have to go quite a distance.

One Q. M. Sergeant was reduced to the ranks day before yesterday for going to a spring almost in our line of march.

I feared there would be a mutiny that day, so many boys hadn't water and weren't permitted to leave the ranks to get any. Hereafter any member of the cavalry losing a horse, save in battle, must go afoot, by order of Col. Wier.

Well, Charlie seems to have had his fill of grass, so I must go back to camp. I have been sitting here on my blanket while he has been grazing. We have to go quite a distance from camp for good grass. . . You don't know what melting weather we have had.

The thermometer has been as high as one hundred and twelve in the shade I believe.

Several men have been sunstruck. There has been no rain of consequence for about two months."

11th. Major Purington returned to us. Had been only to Fort Leavenworth. Could not get beyond the department. Came at breakfast time. I had been out on prairie grazing. Found him here with a tent full of officers. Jolly time. We were so glad to see him, so were all. I believe he has more friends than any man in the regiment.

12th. Saturday. Wrote a letter to Uncle and Aunt Branch. My horse got away suddenly and I did not find him until morning.

13th. Awoke early and found my horse. Took him out to graze. Issued rations to the whole command. Tired at night. Slept out with the pickets, with Charlie Fairchild.

14th. Monday. Read in "Guy Mannering." Rained very heavily most all day. Thunder. Got wet in tent. An alarm. Large detachment sent out. 1st and 2nd Battalions went, Archie and Thayer too. Major was angry that they went. Major, field officer of the day.

15th. Stayed in camp and read "Guy Mannering," good story. Pastured my horse and Brownell's.

16th. Wednesday. Boys returned from Fort Gibson, no enemy there. Enemy four miles below on the south side of the Arkansas, at Fort Davis. Expecting artillery. Boys rested.

17th. Played a little chess. Wrote to Aunt Luna. Slept on the prairie. All the horses of the regiment were out.

18th. Ordered to commence on half rations. Visited Capt. Nettleton. Sick since going to Fort Gibson, weak. At 11 P. M. orders came to march at 2 A. M. Second Battalion in advance. Colonel Wier under arrest and a prisoner, Colonel Salomon commanding.

19th. Kept up after eleven and packed up. The circumstances of the trouble with Wier are these: On account of drunkenness and his seeming determination to starve us out, Col. S., all the officers in his brigade and most of the others approving, concluded to arrest him; sent the adjutant with a detail of 100 men who ordered him under arrest. He refused the order. The detail presented bayonets and took him prisoner. Took him to Col. S.'s tent, where were officers representing most of the regiments. When he saw Capt. Allen of the Battery, he said, "And are you here?" and burst into tears. I never saw so much excitement. All were glad. Before this Col. S. had determined if rations did not come by Monday to march his brigade north. Left the Indians there, marched 39 miles to our old second camp, slept on the prairie as usual. Nettleton came along slowly during the day. Officers began to be frightened after 4 or 5 hours, and ordered an ambulance to go back for him. Just then he came up.

20th. Reveille at 2 A. M. Marched at 4 A. M. Left Co. "A" to keep up communications. Encamped after 12 miles march. Major Burnett left with an escort for Leavenworth with orders and papers about Wier's arrest.

21st. Rested and wrote some.

22nd. Read in "Guy Mannering." Issued rations for eleven days. Horses got away. Looked all over the country until the next day at 4 P. M., when we marched.

23rd. Visited the rich mansion of Louis Ross, brother of John. Splendid place. The destruction seemed terrible. Owned 160 slaves. Good piano. Marched 12 miles and camped at 11.

24th. Marched at 3 A. M. Reveille at 2 A. M. Marched 12 miles. Encamped.

25th. Started at 4 A. M. Marched 7 miles beyond Hudson's Crossing. Met the third battalion.

26th. Wrote a letter to Fannie. Played chess with Sergeant Spencer.

27th. Sunday. Wrote home and read some in "Nathalie,"-by Julia Kavanagh. Very good story.

28th. Mail came. Letter from home. Rather discouraging news. Adjutant Weeks slept with the Major. Such a time talking and carrying on.

29th. Wrote to Uncle Albert Harris.

30th. Wednesday. In camp on Rocky Creek, Spring River. Issued five days' rations, preparatory to marching northward. Boys in good spirits. Wrote to Fred Allen. Saw Charlie in the morning. Read Will's last journal, much better than his late ones. His discouragement about the late reverses. To be sure the present hour looks dark but I have faith in the future. The light will soon break. I have faith to believe that the North will yet be victorious over the South, right be victorious over wrong. I am sorry Will feels so. It looks like an apology for not enlisting. To fear defeat and yet not raise a hand looks faulty.

July 31st. Thursday. Finished a letter to Fred Allen. The Court Martial meetings still continue, Major Purington presiding. The officers are beginning to be more strict and exacting. The discipline cannot but be improved. Went to the river and bathed. Washed a pair of pants and handkerchief and towel. Went up on a high bluff of rocks, a more romantic place than I had seen for a long time. It reminded me much of Old Vermont, or Canada side of Niagara. Marched at three P. M. Reached Baxter's Springs at sundown. Major Miner, Capt. Stanhope and Adj. Weeks ate supper with us, had tomatoes and pineapples for dessert.

AUGUST, 1862.

1st. Friday. In camp on Cow Creek, 40 miles south of Fort Scott. Two men were killed here by Standwaite some time ago. Poor water. The big twenty-five miles prairie just beyond. Rode with the Sergeant Major. Fooled with him considerably. Good time. Capt. Smith played fool, infringing on the Second Battalion. Major Purington gave him a blowing. The mail came this evening. Letters from Fannie and home. They did me good. I long for the furlough time to come. Barnitz received a commission as Second Lieutenant. Pleased all. Wrote a short letter to Fannie. Purington thinks of going on tomorrow.

2nd. Saturday. In camp on Drywood, sixteen miles from Fort Scott. Marched today 22 miles over a barren prairie. Rested for two or three hours in the heat of the day. Mail came in the evening. Received another letter from Fannie. It seemed so good to hear from her two days in succession. Got to fooling with Reeve in the tent along in the evening, and we concluded to take a turn outdoors. We first took hold squarehold. After a long time I brought Reeve to the ground but he whirled me. Boys said I threw. Then he dared me to sidehold. Major and boys watched me. I threw him in a trice. I wouldn't try again for I know his superiority in strength and skill.

3rd. Sunday. Started again at 4 A. M. Marched 14 miles in sight of Fort Scott. Then turned back two miles on account of the scarcity of water. Encamped along a little vale where were little puddles of water. Got into camp a little after noon. Slept some. Got wood for a fire. Helped eat some oysters and sardines. Supper at 5 P. M. Mail came bringing a letter from Minnie. Wrote home. Sent a letter to Fannie. Saw some new acts relating to the formation of regiments under the new law. All Batt. staffs to be mustered out. One more 2nd Lt. to a company. A good berth for some of the staff. Warm day, not much like Sunday.

4th. Monday. "General" blew at 7 A. M. Struck tents and moved to our first camping ground when we entered Fort Scott from Kansas City. I went ahead with Major Miner to lay out camp. Q. M. issued clothing. Drew boots and shirt. Helped get things ready for supper. In the evening Major P., Major M. and Adj. Weeks got news of the fight in the Indian Territory. Standwaite prisoner, another notable killed. 400 proved traitors, having come into camp and given up and then turning on our men. 300 of them killed. Sergt. Major was taken sick suddenly, probably sunstruck. Bill drunk and quarrelsome. Adj. Weeks in tent.

5th. Tuesday. In the morning did little of everything. Wrote to Fannies A. and H. in answer to letter received almost three months since. In the afternoon the service for the burial of three men was performed. Lt. Pike drilled the escort. It seemed his whole ambition to get the men well drilled. He had an escort drilling for one very sick man who had not yet died. Maj. M. and Adj.

W. boarding with us. In the evening attended a variety performance up town. Very good for barren Fort Scott. Got home about midnight. Received no letters, a little disappointed. Mr. Hawkins returned yesterday.

Aug. 6th. Wednesday. In the morning there was a great scare about Quantrell's band. Reported near Montebello, 40 miles east, preparing for a raid against Fort Scott. A report that three companies of the 3rd Wisconsin had been captured. At nine "to arms" blew and to arms the men went. They seized their old rusted carbines, scoured them and were in line for the assembly. They were assembled, mounted under Capt. Smith and dismounted under Major Purington. 3rd came in unharmed save one killed, several wounded and baggage train lost. Rations for five days were issued. Went over to town at retreat, got shaved and hair cut by Charlie Fairbanks.

7th. Watered my horse and took a good bath. Had a good visit with Newt. Adams about officers of our acquaintance and future prospects. Today, as often, I am uneasy for something to satisfy a nervous want of something real to do. Can't be easy at anything. Commenced reading the "Woman in White," by Wilkie Collins. Found the book quite interesting. Could hardly leave it for my meals. There seems to be no stopping place. Every paragraph, every chapter, every book is full of thrilling adventures, well laid plot. Great vigilance against surprise.

8th. August. Commenced "Woman in White" again. Fairly begun when I was ordered off with Capt. Smith to find a camp. Selected one up on the hill west of town. Somewhat fortified. Moved camp in the forenoon. All tired after moving. Had one meal. Continued the story. Our new site for camp overlooks a large tract of country. The horses are picketed away from the immediate vicinity of the camp so that we will be free from the dust, and be nearer water for horses.

9th. Saturday. In the morning had to give up the book which I had borrowed from Robinson. Accomplished very little during the day. Tried to write Will but could not think fast enough, so threw aside paper and ink. Sale of cattle confiscated at the fort. Archie attended. Stock mostly bought by Babcock and Company, who are getting rich from the government. So are many of Kansas officers interested in the many contracts made for the troops, purposely kept here in Kansas. 9th and Battery arrived.

10th. Sunday. In the morning received a little treasure from Fannie at Richfield. Finished the story of the "Woman in White," so well told. Like the style. Inspection at ten A. M. Our staff did not go. I went to the creek and bathed. Issued rations for five days. Delos came up from town and went with me to see Charlie. Had a good visit. Heard Will's journal read. Received a good photograph of Will. Glad to get it. Chaplain preached in the evening, on the parade. Large numbers out to hear him. Good remarks, especially in reference to his visits at home. Enjoyed it.

11th. Monday. Read some in the June *Atlantic*. Nothing especially interesting. After dinner went down for Charlie and visited Delos per engagement. Had a splendid visit, real social time. Got some lemon syrup, talked over our old experiences at home and with "B. F." In the evening went to town to hear Lane and Blunt. Lane did well enough for a border ruffian. Blunt criticised the course of our officers in arresting Wier. Referred to the whole thing as a conspiracy. 1st Brigade did not cheer much till Gen. Salomon's name was heard. Then the boys grew wild with excitement and cheered heartily for him. Blunt found, I guess, that Wier had enemies and Salomon friends.

12th. Tuesday. In the morning molasses was issued to the boys. Wrote a letter home. One boy from Co. G was buried. Wrote to Fannie and Uncle. Lt. Carter died. It must be a sad affliction for his poor mother who esteemed him her pet. Sergt. Daniels was wounded in the thigh by accident. Gen. Blunt held a council of all the officers in the division. Squashed the whole Wier fuss. I hope Wier won't accept the terms. Many officers talk of resigning. Ladies about camp. Arrived yesterday. Mesdames Miner, Burnett, Ratliffe, Taylor.

13th. Wednesday. Did very little in the morning. In the afternoon Lt. Carter was buried. Capt. Nettleton rode up to our tent and told me he would like to see me a minute. I went aside and he said he was going home. I asked him if he were going home for good. He said that was about the only way men could get out of the department at this time. Finally after deceiving me he told me he was going on regiment business. Wrote lines to Fannie and home.

14th. Thursday. Put some stripes on my pants, and gave my poor wardrobe a good looking over and repairing. Should not like playing old bachelor for life—not any. Like company and society too well. In the afternoon orders came for the 2nd Ohio to be ready to march at 8 P. M. with 5 days' rations. Under way at nine P. M. 1st Brigade and 6th and 9th Kansas marched from town at ten with the 2nd Ohio in the rear. The dismounted men and 9th Wisconsin rode in the wagons. Marched all night. I got Major's permission and rode in baggage wagon. Most sick with the bloody flux. All were ignorant of our destination, but supposed and hoped to fight.

15th. Stopped a little while in the morning to feed the horses. Moved on and passed through "Ball Town." Stopped to get some breakfast. Received a letter from home. The prairie took fire several times and kept the boys busy fighting it. Colonel, Capt. Smith, Majors Miner and Purington rested under a tent fly we pitched. Marched again at 3 P. M. Passed Pappinsville. All these places in Mo. are little stingy trading posts. Over prairies and through woods and ravines we went. Sometimes slow, sometimes fast. Tired of jolting. Made a bed of the blankets. 2nd Ohio mounted and in advance under Major Purington. Stopped about 2 A. M. and fed horses. Roasted corn.

16th. Saturday. Kept up our march till morning at nine. Crossed the Osage. At nine A. M. stopped to feed and breakfast. Marched on through Johnstown. All the day the boys made for every melon patch, orchard or beehive to be seen. Had a good eat from melons and apples. Saw very few people. Encamped at sundown. For the first time had a night's sleep. Very little water. Expected somewhat an attack before morning. Ordered to sleep on our arms. I slept soundly, as I usually do. Johnnie Devlin and I devoured a nice large watermelon. Enemy supposed to be six miles away.

17th. Sunday. Breakfasted and under way at 5 A. M. Passed through Rose Hill, a very pretty little town. Hugh Watson and I went ahead and got apples, watermelons, plums and wild grapes. Had a good time. Passed through "Index," another little town. Major rode with us in the wagon all day, good time. Reached "Lone Jack," where the enemy were, at sundown an hour before. A man came up and reported 1500 enemy in our rear. Major Purington with rear guard, watched them and kept near them. Fired a good deal and tried to detain them. Proved to be the enemy retreating the way we had come. Major sent word for reinforcements. Some went but did not follow fast enough till dark set in. Commenced to rain. Command moved. Baggage soon could not go, it was so dark. So the enemy escaped us, so slickly through the gap. General Salomon had advised and entreated Blunt to keep flankers and scouts out through the woods near "Lone Jack." They had intelligence from Warren that they were surely there, and we were passing within a mile. The ground was favorable for their retreat from the town—unseen. They kept a large picket about town and thus fooled our men. Warren could not believe that they had gone. So they left us, as a mouse from a trap. All the officers were enraged and disgusted with Blunt's mistake, still hoped to overtake them. I went out a mile and got an old mare to ride. The history of the fight of the day previous was as follows: The day before, Quantrell, with 1200 men burned Independence and then skedaddled; Capt. Burns from Kansas City, with two companies of cavalry, four of infantry and two pieces of artillery, followed; at night overtook them and shelled their camp. They ran. The next morning Quantrell met Coffee and turned back. Lay in the brush and waited for them, coming through a lane. When the Feds came along they rose up and poured volley after volley into them. They hurried back to the village and there fought desperately. Finally overpowered, spiked one of the guns, destroyed the ammunition and ran. Warren, who had followed Coffee from Butler, watched them here that and the next day, till we came up confident that they would stand a fight. About 60 killed and many wounded on each side. Rebels burned ten of our wounded men in a house used as a hospital.

18th. Monday. After the moon rose, so that the teams could pick their way, we started on. Moved back on the same road we went up. Col. Cloud and Warren's forces took another route and went faster than we. Passed through "Index" and "Rose Hill" and stopped after passing the big mill. Awful place for baggage to cross. Got a little supper. Hard bread and coffee, then moved on— the dismounted men and infantry on foot. The report came in that Cloud met the enemy at Johnstown—so Blunt hastened. Mules and horses tired out. As we marched boys would fall asleep, walk on and frequently tumble down. Major Burnett said he rode the whole length of train and every mule driver but two were asleep—most in their wagons. Train moved on well.

19th. Tuesday. Breakfasted at Johnstown. As usual boys went for chickens, corn and anything to eat. People have felt our march through their country. Report came that the enemy were at Osceola, 30 miles southeast. Continued our march Osceola- ward. Stopped two or three miles from Johnstown and fed mules and ourselves—three hours. Moved on. Report came that Cloud's advance was fighting with rear guard of the enemy. One man killed on the prairie, just buried. Changed our course towards Stubbleville. Reached that place in the morning, sunrise. In the afternoon my horse troubled me so getting away that I got on bareback. Got a saddle and rode all night. Very sleepy. Slept on my horse. Major Miner fell from his horse. Pat Collopy fell twice. It was almost impossible for the rear guard to get the sleep- ing ones awake and along.

20th. Wednesday. Hamlin and Devlin had been missing for two days. Hamlin returned. They had been with Cloud's com- mand. By permission, Hamlin and Watson went ahead intending to overtake Cloud's command, but they had too much the start of us. Went up to the house where four Kansas men's wounds had been bandaged the day before. Sick men and those unable to stand service went to the fort. Warren's command passed. We went with the advance guard of our brigade. In the P. M. Mo. men and Iowa (Warren) turned back. Reached Montebello about 8 P. M. Pedrick, with whom I had been riding, got a supper at an old lady's. Paid 50 cents. Moved on two miles to the prairie. Couldn't find our wagons. It rained hard and wet us thoroughly. So tired we did not feel it much.

21st. Thursday. Went with two Company F men and got breakfast at a farmhouse. Some of the boys had had nothing to eat for 36 hours. Ham and corn bread. Borrowed 20 cents and paid. They asked nothing but we preferred to pay them. Major Burnett, with detail of five started for Fort Scott. Several of us contrived to go too. Got breakfast out three miles, milk and honey. A man came up. We frightened him so he swore he was secesh and made himself ridiculous generally for a union man. Had a secesh horse, taking care of it. Brought him in. In the morning put a rope around a boy's neck and made him take the oath with some meaning. Letters from Minnie, Melissa and Fannie.

22nd. Friday. Slept rather late. F. Brooks back, looking very sleek. Went to the river and washed myself thoroughly.

Changed my clothes and rested as well as possible. The command came in. Boys seem hardy, though the trip has been tough. All the boys are exasperated that they did not catch the enemy. News that Fremont is to have command here, good. We to go home. Wrote a middling long letter to Fannie Andrews. Wrote while Brownell read in "Woman in White." Boys issued rations for five days. Naturally lazed a while myself.

23rd. In the morning did chores and read the papers. In the afternoon went into Adj. Watson's tent. He treated to strawberries. Reeve and Major Miner were in when some one asked about our being mustered out of service. He said he thought we would not be, and then he asked why we wanted to go. He believed if we stayed in the regiment, we would all have commissions. In the evening wrote to Will H. Received letters from Fannie Andrews and Fred Allen, both excellent. Got some new ideas about Will from Fred. News came that Doubleday was coming back to command and that the regiment would be taken to another field. Boys all rejoiced. Some officers were opposed.

24th. Sunday. In the morning found my old contraband missing. Didn't think it worth while to look for it. Cleaned up and prepared for inspection. Archie and Reeve laid out a bed of state pistols, sabres and spurs. Wrote to Melissa and Ma and some more to Fannie. Read some in an old *Independent*. In the evening went out and heard Chaplain preach a good sermon. Romans, 6th chapter, 11th verse. Good remarks. Mrs. Miner was out to hear him. The Mrs. Majors are still here raising sensations. Seemed good to see them horseback riding.

25th. Monday. Went over to Capt. Nettleton's tent and borrowed Longfellow's "Hyperion." Charlie came over in the morning and read Will's last journal and my letter from Fred. Enjoyed both and a first-rate visit about home and "B. F." and other friends. Like Fred's course. Read in "Hyperion." Enjoyed it pretty well. In the evening commenced a letter to Sarah Felton. John Devlin and two other boys of Co. F came in. Were in the late brush on Drywood. One of the corporals was wounded. Had a clever visit with Newt. Adams. Bill tolerably drunk, yelling as usual. Lively talk before sleeping.

Tuesday, 26th. In the morning read some. Finished a letter to Sarah Felton. She is a splendid girl. I wish she would be content to stop study for a year like Fannie A. and Fannie H. In the afternoon issued five days' rations. Had a very pleasant time talking with the boys. Mail came in the evening. None of us but John Thayer, received letters. Rather disappointed. Andy enlisted and left for Mount Vernon. Rather sorry to see him go—good boy.

Wednesday, 27th. In the morning did very little. Read some. In the afternoon Delos and I went down to see Charlie. He was about going to water his horses. Stayed a short time and read a *Lorain News*. Nothing particular. Saw a corpse, a Co. A. man. Went in and saw several sick men. Two from Co. H. are doomed to die. Boys sat about as carelessly as ever, playing cards and swearing. Washed the dishes when I got home. Played ball a little.

Thursday, 28th. In the morning came the detail for the 2nd Kansas Battery. Heretofore officers had said that such a detail should not be made. But the order came to the Colonel for 150 men and the Colonel gave orders to Batt. commanders for the detail and they to their companies. The detail was made but not a man would go. Three or four companies marched to guard house. Finally after several Orderly calls and speeches by Majors to Battalions, the detail submitted. The wrangle about the to-be colonel of the regiment continues. Papers went on signed by ten in favor of Doubleday and nine against. Miner, Burnett and Ratliff rascals— selfish. Major P. sent in his resignation.

Friday, 29th. Morning passed as usual in reading the late papers and loafing. Washed dishes. No encouraging news. Several commissions came over—some very just and deserved ones. In the afternoon came a detail of all well mounted men to go on an expedition into Mo. Archie and I went. 50 men in all under Capt. Welch. 9th Wisconsin, Allen's Battery, and part of the 9th Kansas along under Gen. Salomon. We went as advance. Rode all night. Slept a good deal in saddle. Was very sleepy. Reached Montebello just before sunrise. Went in on all roads, dashing down at full gallop, but never an enemy. Expected to find 1200 there.

Saturday, 30th. In the morning was on picket in the town. Roasted corn for breakfast. Ate and slept on a porch to a jay-hawked store. Slept soundly. Went to the tannery and had a good wash. Got some peaches. Went out about noon and joined the main command, two miles out. Went out a mile where Capt. Welch was staying with a picket guard. Got plenty of melons to eat from a Mrs. Dade, whose husband was in the secesh army, a surgeon. Scouting parties went out ten and twelve miles each way, north and east. Went out and met our command. Slept in a house on floor. Strange.

Sunday, 31st. Word came early to march. Sergt. Co. K and I went out a mile and got breakfast. Three sons in the rebel army. Two good horses, but papers from Gen. Salomon guarded them. Sergeant had got them to cook a few chickens, on which we lunched. At first in the rear, then hurried on and got in the advance. Passed through Nevada about noon. Got some warm bread and butter. Encamped three miles out, where water was abundant but poor. Went out and helped kill and butcher beef. Borrowed some coffee till the wagon came up. Slept out till commenced raining. Got under wagon.

SEPTEMBER, 1862.

Monday, 1st. Reveille in the morning at 3 A. M. Breakfasted and started in the advance. Crossed Drywood and grazed. Got into camp in time for dinner. Sandy cooking, and several officers boarding with the Major. Found a letter from Ella Clark, very welcome. I have a high regard for her. Boys fully convinced that we would soon get mustered out of service. Band went to Leavenworth and home this morning. Boys think can get away in ten or fifteen days. In the evening wrote home. Boys all talking about home visits.

Tuesday, 2nd. Slept till rather late—up in time for Sandy's breakfast. During the day wrote to Fannie Andrews. Delos called in the morning and I read Ella's letter to him. Commented upon it. In the evening Charlie came up and I again reviewed Ella's letter with him. Read some in Shakespeare and the latest papers. Received letter from home. Last one from Minnie E. Tenney.

Wednesday, 3rd. Spent the morning visiting with various boys about the prospects of going home. Boys all in high spirits. Talk of paying Burnett $5 to help us get out. Blunt gone to Leavenworth. When he returns, he will try to get the order made. Wrote quite a lengthy letter to Fred Allen—strange boy. This last letter is better than any I ever received from him.

Thursday, 4th. Read some in "Othello.' Enjoyed some parts much. News came that Jackson had been taken with 20,000 men. Proved a lie. Tried to write a decently neat letter to Ella Clark, didn't succeed very well. Didn't finish in time for the evening mail. A good letter came from Fannie—a little behind time. Enjoyed it all. Read the latest Cleveland papers. News of the morning proved entirely false and we the ones whipped.

Friday, 5th. Went down to the river and washed. Charlie and Delos came up with a letter from Fred Allen, good. Proposed a plan for celebrating C's birthday. Report about camp that N. and M. were to be married. Rode to town. Went and saw some miscellaneous horses. Went to the hospital and saw Merrick and Lewis Emmons. Came back to camp in the rain. Sandy in the guardhouse for insolence. Got supper.

Saturday the 6th. Hugh White cooked for us. Sandy got out of the guardhouse. Hugh cooked first rate. Read and rested. In the evening received a letter from Melissa and a *Herald* from Uncle Albert announcing the marriage of Sister Minnie and giving an account of the Oberlin Commencement. He commended Will Hudson's "The Heroic Age," eloquent, earnest, and good. Read a little after "taps." Two *Independents.*

Sunday, 7th. At breakfast Capt. Seward and Bernard said Nettleton had returned. After breakfast saw him and received a note from Sister Melissa expressing her delight at the visit with "her dear Lu" and giving a description of Minnie's marriage. Sent a nice handkerchief. Read some during the day. In the evening Capt. Nettleton called, invited me to walk and gave me a minute description of his call at Chicago for Melissa; his visit on the road; visit and business with Tod, about colonel etc.; visit at home, and Minnie's marriage. Enjoyed all. Capt. Welsh interrupted us and I went to my quarters.

Monday, 8th. Wrote a short letter to Melissa. Considerable talk among officers about the colonelcy. Tod says Ratliff can not be colonel. So it is thought Major Miner will be the favored one. He says he will either *run* the regiment or be out of it! Considerable prejudice against him among the men on account of his course at Carthage in April and on the march from Flat Rock.

Tuesday, 9th. In the afternoon wrote to Ella Clark. Spent the day much as other days, reading, writing and loafing about hearing the news and waiting for the news. Report that Jackson had been captured. Evening papers contradicted the rumor and gave the Rebels the decided advantage. Driving our men towards Washington. Stirring news from Cincinnati. Battle at Lexington. Raw troops whipped out.

Wednesday, 10th. Word came to Major Burnett that the officers of the 2nd Ohio must be unanimous in choosing a colonel or someone from the regular army would be chosen. Officers met, ballot impromptu, Major Miner 7, Major Purington 7, Major Burnett 6. 1st ballot, Major Miner 7, Major Burnett 7, Major Purington 6. 2nd ballot, Major Burnett 12, Major Miner 8, Major P. having left the room, it being agreed that the one having the least votes should drop out. As agreed they made Burnett's vote unanimous. Miner seemed almost crazy, so surprised and disappointed. At 4 P. M. Major Purington left for Columbus with the papers. At 7 P. M. Major Miner started with his wife. He thought there had been underhanded work, so was going to lay the matter before the governor. If Burnett were commissioned he wished to be transferred. Nettleton stood by him. Very exciting. Officers and men full of wine and champagne at Burnett's expense. King under arrest in his tent, awful mad.

Thursday, 11th. Went down to the post commissary to get provisions. Saw Delos and went down with him to see Charlie. He agreed upon proposal to fill out a program Fred had sent on for the celebration of the 10th, Charlie's birthday, and anniversary of our enlistment. Issued rations during the day. Charlie came up in the evening and read what he had written. Liked it well. A complete farce to fool the boys. No mail for me in the evening.

Friday, 12th. Spent a good part of the day building me a bed. Got some boards at a house near camp. Drove down some stakes, made some crossbars and fastened them and laid boards on top, making a very comfortable cot. Archie, Ed and Reeve full of the Old Nick at night. Nothing of interest transpired. Report that we were bound soon for Ohio.

Saturday, 13th. In the afternoon a brigade left under General Salomon for Carthage. Dispatches from Col. Weir came, stating a fight was soon expected. I went down and got provisions for 88 men going from our regiment under Capt. Welch. No mail again. Read the latest papers.

Sunday, 14th. In the morning washed out some shirts, went to the creek and bathed and cleaned up generally. Mac Murray came up and spent the afternoon. He is a good boy. In the evening borrowed "Agnes of Sorrento" from Q. M. S. Mason and read till about 11 o'clock, by Capt. Welch's permission. The boys were awake late, talking and making a noise. Col. complained about so much noise being made.

Monday, 15th. Okie and I went to town and got provisions for five days' rations. Saw Haynes and went to his tent and took dinner with him. Had a good time. Read a letter from Fred Allen. Went into the hospital and visited Bigelow and Ohio boys. Saw Laundon and walked to camp with him. Full of fun as ever. Found Okie issuing rations. Helped during the rest of the afternoon.

Tuesday, 16th. A rainy, cold and dismal day. Brownell finished a little clamshell ring for me. I polished it up nicely. In the afternoon and evening read "John Brent." Enjoyed it well. Never read a more thrilling story of a ride. The description of the horse Don Fulano, and his powers was grand. The horse seemed the hero of the tale. Went to town and testified against a prisoner taken while out with Major Burnett. I pitied his poor wife, in tears. Believed the man Union.

Wednesday, 17th. Did very little in the morning. Charlie came up for the mail—not arrived. Played three games of checkers. At dinner talked of books read. Saw Capt. Nettleton, returned from Lamar to do some work. Intend to return with him, if Col. Abbey will permit it. Hope Buckshot will get well rapidly enough.

Thursday, 18th. Visited with Capt. Nettleton. Mail came bringing letter from Melissa. Wrote home and to Fannie Andrews.

Friday, 19th. In the morning went to the post commissary for provisions. Met on my return to camp the poor man we had prisoner, with his wife. I stopped and conversed with them. The woman at first seemed angry but she soon quieted. When I bid them goodbye, they invited me to call, if I ever came that way. At 4 P. M. left with detail of 60 men, Capt. Nettleton, Lieuts. Stewart and Niman for Springfield. Marched to the Drywood and encamped at 8 P. M. Lost the command and passed them and went through the woods.

Saturday, 20th. Reveille at sunrise. Boys got the coffee and bacon ready at the creek. Went down with Archie, washed and breakfasted.

As we passed the Big Drywood, we noticed our bed of rough crooked poles. Reached Lamar at 4 P. M. Orders for no man to enter any house or to disturb any property whatever. Some complaining at first but boys soon saw it was the better way. Capt. bought a sheep for breakfast. Noticed several rather tasty girls.

Sunday, 21st. Marched at sunrise. Ate breakfast at hotel. Went back after starting to look for Lt. Stewart. Met him coming. He had been out to stay with some friends and his horse had broken loose. Stopped after 15 miles at Mr. L.'s. Splendid spring, bathed in the cold water. Some of the mixed colored population so plentiful visited the Capt.'s tent. Two quite pretty little girls.

Monday, 22nd. Breakfast at 4:15 A. M. ' Marched at sunrise, passing through Greenfield, a very pretty little village. One encouraging sign, seldom seen of late months, a comfortable schoolhouse. Stopped two miles out of town, by a spring for dinner. Capt., one or two others and myself explored a cave near by. Found the layers of stone filled with shells and all sorts of stones. Several lizards lying about. Learned afterwards that some bushwhackers were watching us from the bluffs above. Here the country changed from boundless prairie to woodlands and hills. Like the variety better. Encamped for the night after riding 7 miles farther. Slept beneath a clump of trees with Archie.

Tuesday, 23rd. Up, dressed and work done and off at sunrise. Our course lay mostly through the woods till within nine miles of Springfield. Stopped at a splendid spring and lunched before striking the prairie. Capt. looked for cover and finally we camped there. Found plenty of peaches and hazelnuts. Archie, Chamberlain and I went with the Capt. in to Springfield. The 8 mile prairie looked more like civilization, good farms and farm houses. The highway to town reminded me of the road to Elyria. Enjoyed all well. All sociable. Passed the road from the north where Fremont's bodyguard charged down the lane. It was indeed interesting to be upon and see the ground where the brave fellows charged so nobly. Entered the village, passing encampments and entrenchments upon elevations on both sides of the road. Springfield a gay little place. Hotel full, stopped at a boarding house. Several officers there, music by them and one of their wives. Excellent. Humorous major.

Wednesday, 24th. After breakfast and taking care of our horses, we went to meet the command. A mile and a half out I waited for the rest to come. Got grapes to eat. Read the morning papers. Stirring news of a week for us. We three boys visited the earthworks. Saw artillery in Pea Ridge battle, one "Betsy" (howitzer) opened the battle second day. Good visit with some of the boys. Four regiments came in, Iowa, Wis., Ind., and Ill. About 25,000 troops in and about Springfield. Arriving all the time and working at entrenchments all the time. Salomon at Mt. Vernon. Hindman reported 40,000 strong at Cross Hollows.

Thursday, 25th. In the morning went to town and did some chores for the Capt. Made out a requisition and got corn. Helped Chamberlain get some clothing and issue it. Got me a blue overcoat, pants and lariat. Wrote brief letter to Fannie A. In P. M. detachment started for Mt. Vernon. Encamped at "Little York," 10 miles. Stayed behind with Porter and a few men and drew rations. I couldn't but notice the difference between the business officers here and at most posts. All pleasant and accommodating. Last night Capt. Nettleton promised me a place in his company as sergeant if I wanted after being mustered out. I was delighted. I should like it well. Overtook the command about an hour after camping. Became quite cold. Frightened a girl—called to inquire our way and surprised them. All seemed frightened.

Friday, 26th. Renewed our march at sunrise after breakfast. Our course lay mostly through the woods, a little over rough prairie. After 25 miles march, reached Mt. Vernon at 4 P. M. Gen Brown's command here mostly Mo. troops, one Arkansas regiment. Made requisition and drew corn. Pretty little town. Took supper with teamsters. Sold my old overcoat to Noah Long for $4, to be paid pay day. News came from Sarcoxie about a fight. Gen. Salomon. Good prospects ahead for a fight. Order to muster out staff has come.

Saturday, 27th. Up bright and early and on our way by sunrise. Marched till about noon, then halted and took a lunch. Found some good peaches and apples. Col. Small, Chief of Commissary of this dep't, passed us in a four-horse rig. Met Capt. Welch and command just before entering Sarcoxie. Seemed good to see the 2nd and 9th boys again. Found all excitement on account of an expected attack—up from 1 A. M. Troops moved to good position for defence. John Devlin missed at Greenfield. Received a note from Melissa. Visited among the boys and accomplished little. Took supper with Capt. Welch and Nettleton. Wier's Brigade arrived in the night.

Sunday, 28th. In the morning went to the creek and washed. 3rd Indian regiment came in. Chilly and misty. In the P. M. Archie, Chamberlain and I went out to hunt peaches. Went three miles, found no peaches. Plenty of good wild grapes. Got some milk from a minister. Written on house "Thou shalt not steal"— pretty lady. Read "Virginia" in Macaulay's Essays. In the evening Chamberlain read Horatius to us—lying under the oak and the fly cover of our tent. Enjoyed it.

Monday, 29th. Spent some time mending up my old clothes. After watering my horses had a visit with Trotter, taken prisoner at Fort Gibson—some interesting facts. 3,000 of the enemy, poor arms and worse clothes, frightened to death for fear of attack. Went out in P. M. for forage, 4 miles—corn. Saw a pretty, modest maiden weave, barefooted, blushed. Went off the road a mile and got peaches, the man a prisoner at Springfield. Wrote home. Order for detail of 25 men and officers for scout. I go. Success and fun ahead I hope. Boys start for Fort Scott.

Tuesday, 30th. Up long before sunrise and prepared for the scout. At 6 A. M. reported to Gen. Salomon. Wanted us to go 30 miles for coal! Boys all mad. When two miles from Carthage, men fired upon the wagons and us from the brush. Drew up into line but they did not show themselves. Passed through Carthage. Kansas train fired upon. Twelve men went back and met them. Reached the coal pit 13 miles west of C., about dark. Bunked with Capt. Nettleton. Rained next morning at 2 A. M. Went to wagon. Got quite wet. Saw Miss Hood and Shirley at their doors. Heard artillery firing. Proved to be a battle at Newtonia between a reconnoitering party of 500 and against 7,000 rebels. 2nd Ohio Battery covered itself with glory.

OCTOBER, 1862

Wednesday, 1st. Up at 5 o'clock. Commenced work at 5:25. Divided into three reliefs. I took charge for four hours. Boys went for provisions to a house three miles and got some breakfast at an empty house. Kept at work—after breakfasting at 10—till noon. Then marched homewards. Bivouacked 2 miles west of Carthage. Slept with A. B. N. My birthday anniversary (twenty-one). Charge of advance guard.

Thursday, 2nd. Renewed our march without breakfast. Scoured the woods for our old friends. Took five men and acted as skirmishers. No bird discovered. Reached camp in the P. M. Heard the boys relate their stories about the fight. Somewhat tired.

Friday, 3rd. Was going to the river to wash when I was detailed for picket guard. My first experience. Reported with 14 men. Relieved 12 on the Granby road and stayed there till 10 P. M. Drawn in to go with command. Whole body moved at 12. Got ready and fell in. N. gave me the command of a platoon of 20 men. Quite an honor! Horse had belly-ache. Bled him most to death. Had to leave him. Saw Sturtevant coming. Had the rear guard.

Saturday, 4th. Rainy and cold early. At sunrise got in sight of the enemy at Newtonia. Got batteries and men into position and fired upon them. The scene of the cannonading of our troops and the enemy was grand. The enemy in force are massed behind a fence and upon the plain near the woods. Our troops occupied the surrounding hills. The enemy at first scatter at the artillery fire, then collect again and commence a retreat. Rabb's Battery, infantry and cavalry follow. We had been support to this battery. Now we change to the 2nd Battery, our own, which had been shelling the town and driven 100 men out. Boys rush into town and soon report 23 wounded of the Dutch retaken. Soon camped for the day. Horses saddled. The enemy fight Rabb. He follows closely and pours shell into them. Boys lay down, half frozen, and slept. One adj. regiment and one Adj. General captured. Took one piece of artillery, a long wire arrangement. Got rails and water and had coffee. Horse grows stronger. Rode about town.

Sunday, 5th. In the morning rode about town and visited the different places of interest connected with the battle. Went into the stable where the Dutch were confined. At noon, after a hearty meal got up by us non-commissioned officers, started south. Capt. Seward came on and took command. N. officer of the day. Encamped on Big Indian, 15 miles from Pineville.

Monday, 6th. Got all ready to start. Ordered to lie still for a day or two for train supply to arrive. Went out on forage detail under Welch and Shattuck, four miles, got plenty of sweet potatoes and apples and honey. Sergt. Smith, Sturtevant and I got up a good meal. Had a good visit with the boys—very warm day. Shattuck said I had been reserved to stay in the regiment. Most of the boys mustered out. A regular officer, a captain, is to be our Colonel.

Tuesday, 7th. Commenced a letter to Fannie after the morning work. Went to the river and washed some shirts with Sergt. Smith, Co. K., a boy whom I like much from short acquaintance. Mail arrived about noon, letters from Fannies A. and H., Sarah Felton, Fred and George Ashman. Went to 9th Kansas surgeon to get medicine for Sturtevant. Finished good Fannie's letter. Sick with carbuncle and I with boils afflicted. I am so disappointed that I can not see her and home friends this fall. Bunked with Capt. N., Co. K. tent. Read part of a letter from Melissa, good sister. Read the late Cleveland papers. We lay and talked about boy and girl friends.

Wednesday, 8th. Commenced drizzling in the morning and kept it up all day. I was detailed to act as Sergt. Major, which pleased me much. Went with picket detail and reported to Stewart at Salomon's headquarters. Went down and saw Battery boys, and Archie, Reeve, Brooks, and Mason. Good time. In the P. M. Major Burnett with detail started back to Fort Scott. Major sick. Our cook among the detail, so we boys had to commence cooking ourselves. Kept raining all night. Battery paid off and very noisy.

Thursday, 9th. Orders came to be ready to march at 7 A. M., we to draw our pay before starting. Hastened breakfast and we were paid during the day. Awful wet and muddy, cold and chilly. Wore overcoats and shivered. Delayed the march. In the evening a Kansas officer of the day became frightened and alarmed the camp. Got saddled and sat two hours in the rain. Boys mad. Some of the boys started for the fort with the sick.

Friday, 10th. Sky clear and quite cold. Lieut. Spencer and I issued a good amount of clothing. About noon orders came to march. After a hurried dinner, saddled and lay about until most sundown. Rear guard. Had to wait till every wagon had started. Very dull business; probably the advance guard was in camp before we started. Every mile wagons were in to the hubs in mud. At midnight halted, saddles on, so many teams had given out. Fed and lay down with oilcloth for a coverlet. Had lent my shawl to Sergt. Randall.

Saturday, 11th. Up before sunrise and got roasted potatoes and honey for breakfast. Marched at sunrise. Passed Wier's and Cloud's Brigades at five miles—and Schofield's. Encamped at Ferguson Springs, eight miles from Cassville. Arrived at 3 P. M. Feasted and rested.

Sunday, 12th. Cleaned my revolver and dried my cartridges. Indians had preaching by their Chaplain. Seemed good to hear singing and preaching even in an unknown tongue. Took a bundle of letters to headquarters. Smith went with me, a right good fellow. Went to spring and bathed.

Monday, 13th. Made the detail to go for forage in charge of Sergt. Smith. Went along in wagon. Got some cabbage and talked with some women while the boys loaded oats. Oh what suffering and misery this war is making. But there is an end to be gained at all hazards. Were it otherwise it could hardly be endured. Went out in the afternoon and bought some apples and lard. Ball and Smith were the company. Pitied the poor woman and her children.

Tuesday, 14th. Saw the Lieuts. play poker a while. Was surprised to see Will Bushnell come up to headquarters boldly with cigar in his mouth. Somewhat changed. In the P. M. wrote a short letter to Fannie A.

Wednesday, 15th. Paymaster started for the fort—9th Kansas and 3rd Wis. escort—made the picket detail. Man wanted to buy salt at most any price—the article is very scarce.

Thursday, 16th. Spent the day reading various nonsensical books. Rather a lazy day on the whole. Capt. Nettleton returned. Whole detachment ordered to "Hazel Hollow" on picket duty. Six miles, advance guard. Slept in a vacant house. Quite a confab with a Kansas Lieut.

Friday, 17th. Aroused at 3 A. M. Killed a calf for breakfast. Quite a time trying to kill a pig. Marched at sunrise. Whole command gone from old camp. Rear guard. At noon arrived at Kritsville. Stayed till 10 P. M. Marched again at 10 and moved till near morning. Lay down a few minutes by a little fire. Before daybreak passed the Arkansas line, Elkhorn Tavern, and stopped for a cold lunch on the old Pea Ridge battle ground. Interesting—trees considerably marred by bullets. Shot, grape, and shell picked up by different boys as relics of the battle.

Saturday, 18th. Lay about two or three hours, then went into camp on the rise near the spring. Marks of a large rebel camp. At noon orders came for the Capt. to go with 50 men to Bentonville, to learn locality and number of the enemy. I went. Started about dusk. Called at a house to know distance. Two or three girls. Looked like a cousin. Shattuck with advance guard two miles ahead. Boys said he was a coward, rode way behind the men. Halted and fed. Heard artillery moving. Capt. ordered me to take four men and guide and learn what it was. It sounded as though it were moving from the southwest. After going a mile or two, we were halted by a picket, close at hand. Ordered one to advance, dismount, and give the countersign. Dared not risk it. Asked who they were. "Federals." Asked who we were. "Federals." "Advance then." What division did they belong to? Gen. Heron's. Never heard of him. What brigade? Would not tell. Ordered them to tell or would march my battalion on them. Didn't care a damn, advance or he would fire. Advanced horseback, a couple of rods. Ordered to dismount or he would shoot. Couldn't see it and shied behind a tree. Told him to listen and I would give the countersign—"Allen." "What! *Allen*—never! that won't do here." Did you understand it, "Allen"? Bang, bang, bang, bang. Boys wheeled and ran. I had sent two back to report to the captain. I wheeled and got behind another tree a rod back. Cocked my revolver and fired once, then wheeled and ran. The bullets followed mighty thick. Met the command and reported the facts. One of the boy's horses was shot in the leg and abandoned. Capt. turned back and went back the same road to camp. Capt. discovered he had given me the "parole" instead of countersign, a mistake that would not happen again for an age, but one that might have caused a great deal of trouble. Started for Bentonville on another road. Slept two hours. N. had cautioned me to be very careful and not approach any force but to learn from families. Proved to be our men—Heron's.

Sunday, 19th. Fed when out two or three miles. Got some apples. When we reached Heron's division, I called at his quarters and inquired if he could give the Capt. any information. Very pleasant. Stylish. A fur coverlet, neat stove and desk, cigars and very fine dress. Said that the rebel pickets were within a third of a mile of ours the night before. Wouldn't pass his pickets, hardly advisable, do as he thought fit. Went through to the town, 100 of our Indians there. Called at two houses and had very pleasant and spicy chats with two girls, one pleasant lady. Southern officers left their "regards" for any "Feds" that might call. Believed the south right. Would fight if a man. Got back to camp at dark and found good letter from home and Fannie. Pleased with the whole trip and incidents. Quite a laugh with the captain. Like Arkansas first rate considering—good farms and orchards—pretty girls.

Monday, 20th. In the morning watered my horse and cleaned up his feet. Capt. N. told me something very acceptable from Col. Ratliffe. Read the *Lorain News* and *Cleveland Herald*. In the P. M. wrote to Fannie.

Tuesday, 21st. Spurgeon went out with forage detail. Bill Smith lost $15. Circumstances as follows: Capt. had given him some money to pay the boys. We lay on the blankets conversing when Sheldon came up, and Bill pulled out his money and paid him. He had showed me the money a little while before. All three lay down, Bill and I side by side and S. a little farther down. All at once Sheldon attracted mine and B.'s attention to a holster, asking if I had lost my revolver. After we had examined, I left. In five or ten minutes Nick called us to dinner. We ate and I went a few rods into the woods, leaving B. by his horse. When I came back B. had lost his money. We looked all about. Soon he told me he suspicioned Sheldon. I tried to find him. Finally found him playing poker, 2 or 3 P. M. Stolen at noon.

Wednesday, 22nd. After breakfast went out on Culver's horse foraging with Spurgeon and Bushnell. Got some apples and a sheep. At one house where we stopped, two sons were forced into the army. The people felt very badly. The old lady, 70 years old, prayed very earnestly and loudly for mercy and protection—quite touching.

Thursday, 23rd. Bill and I did some washing. Johnson, Co. E, invited us to dinner—pork and crackers. Made inquiries about

Sheldon. Found he had not sold his pony—never found it. Claimed he sold it to get "poker money." Said he went immediately to playing poker with Co. F after leaving here. They said it was the middle of the P. M. N. asked him in and saw him. Would not admit it. Read *St. Louis Republican* of the 20th. Surprised to see Ohio so Democratic. Hope it won't influence the president.

Friday, 24th. Got the morning reports and combined them. Helped pitch the tent and clean up. Turned very chilly—appearance of cold weather. News of a fight, Black and Cooper, few particulars, 200 prisoners and 4 cannon. During the night three or four inches of snow fell.

Saturday, 25th. A cold wintry morning. Never remember of seeing snow so early. Snow fell during the forenoon. Afternoon more moderate. Night cold. Built a big fire of brush. Comfortable.

Sunday, 26th. Cold but pleasant morning. Made a forage detail to go out with brigade teams. Several of the boys played poker. Read some in Pope. The Iliad. Gibbs strange fellow. Came into the army a professing Christian, a class leader, today he is playing poker with the boys. I occasionally hear an oath from him. Never saw a man more egotistical. Eats more than any three men. Still a harmless fellow. Good talk about going home with Co. H boys around a big fire.

Monday, 27th. Report that we are to go to Camp Cleveland, boys all pleased. Made picket detail and heard the officers discuss military tactics. Some rather ignorant. A beautiful day, warm and pleasant in the sun. Cold in the shade. Capt. N. officer of the day. Small train came from the fort and recruits for Battery. No news brought about going to Ohio and worse still, no mail. Pity that none of the 2nd Ohio care enough about their fellow soldiers to send their letters to them. Orders to march next morning at 6. Boys played poker till midnight—precious little sleep.

Tuesday, 28th. Reveille at three. Breakfasted and were on the move at 6 in the advance—bound for Maysville. Capt. kept me running a good deal. Passed through Bentonville about noon. Saw several whom I had seen on my other visit there. Passed along two miles. Got plenty of rambow apples at an orchard. Encamped in an orchard. Had to go two miles for water. An old man showed us protection papers, signed by Curtis, given because he went for the old Constitution.

Wednesday, 29th. Up at daybreak. In the rear guard. Waited several hours for the train to get by. Stewart and Jacobah came up and joked. Read a *Leslie*. Very slow work today, so many halts. Can not admire Capt. Seward. Had the impudence to keep me carrying water for him to drink. Lingered to guard a sutler, whose stock he tried—the miserable poison. Advance guard fired upon near a mill, three stories. Got into camp at Price's old headquarters three miles from Maysville—an old Free Love Institute, they say. Had a little conversation with our guide of the 1st Arkansas. Bill and I went to work to get supper—soon others joined us.

Thursday, 30th. In the rear guard again. Till noon getting to Maysville, a little place, mostly forsaken, a few old people. Tried to catch a hog. Didn't succeed. Letters from home, Sept. 30th, and an *Independent*. Read *Lorain News*. Little article about N. and me being taken prisoners.

Friday, 31st. Reveille between two and three A. M. Breakfasted and off in advance at five on backward track. Reported that our rations had run short, a train been captured, etc.—again that we were to join Schofield, etc. Nothing of interest till we reached camp 10 miles from Bentonville, near where they were fired upon before. I had gone ahead to see if there was a spring up a ravine, advance a little ahead—halted—suddenly, "bang, bang, bang." Drew revolver and waited. Nothing appeared. Saw Hoppy, Co. B, rnnning by—followed. Heard him telling a woman to show him where to find the rebels. I told him we knew enough and two of us rushed up the hill and others followed. Burr, Co. G, rushed ahead. I saw nobody, soon heard shouting—Burr—saw him and followed. Got off half a mile. Foolishness to pursue so far with such a start. Followed a distance and was returning when we met Capt. Welch's command. Scouted the woods some and went to camp. One man was overtaken, his arms taken and himself shot. Got dinner at the house. Considerable excitement.

NOVEMBER, 1862

Saturday, 1st. Lay in camp. Men save ours were mustered for pay. The boys went out and got the body of the Butternut, and buried him in the cornfield—shot in the neck. Wrote home. Bought a jacket of T. R. S. Saw Major P.'s ring we boys have bought for him—nice. Went to bed rather early. Commenced a letter to Fannie. Interrupted to go out scouting. In the P. M. Capt. Welch with Stewart and Lisering and 25 men went out seven or eight miles expecting to find some bushwhackers seen by a 9th Wis. Found nobody. Stopped at three houses and got horses. One girl, husband pressed into rebel army, plead so earnestly for her pony. It was touching. Finally the captain gave it back. Reached camp at 1 A. M.

Sunday, 2nd. In the morning read Oct. *Atlantic*. In the P. M. finished Fannie's letter. Detail came for Lt. or trusty Srgt. to go out with 30 men as escort to brigade forage teams. Officers said they proposed sending me. I agreed if they wished it, to start at 7:30 A. M.

Monday, 3rd. Orders to march at 7. Up at 3 A. M. Breakfasted and in saddle at 7. Advance guard. Marched 8 or 10 miles to Osage Spring 5 miles south of Bentonville, Ark., on Burns' farm. Got the lady to bake some bread. Went out and killed some chickens. Quite tired at night.

Tuesday, 4th. During the day got a report of horses in detachments. Bill and I washed some clothes. Before dark orders came for a company of 2nd O. V. C. to report to Col. Weir with 3 days' rations. Capt. N. went with 40 men, I along. Reported and after waiting an hour or two returned till daylight the next morning. Got a good sleep. Caught some cold from damp clothes.

Wednesday, 5th. Up at 3 A. M. After breakfast started for Jones' Mills, with two companies of 6th Kansas. Some 10th Kansas—two howitzers. Pitched tents and made ourselves comfortable.

Thursday, 6th. In the morning went out with four men to forage three and one-half miles south. Load of oats for 6th and 2nd. The owner just up from Vanburen with two bushels of salt. Seemed to have considerable information, so took him in to Capt. Quigg. One of the boys met me with my horse to go with Capt. and 20 men on scout. Had to gallop a good distance to catch up. Within seven miles of Fayetteville, fifteen miles distant from camp, took a prisoner from Col. Armstrong's conscripts. He was at home—on furlough—been sick. Out with horse saddled, talking with his wife washing by the clear stream of water. She seemed a very pretty lady, pitied her—innocent looking man. Before reaching Fayetteville two miles out, Capt. sent me with three men, Porter, Morgan and Shaw. After going a mile, found a fire; soon spied two mounted men with glistening guns around a point of woods, watching us and quietly disappearing. Sent back word. No answer and went on. After half a mile we got within sight of them, but did not know whether to shoot or not—no instructions. They took a final look and went pellmell down the hill. Sent word to Capt. No instructions again. Neared town—women and girls at windows and doors—perfectly ignorant! Didn't know that there were any secesh in town. Passed by a large house. Big negro woman stood on the stoop, showing her teeth and pointing to town ominously, and shook her head. Such were appearances. By the tannery stood a grey horse, looking like the one the picket was riding; were discussing whether to take it or not, when two men came out, citizens apparently; said there were but two or three dozen in town. Capt. halted his command and overtook us and asked what we had learned. Told us not to go further for the present. Turn back if he whistled. After enquiries whistled and turned back. Porter and I kept in the rear in hope that they would follow us. Three miles out saw a man at a house near by. Rode out and learned that he had charge of a hospital at F. Had no papers to show it. Took him to Capt. He brought him to camp. Rode along beside him all the way in. Had been in the service one year last May, on Raines' staff. Dressed in a field officer's uniform, coat, black pants, neat gloves and cap and patent leather boots. Was perfectly sanguine of success eventually—perfectly posted in regard to our movements. A lady was out riding with him, out to see some sick. Very indignant. Waited at a private house with him for supper, while Capt. went to camp and back. Ladies very much pleased to see him.

Very sure he is an officer of rank. Said he had no commission as
surgeon. Showed an appointment as assistant surgeon by surgeon
of 8th Div. Mo. State Guards.

Friday, 7th. Capt. Quigg after examination released "Dr.
Brissel" without a parole. Capts. Lucas and Nettleton and all the
boys think the man fooled us—black hair and whiskers, good looking and very gentlemanly. Heard no mean expression. When I
bade him good morning, three miles out, he shook hands with me,
and said if we ever got into trouble, he would be glad to do what he
could for us. At 11 A. M. got orders to march with two days' rations, at 12 M. Had no bake kettles and no rations but beans and
flour. Got me a canteen full of bean soup. Ready at noon. 25 2nd
Ohio and 25 6th Kansas. Had charge of platoon of twelve—our
boys. Went west, trotted most of the time. Got to the tannery at
3 P. M. 13th at work getting out the hides from the vats. Soon Col.
Cloud with 250 or 300—and all went to work. A grand scene.
Would like to see it represented in *Leslie*. Burned up twenty or
twenty-five thousand dollars worth of property. Started in about
dark—southwest. Went 15 or 20 miles, mostly on a trot. Then
stopped at a field of corn and lay down by fires till 4 or 5 A. M.
Changed platoons to get 2nd Ohio together. Capt. N. with Kansas
platoons.

Saturday, 8th. Still southwest to Rhea's Mills ten miles and
then breakfast—fresh beef and no salt. Col. Philips here two
nights before, two of his Indians shot. Two girls wounded severely by rebels firing into a house. After breakfast went to my
own men with Capt. Gave Capt. Lucas detachment—the advance.
Direction southeast. Rode 7 or 8 miles to Cane Hill—Boonsboro—
hilly country. Pickets fired upon at Cane Hill. Captured a secesh
saddle and equipments. Went into town. Col. made inquiries and
moved on. Col. always with the advance. Went a couple of miles
and bang, bang, went guns. Soon 60 or 70 men showed themselves
in the woods on a hill half a mile to our left. Sharp's rifles and carbines came into play—no effect—distance too great. Howitzers
came up, cavalry fell back into the woods and shell went whizzing
over the cornfield. They skedaddled. One fellow whom 8 or 10 men
started for, ran forward and threw down the fence and then ran
back behind a tree. Blue overcoat. Did not take him. Bold fellow.
They took two or three prisoners. After some delay, Col. learned
that the rebels, 400 or 500, were one mile farther on. Went on a
mile, saw pickets on a distant hill. Sharpshooters advanced, and
then command moved forward. Found camp just vacated—fires
still burning. Went over the Boston mountains. Over the mountains at the foot, our extreme advance came in sight of rear guard
of the enemy. A charge was ordered and away we flew with loose
reins and set spurs, up hill and down hill, across and back again
Cove Creek, a very rough road. After three miles we began to see
stirrups, blankets, corn and a thousand things strewn along the
road. The Col. was up with us. He commenced yelling, which
was kept up by all the men. More things scattered along. After

ten miles in the midst of excitement, back came a volley of shot and bullets from the bush at a point a little elevated just ahead of us. The extreme advance fell back a few rods. Up we rode upon a charge into the bush as we were ordered. We rode up and fired away. Still farther up into the road we were ordered. We hurried up and formed along the road facing the bush. The bullets whistled merrily for a season. Not over 20 or 25 were up. We fired all our rounds, then a sabre charge was ordered. We had our sabres drawn and ready for a charge, when Capt. Lucas' horse was shot and the rebels were running by a byroad. The color-bearer was shot through the head and colors captured, 13 stars—two others were reported killed. Waited for signs of the enemy, but in vain. Went down and helped about unloading wagons and burned them. None of us harmed. Started back. Returned 4 or 5 miles and camped. All the boys got some little trap—baggage and equipments of Mo. Provost Guard commanded by Provost Gen. McDonald. Private correspondence of Col. Sevier of Marseilles, Mo. One excellent letter from his Aunt Phil on the war.

Sunday, 9th. Recrossed the mountain, after a breakfast of hoecake of meal captured from the enemy. Went by another road direct for Fayetteville. Very rough roads and poor country most of the way. Encamped in sight of the town.

Monday, 10th. After breakfast—poor beef—went into town. Advance with secesh flag and a dozen rushed to it and showed passes from Raines and McDonald—one had taken an oath to shoot every picket, straggler, messenger or pilot he could. Citizens came in for protection. Several recruits came in with guns. 6th sang John Brown and Dixie. Got back to the Mills at noon—tired out and chafed up badly—without anything to eat to speak of but fresh beef—and that seldom enough. On a trot most of the time—tried to rest some. Letters from home and Fannie.

Tuesday, 11th. Capt. went to camp and left me in charge of Det. Wrote letters home and to Fannie. Felt most sick during the day. Did little. Read the *Independent* in the evening.

Wednesday, 12th. Lay around most of the day, feeling most sick. Went into the mill. Capt. returned and Bushnell and several boys for a visit. Said Major Purington sent his love at three different times to me. Made me feel good. Sky clear again. Yesterday cloudy and cold.

Thursday, 13th. Felt most sick. Had a slight chill—I suppose—afterwards feverish. Moved camp late in the afternoon on account of a report by an old man who came in with two conscript deserters to join our army, that a force of cavalry of 9,000 were moving north, then at Cane Hill. Before midnight orders came to join our commands. Got breakfast and saddled at 2 A. M.

Friday, 14th. At 2 A. M. moved a mile to the other mill, then lay down by the fire till sunrise. Marched most of the day in the woods, southwest. Found the command encamped at some good springs. I felt very tired and sick, sore throat and chill. Went to

bed early. Capt. Seward came in. Had been with 200 men, some
2nd O. to Cane Hill. Had a skirmish with enemy. None hurt.

Saturday, 15th. Alarm at 4. Saddled and packed up. At nine
in line on account of firing heard. Proved to be Capt. Greenough
fighting a scouting party. Enemy moved camp about a mile to the
prairie west, a little nearer the other brigades. I still felt pretty
bad—another slight chill. Lay down by fire but could not keep
warm. Fever some worse in the night.

Sunday, 16th. It commenced raining early and kept it up all
day. Felt weak and miserable. Still did my duties as sergeant
Maj. Some seventy odd contrabands came in from Indian Territory—Creeks. A good many had arms. They had a skirmish with
bushwhackers. Seven of their men killed.

Monday, 17th. Made the accustomed details. Papers from
home, *Herald,* the 8th. Archie gave me a bottle of pickles. Lay
still in the tent. Boys got a stove and had a good fire. At night
feverish again. Very hot fire.

Tuesday, 18th. Still rainy and muddy. Lay in the tent unless
obliged to get out. Almost homesick. Body guard came back.
Sore throat.

Wednesday, 19th. Wrote short letters home and to Fannie.
Cleared up about noon. Bought a pack of envelopes and a little
ᐱndy. Moved camp up on the hill to the Masonic Hall. In the
evening had a chill, took some quinine.

Thursday, 20th. Another pleasant day. Made a detail of 20
men, one sergeant, two corporals, picket, 15 for forage. Chicken
broth and dumplings for dinner.

Friday, 21st. Took three powders and at night had another
chill. Drank some capsicum tea. Slept pretty well.

Saturday, 22nd. Took a blue pill and three quinine powders
during the day. Kept very quiet. Went to bed early and rested
well. Still did my usual duties. Letter from home.

Sunday, 23rd. In the morning commenced Macaulay's "Warren Hastings." Kept still during the day and commenced to feel
like myself again. Had a good visit with A. B.

Monday, 24th. Read 15 or 20 pages in "Hastings." Made the
details. Got my horse shod during the afternoon. Rebel Captain
and 25 men with flag of truce came in with sealed orders for Gen.
Blunt. Some shrewd fellows they say.

Tuesday, 25th. Went over to see secesh but they had gone.
Shattuck went on detail as chief of commissary. Capt. Seward said
I must make out morning reports after this. Major Purington received orders to proceed at once with his command to Evansville.
Blair's Battery practised with artillery—shell. Major and detachment started out on a scout, an odd old genius on a white horse as
guide. Went by a byroad. When 4 or 5 miles from Cincinnati,
crossed a byroad where 400 or 500 had passed. I had charge of
advance. Before going a half mile, saw two "butternuts." Wheeled
and ran like fun. Followed about a mile and learned from a family

that 4 or 5 had passed not more than ten minutes before. Reported back. Followed most of the time at a trot. When we had gone two miles, we struck the main road and here the rebels fired at us from the brush. I had 20 men. All wheeled but 3 men. Soon rallied. Moved on a few rods and saw 15 or 20 in line by the bushes ready to fire. They fired and we in line fired in return. Soon Major sent word to reload. While reloading the rebels crossed the byroad to the main road. We followed a few hundred rods and were ordered to halt. Soon some of the 3rd Wis. came up, and passed dismounted. When 5 or 6 rods ahead a volley was poured into them, wounding two. Two days after, we heard that they were 400 of Quantrell's men and that they ran to Cane Hill, also that 4,000 went over the mountains. Also that we killed two men. Bivouacked without fires.

Wednesday, 26th. Capt. Welch came up with 15 men and Capt. Greenough with 50 men, increasing our force to 180. At daylight moved on south. Passed through Cane Hill and followed the Division train, which we supposed the rebs were after. Officers feared that they had run into the rebel camp at Dutch Mills. Found them on 3 or 4 miles. Went on with them 3 or 4 miles, then went on alone till within a mile of the mills. Then Major and Capt. Greenough went on alone and discovered two regiments in direction of Cane Hill moving north at a trot. We turned back by untraveled roads and reached camp at 9 P. M.

Thursday, 27th. Up at 3 A. M. and ready to march at sunrise. Went as advance of whole division. I had charge of advance, 20 men. Moved south till within a mile of Rhea's Mills. Fed ourselves and horses at Cin. and went on. The scouts were in advance most of the time, saw no enemy. Got some nice apples at a house. Went into camp on the hill and went out as picket on the road to the south. Slept without fires.

Friday, 28th. Started out at 5 as advance, but soon were ordered back, as rear guard. Division moved by another road. While at Rhea's Mills we could hear the cannon roar. How aggravating. Moved on to Cane Hill. Learned that quite a battle had taken place there and on the mountain beyond. Went to a house and got some provisions. Built fires and rested, after some fresh pork and meal cakes.

Saturday, 29th. Other brigades returned to Cane Hill, where we had been retained as reserve. Our brigade was ordered back to Rhea's Mills. Moved back and camped north of the mill. Got the mail from the train just arrived. Six letters, two from Fannie, 3 from home and 1 from Will. Happy boy. Several papers.

Sunday, 30th. Had to make out morning report and field report and details. Was kept quite busy all day. In the evening wrote to Fannie A.

DECEMBER, 1862

(Still in Arkansas, near Bentonville)

Monday, 1st. Day cold, like snow. Kept quite busy all day. Did some washing. In the evening wrote home a hasty letter.

LETTER FROM L. H. TENNEY TO HIS MOTHER AND SISTERS

Camp at Ray's Mills, Arkansas, Dec. 1, 1862.

My Dear Friends:

I guess you wonder a little why you don't hear from your soldier boy. Well, I presume you will wonder often if we stay in the field and keep up our scouts and marches. Since last Tuesday, my regular day for writing and the day I intended to write, I haven't had a minute's opportunity for writing until yesterday, and then I was busy till night, when I was too tired to write.

Tomorrow another train leaves for the Fort. Several sick boys return. I should have liked to go back for comfort, but after all as long as there is a man in the Regiment in the field, I want to be there, too, though there must be some suffering and sacrifices.

Today I had an opportunity to go into the Brigade Commissary as clerk and get $12 a month extra. Lt. Shattuck, brother of Nina, is acting Brigade Commissary and wanted me to help him. N. thought I hadn't better go. I don't care much. Should have liked the little spondulics though.

Sunday night when we arrived here I found six letters, three from home, two from Fannie, and one from Will. I guess I was happy that night and as usual dreamed of home. Thede, I thank you very much for your good long letter. You did me proud. Please do so more.

I see by the papers that Col. Ford has received his just deserts. I enjoy all the particulars of the home circle visits, calls and town gossip. It is always my Thanksgiving Day when my letters come. My letters both received and written have been quite irregular of late and I presume will be in future.

During the last week we have been on our horses most of the time. My ague left me just in time. Tuesday and Wednesday our detachment was out on a scout down below here a little. We had the pleasure of overtaking 400 of Quantrell's men Tuesday night and turned their course from the north southward on double quick. The Major had 115 men. I had the pleasure of being in the advance and had two or three little skirmishes with the rear guard. None of us, how I don't know, was hurt. Afterwards some of the 3rd Wis. were sent ahead of us and when a few rods in advance were fired into from the bushes and two of the men wounded.

I suppose you have heard by this time of the fight at Cane Hill and beyond. Thursday our detachment went in advance of the whole division but Friday we were rear guard and the Brigade was left at Cane Hill as a reserve. It was aggravating to hear the roar of artillery and not partake. There will be some hard fighting if we go over the mountains.

I have no ambition to die immediately or anything of that sort. I guess life, real life, is precious to the most wicked, but I do long to have our armies hasten on to victory or defeat. If Schofield's forces join ours, I believe our success will be sure, though earned by a good deal of sacrifice.

Lt. Shattuck has been acting Adj. but has gone now. So I have enough to do his duties and those of Sergt. Major.

I have just been out doors and I could see the "fire on the mountains" along our line of march over the hills from the North.

Tonight the air is cold and the fire in our little stove is comfortable and cozy enough. We are getting well used to bivouacking in the open air with few blankets and no fires. When out scouting we go without fires so as not to let the enemy know our movements. Sometimes we can't get much sleep,

THE TENNEY FAMILY, OBERLIN, 1855

though. Don't you believe I occasionally long to creep into that soft bed at home and to sit down at our little supper table? Oh no, never!

Please excuse another hasty letter. The *Independents* have come as usual. I presume we will remain here a few days and then go over the mountains. I hope so.

The boys are all talking as loudly as can be and I can't think overmuch straight.

With much love,

Luman.

Tuesday, 2nd. Saw Shattuck. $9.00 extra. Refused. Up early with orders to report with the train to Fort Scott. Most of the boys glad. Marched to Cincinnati (Ark.).

Wednesday, 3rd. Met the train coming down—some delay. Sorted out the mail. Several letters for me, Fannie, Lucy, Fred, Charley. Marched to our old camp on Lindsley Prairie.

Thursday, 4th. Marched to Maysville and camped in town. Cold and uncomfortable. Went to the Secesh hospital and got supper of the family. Good visit with the surgeon. Invited me to stay over night.

Friday, 5th. As we neared Cowskin a good many bushwhackers showed themselves, but at a distance. Camped three miles north of Elk Mills.

Saturday, 6th. Up at 3 A. M. and off at daylight as usual. Reached Neosho at 8 P. M. Charlie and I got supper at a private house, secesh. Got into a little fuss with Mart Cole in regard to forage. He pushed me off the wagon and I reported him. He was tied up to a tree for an hour. The Major asked me why I did not knock him down. Afterwards I was put under arrest for investigation.

Sunday, 7th. Up and off as early as usual. I carried a carbine and rode as usual in the ranks. Saw a large flock of wild turkeys. Advance ran after three "butternuts." Took two horses. Saw any number of rebels around Diamond Grove. Encamped four miles west of Sherwood.

Tuesday, 9th. Saw a good many rebels about Turkey Creek. Camped 30 miles from fort.

Wednesday, 10th. Maj. P., Capt. S., Capt. N. with 25 men came into the fort. Arrived about 2 P. M. Got supper at Mrs. Harris'—very kind. Other detachment came in. Several boys drunk.

Friday, 12th. Issued clothing in the morning. Bathed. Marched in P. M. to Fort Lincoln. Took charge of 10 soldier prisoners.

Saturday, 13th. Marched at daylight. Had a cold ride, chilled through. Reached Twin Springs in time for supper, before dark. Slept soundly under tent. Rained a little during the night.

Sunday, 14th. Reveille at 4 and off a little before sunrise. Reached Spring Hill at 4 P. M. Charlie Ball and I went out to a house and got supper. Kept us till dark. Got cider.

Monday, 15th. Reached the Kansas river about noon and got crossed before dark. Went five miles to the edge of the prairie and camped. Pleasant place.

Tuesday, 16th. Went on as usual 18 miles and waited for the Major to meet us. Went in and camped between the fort and town. Went down to the Planters House for supper with Sergts. Love, Pierce and Archie. Had my hair cut. Went with Love to theatre. All the officers there. Play was Willow Copse. Very good, also a farce.

(Fort Leavenworth)

Wednesday, 17th. In the morning took the prisoners to the fort and hurried over to Col. Burris. Rode up to south part of town and found Cousin Austin's. Stayed to dinner. Had a good visit. Made me promise to call in the evening if we stayed in town. Went over in the evening. Lost my way. Found Mr. Buckingham of the *Bulletin* there. Read some of his letters for Augusta for the Baptist benefit. Augusta played on her guitar and sang, also on the piano. Enjoyed the evening very much indeed. Leona a very pretty girl. Had a lunch and apples, good feather bed. Had nice peach sauce.

Thursday, 18th. After a good breakfast, cousin went up to camp with me. Officers gone. Went back to town and the Planters. Introduced him to Capts. Seward and Welch. Went about town with him. Enjoyed all. Went to fort and helped in turning over property. In the evening went with Bill Porter and Nichols to theatre. Officers there. "Pizarro." Rolla played well. Wanted to go to Festival but dared not.

Friday, 19th. Up at 4 A. M. Off on foot for the ferry at 7. Boys started with the Indian warwhoop. All in good cheer. Quite a long walk. Bid Kansas goodbye before noon and were off on hog cars at Weston. At St. Joseph got a lunch, pie, bread and ham. Got some hay. Bill and I fixed a bed. 34 in a freight car, all lay down, piled top of one another.

Saturday, 20th. Reached the river about noon. After some delay were ferried over and marched to the cars. Then waited in a cold wind and occasional sleet for two hours, then marched through the town east to barracks. Got some coffee and hard bread. In the evening had a good fire. Most of the boys up town. Capt. invited me to Quincy House but preferred to stay in camp. Quincy a very neat town—city.

Sunday, 21st. After cleaning up in the morning went up town with Brown. Promenade about the leading streets. Then left him and went to the 2nd Congregational Church and Sabbath School. Seemed very much like home but not so full and interesting. Heard a very practical sermon on the use of wealth. The congregation seemed very intelligent, aristocratic and up with the times. Seemed good to see some civilization again. Took dinner with A. B. at Quincy House. Wrote home. At 2 P. M. went to depot and loaded into freight cars. Off at 4 P. M. At Springfield at 9 P. M. Took passenger cars.

Monday, 22nd. Arrived at Lafayette at 10 A. M. Went to a bakery for dinner. Pie and bread and butter. Remained till 2

P. M. Herb. Kenaston came aboard and went with us to Indianapolis. Had a good visit with him, not much change. Told a pleasing incident about correspondence with Mary Dascomb. Arrived at
Indianapolis at dark, only an hour or two delay. Lunch.

Tuesday, 23rd. Arrived at Dayton at 2 A. M. Went into a
hotel. Landlord very insolent. Turned down the gas on the Major.
Major told him he was the meanest man he ever saw. He intimated
that he was secesh. I told him to say he was half secesh and we
would clean him out so soon he wouldn't know it. Kept the light
burning. Boys stole a good many things. Went around Dayton a
little. A very neat city. Liked it well but couldn't go the "Vallan-
dighamism" of the place. Arrived at Columbus at 3 P. M. Remained with baggage to take care of Major's things. After dark
when I got to camp, stayed with Bill.

Wednesday, 24th. Went and saw the boys and Col. Abbey.
Moved my things over to his quarters. Spent the day looking
around and seeing the boys. In the evening wrote to Fannie Andrews.

Thursday, 25th. Rather a quiet day for Christmas. Wonder
how the folks at home have spent the day, happily I hope. Received a note through A. B. Went over and had a good visit with
him. Told me some encouraging things. Not much faith! In the
evening wrote some. Saw Dwight Burrell. The day has been
cloudy and damp. I have caught cold by some means. The air is
getting colder this evening and the wind getting into the north.
Washed up and changed my clothes. Where will another Christmas
find me and the whole army?

Friday, Dec. 28th, 1862, till Jan. 1st, 1863. Received and answered home letters. Kept at my old duties of Com. Sergt., not
very arduous. Delos went home, having received a telegram that
his presence was needed there. They had a real family gathering
of friends from east, south and west. Came back the 31st and made
us most homesick. Wrote a letter, a good one too, to Will, intending to send it by C. G. F. but he did not let me know when he left,
so I destroyed it, getting too old.

Well, the year as a whole has passed much more rapidly and
pleasantly than I anticipated a year ago. To be sure I never could
be satisfied to spend a life in such service, still I have rather enjoyed
the life I have been leading, because a sense of duty prompted me to
it. My sufferings have been light indeed.

Of one thing I am sure. Had I spent the year at home, though
I would have enjoyed it much, I would have been a poor, frail, sickly
boy longing for death to come quickly and suddenly. Nearly so I
felt January last. I hoped that health would come quickly or that
by the fate of war my life would be sacrificed. A lingering death
I have always had a horror of. Even now did I know that my fate
were to die of consumption 8 or 10 years hence or to be shot in
battle in six months, I should prefer the latter I believe. In fact, I
have no desire to live a frail *dependent* boy any length of time. I

presume this feeling has influenced me greatly in going upon so many expeditions, when I have been where I need not have gone at all. I have felt that this time I can go as well as any one else and if I fall, the world loses nothing, if somebody else fell, the contrary. Still I never went where bullets were flying but I thought seriously of my past life, my preparation to die. Sometimes there would be a hesitation, but only for a minute.

February, Independence.
March, Platte City, Fort Scott.
April, Carthage, Horse Creek, Neosho, Cowskin Prairie.
May, Fort Scott, Iola.
June, On the march to Indian Territory.
July, Cabin Creek.
August, Fort Scott, Lone Jack.
September, Springfield, Mo.
October, Sarcoxie, Grandby, Newtonia, Coalbed.
November, Arkansas, Pea Ridge, Bentonville, Maysville, The Mills, Osage Springs, Jones Mills, Fayetteville, Tannery, Boonsboro, Boston Mountains, Cane Hill.
December, Fort Scott, Leavenworth, Ohio.

JANUARY, 1863.

Columbus, Ohio

Jan. 1st. In Camp Chase. Charlie went home and D. R. H. returned to camp. Saw D. R. and John Devlin. Brought a note and stick of candy from home.

2nd. Friday. Issued bread and beef. Read some. In the afternoon rode to town. Went up into the Senate and heard the big-bugs spout. Went to Quartermaster and selected some pants. Crabbed fellows.

3rd. Saturday. Besides my daily work, did little. Took up checks and distributed them. Col. Abbey made me a present of a pair of government pantaloons. I was pleased with the kindness. Heard that Phoebe (Haynes) was in town.

4th. Sunday. Stayed at home and read the *Independent* and newspapers. Passed the day very quietly. Wrote a letter home.

5th. Monday. In the morning George Fairchild called. Pleasant visit. After my work Rob and I rode to the city. Took up my pants for stripes. Got me a vest. Called at Neil House. Phoebe not in. Sorry. Muddy, and I had a servant black my boots! Rode back disconsolate and disappointed.

6th. Delos returned from town and told me of his visit with his sister. Sent my regards and explanation. John got into the guard house for being away without a pass. R. and I went to Mr. Bateham's, met Libbie Kinney, Will Rice and sister, and Miss Cohen. Went to meeting in the evening, concert for prayer. Walked home. Letter from home, wanting me to come home.

7th. Wednesday. In the morning rode to town and took a telegram for Lt. Abbey to his wife. Went and got Rob's boots and tried some on. Then rode back to camp again in time for supper.

Jan. 8th. Thursday. Saw Delos a few minutes. Wrote to Fannie. Read some in "The Canoe and Saddle" by Winthrop. Don't like this as well as "John Brent." Commenced getting bread from baker of 2nd O. V. C. (A. B. N. and Melissa Tenney married today.)

9th. Friday. Got the rations up from the post Commissary, ready for issue the 10th. Was kept quite busy. Finished "Canoe and Saddle" and read in January *Atlantic*.

10th. Saturday. Robinson and I issued rations for ten days. Col. Abbey went home on the morning train, also Dan Arnold. In the afternoon had baked beans. Capt. Nettleton returned. Left Melissa with his friends near Delaware. Charlie F. returned.

11th. Sunday. Stayed at home again and read the *Independent* and home letters telling of M.'s marriage.

12th. Monday. Capt. N. called for me. Went into the house and stayed till noon, then went to the depot and met Melissa and S. R. N. Went with them to N.'s Aunt's. Plain people. Returned to camp and went down with boys to Mr. Rice's. Melissa there. Very good visit. Miss Cohen there, too. Libbie expects to go home Friday. (S. R. N. was Stiles Nettleton, brother of A. B. N.)

13th. Tuesday. Spent the day very quietly at home. Worked as usual. Last night Chester treated to the oysters. Buglers expect to be mustered out, very jubilant over it. Wrote a letter home.

14th. Wednesday. Met D. R. in the morning. Gave me a letter from Ella Clark. Went over to Co. H. and read it to the boys. The best I ever received from her, I think. The boys seemed pleased and surely I was.

15th. Thursday. The Buglers went down town and were mustered out. I was not there to get the promised oysters. The others did. D. and John called on Melissa.

16th. Friday. After work went up town in the afternoon. Saw Melissa. Libbie was there. Had a good time. Rode back about dusk. Libbie has concluded to wait until I go home. Good for me.

17th. Saturday. Tried to get my pass signed so as to get away Monday. Drew the rations from the post for the next ten days so as to get away.

Jan. 18th. Sunday. In the afternoon rode to town to see Melissa. By invitation stayed to tea and then overnight. Had a first rate visit with Melissa during the evening and wrote a little to Theodore. Intended calling at Mr. Rice's, but Melissa promised to call and see Libbie.

19th. Monday. Went to work early and got rations issued by noon. But I could not get my pass signed so as to leave. Got memoranda of all stores received and accounts at bakery and compared all accounts, which proved correct.

20th. Tuesday. Got my pass and started in the rain. Called and told Libbie all ready. At 1 P. M. left with her for home. How good it seemed! Could hardly wait for the slow cars. Pleasant company. At home at 8:30. W. N. and D. R. at depot. Found Minnie and John at our house. What a blessing to be home again.

Oberlin, Ohio.

21st. Wednesday. Stayed at home in the morning. D. R. called. Played a game of chess with Minnie. Saw Ellie. (Mrs. Albert Bushnell.) In the evening called on Fannie, the dear girl. What happiness for me, a poor soldier boy! She has not changed much. The same beautiful, perfect creature of 15 months ago. Home at nine.

22nd. Thursday. Had a good visit with Ma. In the afternoon met the "B. F." at Will's. Adjourned to Thursday lecture by Prof. Fairchild. Liked it well. In the evening called on Fannie. Home early with Ma.

23rd. Friday. Minnie came down and played chess. In the evening met the boys at Fred's and had a very sociable time. Went to church and heard Fred play on the organ—good.

24th. Saturday. Spent a portion of the afternoon at Fannie's. F. Henderson was there and we had a good time. Got home early and read in "Fantine" and visited with Ma. Read some in the February *Atlantic*.

Jan. 25th. Sunday. Met M. at Infant Sunday School. Went to Sunday School with the girls, then to church. Pres. Finney preached. Made some hits about the new chapel. Afternoon sat alone and heard good Dr. Morgan. Minnie at our house to tea. After a nap went over to Mrs. Holtslander's. Apples, pears and cider. Went home with Minnie. Heard John relate about the Chaplain's sermons.

Jan. 26th. Monday. In the morning read. At 1 P. M. went up town. Got chess and called at Fannie's—played some. F. Henderson stopped in. Good visit—played on piano. Went to Young People's meeting and enjoyed it much. Called on Libbie and played chess. Beat Hattie at checkers. Went to Minnie's. Had some nuts and heard Ellie and John play and sing. Rich treat.

27th. Tuesday. After breakfast went up to prayer meeting. Met Minnie at the corner. Called with Minnie on Henry Lincoln, Prin. Fairchild, and Haynes. Went to the new house and then home. After a lunch played battledore and game of chess. W. N., F. D., and D. R. called, good time. Took tea with Fred. Charade party. F. D. A. and H., M. and J., Ella and Libbie acted Masquerade and Mendicant. Music.

28th. Wednesday. Went to prayer meeting at nine. Had a nice fall at Goodrich's. Went to Minnie's and played chess. Ellie and Minnie came down. Played battledore. Good time. In the evening by invitation went to Libbie's. Small party. Had a very pleasant time. Pins and backgammon. Got home at 11, in bed by 12.

29th. Thursday. Went to Minnie's at nine. Found E. and M. about to go to the skating pond. Went as far as shop. No ice. Went down by the mill with E. Ice good. Called at Chester's, Bigelow's, Ella Clark's and French's, Mrs. Kenaston's and Johnson's. In the evening saw Fannie. Went down to F. Henderson's. Bid F. goodbye at 9:30 P. M. Hard. Found Theodore at Prof. Ellis's. Heard them sing awhile, then home. Bed at twelve.

30th. Friday. Concluded to wait until 2 P. M. Called with Thede at Maria's, Fannie H. and Fannie A.'s and said goodbye. At two rode out to Cleveland. Time for Holland's lecture. Ma and T. came on train. Lecture on "Fashion." Very good. Visited with Uncle and Aunt. Thede went to the Bazaar.

Jan. 31st. Saturday. We went to Camp Cleveland and saw the boys. Then to Auntie Jones' to dinner. Down to Alfred's, Mattie's and back to Uncle's. Then with Thede went to see Lizzie Cobb. Not at home. Called on Mrs. H. Cobb. A pleasant time. Off at 6:45. C. G. at the depot. Put up at the National for the night.

FEBRUARY, 1863

Columbus, Ohio

1st. Went up to Melissa's after breakfast in the rain. N. there. Stayed to dinner. About 2 started out with N. in a drizzle for Camp Chase. Rather tires me walking. Enjoyed rehearsing my good visit home with Ma, F. and other friends.

2nd. Got the rations up from the post and Okie (MacDowell) helped me issue them. Thede came down. Helped me clean up about the commissary. Felt rather tired when night came. Wrote two small sheets to Fannie and then retired. A cold night.

3rd. Tuesday. Commenced taking care of my cream mare. Thede tried her gait. We cleaned her off nicely. Was kept quite busy all day straightening accounts in commissary. A cold, chilly, piercing day. Suffered considerably. Seems good to have Thede with me.

Tuesday, 4th. Let Thede go to town on my mare. Read "Tom Brown." Became quite interested. There seems so much reality in all the sports and tricks. In the evening went to tactic school at Co. K's quarters. Like it well.

5th. Continued the reading of "Tom Brown." The talk of consolidation is making the boys very much dissatisfied. There will be more deserters. In the evening recited my lesson.

6th. Called at the captain's quarters. Told me Fannie Hudson was coming that day at noon. Am glad. Would I could see Will, too.

7th. After my morning work, issuing bread and beef and tending to my horse, Thede went to town for the girls. Called at Capt. N.'s quarters in the P. M. to see them. Good time. No lesson in the evening, so many of the boys away at theatre. I went over to Chester's. Played checkers and dominoes.

Sunday, 8th. Spent the day very quietly in camp. Finished "Tom Brown" and read some in "Sermons on the New Life," and in my Bible. Archie called for me to go to town with him, but I had some invoices, etc., to make out, so stayed in camp.

9th. In the morning moved up to the commissary to make room for Lt. and Mrs. Abbey and child. Brougham came and I went to town with him in the evening. A lunch in town and then to Melissa's. Major P. and Reeve left for Kentucky. Met Brougham at 10 at Winard's and went to Mr. Crarey's for the night.

10th. After breakfast we four started out to visit the penitentiary. Called at Mr. Rice's. Got Mary and Mrs. Hickox and went to the Asylum instead. Was deeply interested and affected. So many pretty and talented little creatures among the sufferers. Saw Fanny H. off at 1 P. M. Uncle dead. Went with Brougham to Penitentiary, then to camp for the night. Answered a good letter from Fannie.

11th. After breakfast B. went with me to commissary and then to town. Drew and issued rations for ten days. Rained in the afternoon. Did the work alone. Thede went to town and brought me back Irving's "Life of Washington." Commenced it. Case inquired about Thede enlisting in his company.

12th. A dark and unpleasant day, rainy. Saw some of the boys and talked over the invitation to Mr. Rice's. Thede got the papers made out for muster. Had to get me to sign Ma's name allowing him to enlist. Covil examined Thede's head. Made it out a good one. Let him look at some writing.

13th. When Chester came over we talked about going to Mr. Rice's in the evening and concluded we wouldn't go, so went over to Capt. N.'s and got him to give our regrets, etc. Saw the other boys before dark and none of them was going. I prefer staying in camp, a soldier's home.

Saturday, 14th. Was kept quite busy in the forenoon, issuing bread and beef for two days. Thede got a pass from Capt. L. and left for a visit of a week at home. I wish I could be there with him. Home is dearer to me now than ever. Will God ever bring us all home on earth again? If not, may He in Heaven.

15th. Thought some of going to camp, but concluded not to. Made some taffy and read some in "Ravenshoe." Called at Captain's quarters and had a good visit. Seems lonely without Thede after being with him so constantly for a week or two. How hard it is for mother to be entirely alone. God bless her.

16th. After breakfast exercised my horse a little bareback. Enjoyed it well, though it was hard work. Got her shod. Finished "Ravenshoe." Rather pleased with the story. Mud deeper than ever. A poor woman told us how she had $6.25 stolen from her. Has two little children, dependent upon her daily work.

17th. After breakfast fixed up a little and went to town to see Melissa and get second volume of "Life of Washington." Received an excellent letter from the fair Rowena. In the P. M. and evening wrote to Ella Clark and a little to Fannie. I like Ella Clark very much. She is talented and good and true, I guess.

18th. After a late breakfast, at which John Devlin partook with me, and my morning work over, I finished my letter to Fannie and got out Cream to take letters to town, when I saw Chester homeward bound, so I stayed. Read in "Life of Washington" and played some at checkers. Received letters of Dec. 1 from home and F. Violins and guitar going in the evening in the Q. M. D.

19th. Robertson came at 3 A. M. I got up and read Irving's "Life of Washington," Vol. 2. Bob brought me a nice little box to keep my things in. After my work read most all day. In the evening wrote to Sarah Felton and Fannie Henderson. Talked with a little girl begging and with our washerwoman. Has a hard time.

20th. Brought up the rations from town. Got another volume of Irving. Met Capt. when coming back. Expecting Sarah Jewell. Oberlin boys came back over their furloughs one day. In the evening read till late.

21st. In the morning we issued rations for eight days. Then cleaned out and chopped wood. Thede came bringing a line from home. Seemed to have had a good time. Glad to see him again. He will be a great deal of company for me. Fannie Turner came.

22nd. Snowing in the morning and all day. Thede came over and stayed with us to breakfast, 10 A. M. During the day read 3rd volume of Irving. Stormed so I did not go to town. A year ago we had the little affair at Independence. Oh what a time in rain, snow and ice at Kansas City.

23rd. Cleared off pleasantly. Busy in morning getting memorandum receipts of the stores for the month. Afternoon rode to town and beat Melissa at a game of chess. F. gone. Had a good time. Spent the evening. M. and N. went to theatre to hear Macbeth.

24th. The mail brought me three letters, one from Lucy, one from home and one from Fannie. All good and cheering. How much I prize my letters. Back and forth to Post Commissary. In the evening beat Capt. N. two games of chess. Read some. Finished 4th Vol. Thede looks well in "sojer" clothes.

Wednesday, 25th. After breakfast wrote to Fannie. Thede took the letter to town. Found tea, candles and coffee in McGuire's box—the thief. In evening at quartermaster's. Ate apples. Got beaten at four games of checkers. Read in Irving. Am rejoiced at the reaction against the Copperheads. God still rules.

26th. In the morning came letters from Will Hudson at Lebanon, and one of Nov. from home. Had quite a visit with Lt. Abbey about Pa. In the evening took my letters from Fred and Will and reviewed them with Charlie. Played four games of chess with McAulis. Beat three times. Finished the "Life of Washington." Had some taffy.

27th. After breakfast played two games of chess with Case. Got beaten. Ordered to move to Covington immediately, then countermanded. Wrote to the boy William. God bless him and lead him. Thede came over. Went down and looked at a horse he thought of taking. Read in Scott's "Waverly." Music in Q. M. D.

28th. Got up the rations and issued for ten days. Overlifted and strained my back and sides, makes me lame. After we got through I cleaned up. Charlie Crarey came down, got all the business straightened up, thinking I would go home Monday morning.

MARCH, 1863

1st. Stayed at home in the morning. Snow. Chester came in. Made a little taffy and ate apples. Read the *Independent* and *Cincinnati Commercial*. Col. Abbey was in and told his usual number of stories. Knew Pa well. Wrote a short letter home.

2nd. Helped about the meat and bread. My back gets worse. Mason has given me some liniment which he warrants sure cure. Invited to Mr. Rice's. Charles, Tully, and Theodore went. M. and I couldn't. Commenced a letter to Fannie Andrews and wrote a short letter to Fred.

3rd. The Convention of Govs. took place. I was too lame to venture out. It stormed awfully, snow and rain, and the boys suffered considerably. 2nd Ohio out en masse, as escort. No letter from Fannie. Finished her letter and wrote to Lucy Randall. Played checkers with McAulis.

4th. After the work in the morning repaired to headquarters and heard Andy Johnson of Tennessee and Gov. Wright of Indiana. Both spoke well, said much to encourage us soldiers and discourage traitors. Received good letters from Sarah Felton, Ella Clark and home. Went over to see Charlie. Wrote a line to Delos.

5th. My back quite well. Not much going on during the day. In the evening the boys mostly went out to town and mobbed the *"Crisis"* and then went to the *"Statesman"* but did no damage. Medary and the press were in Cincinnati. The boys carried off all the books, etc., they could find.

6th. In the morning the colonel called the officers together and stated in tears that he should resign if the thing were not ferreted out. I was in Case's tent. C. and H. burned their property. Officers feigned a search but found nothing. In the evening officers held a meeting and passed resolutions. Medary received at the cars by democrats.

Note—The episode briefly referred to under date of March 5, 1863, was of this nature: At that time Samuel Medary, formerly a state official of considerable prominence, was conducting a weekly newspaper called "The Crisis" at Columbus. This periodical was perhaps the most bitter and dangerous and disloyal "Copperhead" sheet published in the North. Its utterances distinctly encouraged the Rebellion, instigated desertions of Union soldiers and thus promoted disunion, prolonged the war and increased the slaughter of Union troops. On the night of March 5th, a considerable number of Second Ohio boys mysteriously got through the guard line of the Camp Chase encampment, went quietly down town, threw out pickets for protection from the police, entered "The Crisis" office and thoroughly gutted it, throwing the type, presses,

Saturday, 7th. Finished my letter to Ella. Col. Abbey went to town and sent a barrel of flour to mother. Good. A Democratic mass meeting to consider the best way for democrats to protect their property. Finished "Mistress and Maid."

8th. Spent the day in camp. Thede came over and we made a little sugar candy. Read some in "Currents and Countercurrents," by O. W. Holmes. Wanted to read Motley, but Charlie had sent the book back home. Thede and I wished we could be at home two or three hours. A dark and cloudy day.

9th. Melissa sent word that she was going on the P. M. train. So I rode up and bade her goodbye on the cars. Seemed sad to have her go. Have enjoyed having her here so much. Thede got a letter from home. Sent a letter to Ma. Roast beef for supper. Went down and saw the boys in the evening.

10th. After breakfast got up the rations and got shaved. Read some in the *Ledger*. Bought some maple sugar. Took a little down to Thede. In the evening wrote to Sarah Felton and a little to Fannie. Got a good letter from Minnie and Mother. Checkers with Mason and Mac.

11th. After getting up beef and bread, issued rations for 10 days. Drove round in wagon and distributed the potatoes. Through in good season. In the evening played checkers and finished my letter to Fannie. Received a good letter from her, also one from Frederick.

12th. Capt. Nettleton called and gave me a line from home and told me about his visit. Read two or three good lectures in "Currents and Countercurrents." Went down to Co. H in the evening. Visited with the boys.

13th. The Capt. called and asked me to join his school. Got a book and went over in the evening. Then had some maple sugar. Washwoman came in. Pity the poor woman. Her husband has returned and I fear will cause her trouble.

14th. Robinson went home to make a chest for H. quarters. Went over to Capt. N.'s and saw T. E. Davis, Morey, E. W. and Joe Dewey. A letter from Major Purington inquiring about his papers. Got them out and commenced work. Covil said he would do it if I would help him. Evening attended class.

15th. After the morning work was done, bathed all over. Thede and Lu Emmons came in and stayed some time. Wrote a line to Major Purington and a letter to Cousin Augusta Austin. Read an excellent sermon in the *Independent* on the differences between the good and bad. Day passed very quietly.

16th. Theodore was over awhile after the morning work.

---

paper, etc., out of the back windows into the Scioto River. Then as quietly as they came they returned to camp, still unobserved by the sentinels on guard at camp, and went to bed. As mentioned in the subsequent entries in the diary, it proved impracticable to identify any of the participants and nobody was punished. The then Colonel of the Regiment, August V. Kautz of the Regular Army, and a son-in-law of then Governor Tod, was naturally greatly wrought up over the circumstance.—A. B. N.

Good visit, letter from home. After class in the evening played two games of chess with Chester. One draw game and beat him once.

17th. Day passed very quietly, like others. Soon Camp Chase will be very pleasant, as soon as the sun comes out and dries up the mud. More orders to march, I believe. No arms yet. Some talk that we will be kept in the state to help enforce the coming draft. Boys would like to go at the *"Crisis"* again.

Wednesday, 18th. Day passed about as usual. In the morning answered Fannie's letter. In the evening at class and at chess with Capt. and Case. Washerwoman was out. I pity the poor laborer for her daily bread and two poor little children. God help the poor in these times.

19th. In the morning cared for Rowena and gave out the bread. Read "Thirteen Months in the Rebel Service" by Stevenson, very interesting. No lesson in the evening. Capt. and Lt. Case gone home. Studied mine but did not care much about reciting. Wish I could go home now, too.

20th. Issued bread and beef after breakfast. Then got up rations to issue for the remainder of the month. No lesson again. Read some and played checkers. C. G. slept with me last night and did not wake up, so has had to work all day. He received a letter from Fred.

21st. John Devlin went down to Oberlin without a pass. Will probably be punished. Took a letter for C. G. and brought another from Fred which C. G. showed to me. Both good. Issued rations for 11 days. After going round with potatoes, felt rather tired. A sore toe, miserable corn.

22nd. After morning work, Sergts. Drake and Arnold and Capt. Tod and I rode down to Alton. Very pleasant. Drake is a good boy. Seems to have a heart. After dinner saw Col. Ratliff and got permission to go home three days. Oh what a happy boy. How good it will seem to see Ma and girls and F. Thede has a pass, too. C. G. and Tully (Norton) rode to town with us. Stayed at the National.

23rd. Awakened at 3:30 A. M. Off at 4 A. M. Reached Oberlin at 9:15. So good to see the dear friends. Minnie and Ellie came down. At 11 started for Elyria with Delos. Very muddy. Took dinner with Floy. Aunt Mary looking well, pretty little baby. At 8:15 saw Fannie, the dear girl, good child! Home a little after ten. How hard to return to camp again.

24th. In the morning did some errands. Played chess with Thede and Melissa. Oysters for supper. Thede goes back tonight. I could see he dreads it—so do we. In the evening went to N. P. (North Professor street—Fannie Andrews' home). Had such a good visit. Called at N. P. 2 a few minutes. (Fannie Henderson's home.) Had a pleasant tete-a-tete with F. The more I see her, the greater is my love and admiration. Called on Fred and Fairchild. Thede returned to camp. Pictures. Sweet Home!

25th. After reading some in the morning, went down to Minnie's. Heard Ellie sing. Beat Minnie a game of chess. John beat me twice. Stayed to dinner. Did some chores and went down N. P. in the evening. Read and visited. Happy enough. How glorious it will be when war ceases, we victors and peace comes again. F. sang so sweetly.

26th. In the morning played battledore with Melissa. Scored 711 and 637. Made us feel large. D. R. and C. G. who came in last night, were down an hour or two. Went to town. Met Minnie. Called on Lucy Randall at the store, then at Mr. Fairchild's and at Mr. Lincoln's door. C. G. and I went to F. A.'s F. H. came up. They played for us. Said goodbye all around. Left at 6:30 with C. G. and Mrs. Norton. Tried to be cheerful.

27th. Got into Columbus at 1. After a cup of coffee and lunch, walked out to camp. Delivered letters and packages. Wrote hastily to Fannie. Commenced instruction on Outpost and Picket. Got a lesson and recited in the evening. Read some in "Guide to the Savior." My heart received new life in my visit home with F. and Mother. So anxious for us to do well. May we not disappoint them.

28th. Tended Rowena, my saddle mare, and got rations from the Post Commissary. About noon Bob came. Glad to be relieved. Letters from Lucy R., Ella Clark and Sarah Felton. All very good and quite acceptable. In the evening went to class. After it, beat Capt. N. three games of chess. Boiled eggs. Sleeked up the commissary for Sunday and chopped wood. Unusual.

29th. After breakfast cleaned up and changed my clothes. Thede brought a note from home through Tully. Got a lesson and recited to Capt. N. Our new Chaplain, Brown, has been very busy visiting the companies. Hope he may do much good. How we need some religious influence. I long for a closer walk with God. Read Independent and "Guide to the Savior."

30th. After issuing the bread and beef went to Columbus with Chester. It was a delightful ride, the air so mild and warm. Went to the Blind Asylum to see about a collar. Went to a bookstore and bought "Les Miserables." Got back about 5. Studied and recited lesson in evening. After recitation wrote to Lucy Randall. I pity the poor girl. She has the dark side of life.

31st. Got up rations for the next issue. Read some in "Country Living and Country Thinking," by Gail Hamilton. Was particularly interested in "Men and Women," a good deal of sense and truth. In the evening wrote to Ella Clark.

APRIL, 1863

1st. After breakfast and morning work, issued rations. Then cleaned up nicely. Practiced my horse some at jumping. Is learning nicely. Read some in Gail Hamilton and "Les Miserables." In the evening attended class at Co. H and wrote to Fred Allen.

2nd. After issuing bread, got out Rowena and tried her at jumping. Did first rate. Charlie came over and read me Delos'

THE ANDREWS HOUSE
BUILT IN 1853

THE ANDREWS HOUSE

As It Looked After Being Remodeled in 1902

Journal. Enjoyed it well. In the evening attended class and played three games of chess. Was beaten once and beat twice.

3rd. Rumor about camp that we will leave Monday. We are ready. Arms have come and good ones, too, I guess. Received and answered letters from home and good Fannie. Did me good. No school in the evening so stayed at home and wrote. Snowed in the morning. Pleasant afternoon.

4th. Went up for the bread and beef. Visited the barber shop. Sleeked up. Examined our new arms. Like them well. We ought to be able to accomplish something with them. At school in the evening. A. B. has telegraphed for Melissa. Hope she can come tonight. He goes to town. Beat and was beaten one game of chess.

5th. Orders for our Battalion to move today to Cincinnati. Received orders to go along a little while before starting. Went up with the Battalion. Drew my pay. Went and called on Sister Melissa in P. M. and evening. Sent $125 home. Wrote to Fannie and home. Left on the cars at eight. Rather tiresome ride. All glad to go into the field but sad at leaving again.

Monday, 6th. Got into Cincinnati at 8 A. M. Stopped a mile from the depot. Watered and fed horses. Then marched down town to the market. Dismounted and were given a very good dinner and breakfast. Election in the city. Crossed the river and passed through Covington to the barracks. Dod and I stayed at the stables in an old building.

7th. After doing stable duty, went up to Co. H and got some ham, bread and coffee. Read the morning paper and wrote to Delos. A little after noon received orders to march. Fed, packed up and marched down to the boat. Saw Al Bushnell. Other battalion along. Took supper with Capt. Stewart on the boat. Had a berth with A. B. Good sleep.

(Ohio River)

8th. Had a very pleasant morning ride up the smooth, glassy water in the sunshine. Reached Maysville at nine. The people received us with open arms. All seemed very hospitable. Waved handkerchiefs and flags and invited the boys to breakfast. Never were treated so well before. Took dinner at hotel with Thede and Burt. Horse at stable. Marched at two. Rode with Drake. Had a very pleasant visit with him. Beautiful rolling country, grass green. Encamped at Lewiston, 7 miles from Maysville. Slept out with Drake. Cooked ham and made tea for supper. Many boys and officers drunk.

9th. A little after sunrise, went to breakfast at a private house. So many slaves about here, more than white folks by far. Started on at 8 P. M. After nine miles passed through Flemingsburg. Men, women and children were out with flags and handkerchiefs. It did our hearts good. Passed through Tilton. Drake and I stopped at a house and got dinner. Went on to Sherburne and camped. Chamberlain got thrown and hurt badly. Got wagon for the boys.

10th. Renewed our march soon after sunrise. Got some biscuit for lunch. Drake and I rode together some again. Got into Sharpsburg a little after noon. We of the commissary put our horses in a shed and slept in a hayloft. Issued one day's rations. Such a green Com., never saw. Ate supper at a sound Union family's Hart's. Sarah very pretty little girl. Saw quite a scene at the hotel about a slave. Four or five girls crying.

11th. Left town soon after breakfast. Two negro slaves were snatched from the horses—oh how shameful! Am glad I did not witness the scene. Afterwards several such incidents transpired. How shocking. Major Burnett delivered up one on the word of two Ky. officers. Met the Third Batt. at Mount Sterling. Very pretty country all the way. Letters from Fannie, Will and Fred. Wrote to F. Chaplain at supper. Drake most sick.

12th. After breakfast, Col. (Abbey) and I got a team and rode horseback to town for rations—got 3 days' rations. These troops from the Potomac never received any company savings. Marched at noon after giving rations. Ordered to Stanford, 50 miles south of Lexington. Reached Winchester about dark. Got some eggs and biscuit. A darkey came in and had a good visit. Intelligent though uneducated.

13th. Ordered to remain here at present. Prospect of staying in "Sturges's" division in east Ky. Don't like him on account of Mo. notoriety. After breakfast cleaned up my revolvers and loaded them. After noon, wrote home and went down town. Pitched quoits over at Co. H. Charlie came over and we reviewed old letters of mine. Saw the boys gamble. One little 15-year-old had $120 won.

Kentucky

14th. Ordered on to Stanford. Started right away after breakfast. Passed many large massive residences along the road. Excellent fences and beautiful farms. Saw a great many negroes, generally well dressed, but very wishful. Drew and issued rations at Lexington in the evening. Saw West Hospital. Rode through the city, twelve or fifteen thousand. H. Clay's monument, 150 ft. high.

15th. Rainy during the night and drizzling in the morning. Went on, leaving the teams. Drew ammunition. Rode along some with A. B. then with Chester. Passed through Nicholasville and Lancaster. Crossed the Kentucky River. Mountains for several miles. Grand scenery. Reminded me of the Alleghanies. Reached Stanford, 45 miles, about 10 P. M. Went on two miles.

16th. Got up and foraged eggs for myself and oats for my horse. Box gone. Team tipped over last night three times. Very dark. Slept with Thede. 103rd camped near by. Many boys came over, seemed good to see them. Issued beef. Boiled beef and had tea, crackers and gingerbread for supper. Like old times. Thede and Charlie on picket. Occupied their tent alone. Wrote to Sarah Felton.

17th. In the morning got breakfast and brushed my clothes. Went to town with the Lt. to get five days' rations. Saw Gen. Carter, a man slightly gray, whiskers and a good kind look. Took dinner on Co.'s account. 3rd Battalion came in. Saw Bob. Issued rations before dark. Wrote to Fannie in the evening. Ordered to march to Somerset at 10. Up till 2 A. M. Then slept again till morning.

18th. Got started at sunrise. Rode along with Drake a good deal of the way. Had to leave some rations. Met a messenger for more forces. Fear of rebels crossing the Cumberland. Very warm and sultry at noon. We stopped twice and napped. Very rough and sterile country. Houses deserted generally. Got into camp at sundown. Slept with Thede and C. G. Had a good visit with Henry Drake on religion. Did me good.

19th. Train stopped back twelve miles. No grain or feed for our poor horses. Ordered to march at 11. Train arrived at noon. Got rations and started. Took a good bath. All the forces, 1st Ky., 2nd Ohio and 45th Ohio moved to the Cumberland. Pickets could be distinctly seen across the river. Rode with Lt. Abbey, and Drake. Got some forage. Moved camp. Went to church in the evening. A chaplain preached. Rather tired tonight.

20th. Passed the day very quietly in camp. Took my washing over to a house. Called at large white house to see if we could get a beef creature. Made a good many inquiries. Got shaved by one of the boys. The day has been very warm. The train brought in a good supply of forage. Everything passing quietly at camp.

21st. Took my horse out to graze in the morning. A good long letter from Fannie. Saw Delos' journal. Ordered out on a reconnoissance. Went to the river. Major P. and several of us went down the bank about two miles. Pickets visible. Quite romantic, a narrow path between deep river and high perpendicular bluffs. In the evening wrote to Fannie. Have been happy all day.

Wednesday, 22nd. Finished Fannie's letter and mailed it. Pitched quoits awhile with Charlie Fairchild. Read in an old *Atlantic*. "Old Age and Hundred Days in Mo." Boys went out and got a beef from 1st Ky. Issued rations from what we had. Received some from 3rd Battalion. Stayed out doors till tattoo. Commenced raining. Wrote a letter home. Got a Cincinnati paper of the 20th.

23rd. In the morning Dod killed the beef. Issued some rations. Received letters from home and Lucy Randall, also one from Charlie Crandall. Does me good to hear of him, an old schoolmate. Pitched quoits with Henry Drake. In the evening played three games of chess with Capt. Nettleton, all success.

24th. After breakfast had a visit with Henry Drake. Examination for commissions. Henry went in. None in before allowed. A very pleasant day. About noon rations came. Issued in the P. M. A little slave child buried. Exercises by the chaplain. Serious thoughts. An immortal soul gone out of a poor slave.

Wrote to Will in the evening. Read *Independent*. Letter from home.

25th. Played chess with Chester. One game ahead. Was down to see Charlie, writing to Will Hudson. Mr. Brown preached in the evening at the church. Read Fantine in "Les Miserables." Much more interested than at first. Splendid. In the evening wrote to Delos. This is his birthday. "B. F." anniversary.

26th. Spent the morning cleaning up the tent clothes and boots. At 11 A. M. went to hear Mr. Brown preach. Was much pleased. Quite disappointed. My only objection was that I had seen him smoke. Read some in *Independent*. Orders to march at daybreak, so went to bed rather early.

27th. Up at 4 and an early breakfast in anticipation of marching. Infantry came in a little before noon. Saw Wattle. Got dinner and then started. Bob, Col. A. and I went. Covil and Dod stayed. Marched by way of "Fishing Creek." Very high banks. Country quite mountainous. Fun to see the infantry fording. Encamped at 16 miles. Got a ham and had tea and crackers. Rained in the night.

28th. Up at daylight, breakfasted, fed and started on at 6. Gen. Carter passed by. Went but two miles and waited an hour or two. River not fordable. Returned and bivouacked on the ground of the night before. Went out foraging corn, hay, and cornbread and milk. Saw two idiots. Rained again. Got somewhat wet. Two of the 2nd O. V. C. companies on picket.

29th. Went out for oats. After breakfast started back to Somerset. Let our horses eat and then followed. Drake, Ritter, Bob and I stopped half way and got a cup of tea. Found reinforcements at S. Issued pork. No mail for me. "H," "E," and "M" ordered over the river. In the evening got my coat fixed—mended. Got my washing. Wrote to Fannie.

30th. After breakfast, mustered. Issued two days' rations. Lt. Abbey started for Stanford for rations. Bob, Ritter and I overtook the column five miles from Mills Springs. 103rd, 27th N. J., 112th Ill. crossed at the upper ford. Commenced crossing at Mills Springs at 10 A. M. Unsaddled and got tea. Skirmishing over the river. Saddled up and hastened to the river by order. Swam the horses, ferried the men. Amusing to see the horses. Several drowned. Hard to get them across. Lay down on the bank. So much noise, could not sleep much. Crossing all night. Fannie's birthday (nineteen).

MAY, 1863

1st. Commenced moving across at 4 and all the regiments over by 9 A. M. Some fortifications on both sides of the river; Zollicoffer's old huts still there. Moved on and overtook the 1st Battalion at Monticello. H, E, M in advance of column continually. Skirmishing. Four miles beyond M. found the rebels in force on two roads leading to Albany and Traversville. Howitzers, 1st. Ky.,

45th O. V. I. on the Albany roads, 2nd O. V. C. on Traversville. In line near the woods. Co. D dismounted to fight on foot. Rebels broke. Pike fired 5 rounds at them, 500 or 600 yards, wounding some. Gave my canteen to one wounded man. Pursued two or three miles, ordered back. Several prisoners. Ate supper where one wounded 1st Tennessee man was, Andrew Johnson. Marched back to Monticello.

2nd. Major Purington ordered on a scout with 150 men towards Traversville. 7th on the Albany road, I went along. Learned there were 900 rebels in the fight yesterday. Cheke among them. Went to a house and saw another wounded man, wounded in the charge near Monticello, hit in thigh. Rode four to eight miles, leg bleeding, Arthur Brannon of Lebanon, Ky., Shewarth's Regt., wished the war had never commenced, still willing to fight. Citizens represented nearly 100 wounded. All demoralized. Officers could not get them to stand ground. Got into camp at 8 P. M. Rained during the night. I got wet enough.

Sunday, 3rd. Wet and muddy, disagreeable. Went to Post Commissary and drew rations, 948. Issued to the men in the P. M. Mr. Brown came, bringing the mail. Two letters for me, one from Fannie and one from home. Both did me much good. Fixed up our oilcloth as a tent. Thought it very nice. At dark a thunderstorm arose. Had a candle to read by. Soon discovered a stream ran through the tent. Blankets wet—soaked and half suffocated. Rebels gone to Traversville.

4th. Sky clear and sun roasting. Blankets steaming. All felt miserable, so wet and such a dreamy sleep. "Boots and saddles" before breakfast. Went to commissary for rations. Could get none. Whole cavalry force went out, some on each road. When at Otter creek learned that the rebels had left Traversville and gone to Jamestown, bound for Knoxville. Turned back, heavy thunder shower. Wet through in places. Got forage. Got supper and slept just inside of our lines. Slept on a porch.

5th. Rode into camp bright and early. Made a tent again and got some coffee. Cloudy and dark. Got dinner at a wealthy planter's. We were all disgusted, so much superficiality. So little soul or mind. Marched towards the river. Ordered back to Somerset. Various reasons given. Many speculations. Got rations after stopping for night. Went two and a half miles and dealt with drunken Lt. Was angry and threatened him.

Kentucky

6th. Reached the ford at Waitsboro at noon. Troops were crossing. One boatload of 27th N. J. drowned, 32 persons, Capt. Alexander. Pitiful sight. Camped on the hill. Rainy and chilly. Issued about half rations. Saw an old lady, "Aunt Betsy," 115 years old, good mind and good heart. Enjoyed hearing her talk. Rheumatism, ready to die when God calls.

7th. Weather still bad. After breakfast ordered to the river. No chance for us today to cross. By orders of Col. Kautz, I went to the Div. train and helped myself to one day's rations. Lt. crossed over. Robinson, Drake and I got permission to swim our horses and cross. Saddled and went round by the river road to avoid pickets. Glad to get back into a dry bed again.

Friday, 8th. Clear but uncomfortably warm. The regt. came in during the day. Issued four days' rations in the morning. Conflicting reports about a battle on the Potomac. Hooker whipped! Richmond taken! etc. All very anxious to get reliable news. Col. Miner in camp. Received no letters from home and Fannie. Wrote in the evening.

9th. Killed beef for Sunday. Read considerably in "Les Miserables." Reviewed "Fantine." Never read a book which contained so much truth and sense on every page. Rob and I took a good bath and changed our clothes. Wrote home.

10th. Issued beef in the morning. After cleaning up and inspection, Mr. Brown preached. Small audience but good sermon. Psalms 2-11. He seems to study his sermons. Took dinner with Capt. Nettleton and Lt. Case at a widow's in town. Very genteel and pretty lady. Read. Went to the woods and let Rowena graze.

11th. Issued five days' rations in the morning. Watched the boys play chess. Had a good visit with Thede and Charley. News in papers a little more encouraging. In the evening heard Co. H boys sing. Enjoyed it much. Capt. Nettleton and Col. Ratliffe told me some news.

12th. Sent a letter to Minnie. Played chess with Chester and Lt. Case, on the whole did well. Short talk with Bushnell. Could have done better in Arkansas. Let our horses into a field to graze. Read the *Commercial* of the 10th, some in *Gazette*. Drove up a beef from town.

13th. Took our horses out. Issued beef. Cleaned up and went over to town. Col. Abbey bought me a good woolen hat. John Ritter moved over to town—Div. saddler—good place. Took Thede some cheese. Diarrhoea. Sorry. Played chess with A. B.—got the worse. Rainy evening. No letters.

14th. Went down to H Co. after morning work and played chess. Beat Capt. N. three times and John Devlin four times. Cleaned up my revolvers. Col. Abbey appointed acting Brigade Com. Says Thede can be detailed here. Good. He has been sick with diarrhoea. Getting a little better. In evening read in "Les Miserables." Has been a pleasant day. Girl of McGuire's buried today. Alarmed last night. Morgan coming.

15th. Theodore brought over a letter from Melissa. Good. Reported this morning for duty. I am glad we can be together. We now belong to the 1st Cav. Brig. 4th Div. 23rd Army Corps. Another beautiful day. Morgan expected. Thede and Dod got two beef creatures and butchered. Wrote a letter to Minnie. Read some in Victor Hugo.

16th. Played at chess in the morning with Chester and Case. Co. returned from scouting. About noon rations came. Issued to the boys. Rushed them through rapidly. Had a shave and spent the evening in quarters. Read the *Cincinnati Commercial.* Wrote to Lucy Randall and Fred Allen.

17th. In the morning, Rob, Thede and I went to the creek and took a bath and changed clothes. Read some in "Guide to the Savior." At 5 P. M. Mr. Brown preached from "And shew thyself a man." The companies were out. Gen. Carter and staff were present. Good sermon. Letters from home and Fannie.

Monday, 18th. Got Victor Hugo and finished it. An interesting and profitable work, a few exceptions. Capt. Hayes and A. B. called a little while. Gave them some pickles and H. bread and butter. In the evening wrote to Fannie. A delightful day. What a blessing, such weather and good health. Thede has a troublesome boil.

19th. Finished a letter. Henry Drake brought me a letter from Will Hudson. Good but rather discouraging. Beat Capt. Nettleton at two games of chess. Horse shod. Mike took him out to graze. Put up a fly for commissary. Read the *Lorain News* and also *Herald.* Compliment to Case. Favorable news from Grant, Jackson and Alexandria Banks.

20th. After breakfast Mike and I took out the horses to graze. Went with Co. G. Took a book along to read, "The Slave Power," by Cairnes. Very sensible. Got dinner at a house. Avoided the order by having dinner on the porch. Returned about 3 P. M. Mike got a chicken. An excellent letter from Sarah Felton.

21st. Played some chess with Thede. Beat Chester two games. Thede and I one apiece. In the afternoon issued rations of sugar and coffee. Pork, bread and beef in the evening. In the evening two papers came, *Independent.* Commenced letter to Sarah.

22nd. After breakfast sleeked up. Charlie blacked my boots. Bill shaved me. Played two games of chess with Capt. N. Even games. Wrote to Sarah. Received two papers. Very warm day— uncomfortable. Major Purington's horse died. Seems to have very bad luck.

23rd. Drew rations for the 7th Ohio. Got rations over for the remainder of the month. Potatoes and beans. Thede went out a mile or so with the horses and came back used up. Looks miserable. Eyes glaring and face emaciated. Made me frightened. Had the doctor look at him. Gave some rhubarb, uneasy during the night, cramps. Slept with him. Wrote to Fannie.

24th. In the morning early issued potatoes and beef. Thede felt a little better. After breakfast got water and helped him bathe. Bathed myself and changed clothes. Read *Independents* and *Congregationalist.* Word that chaplain would preach at 5 P. M. but ne'er a sermon. Report came that Grant had defeated Pemberton. Wrote home. Made thickened milk. Slept with Thede.

25th. After breakfast, just as most of the Cos. had started to graze, word came that rebels were crossing at Fisher's Creek in force and had captured pickets. "Boots and Saddles" sounded and we were soon under way for the ford. Issued rations first. Rebels gone. Followed trail some distance and rested at the Brewery. Got back into camp before dark. Got some supper. Cleaned my horse. Wrote a little and retired.

26th. Charlie came over in the morning. Finished letters home and to Fannie A. Yesterday was birthday of Fred Allen. Wrote him a congratulatory letter according to program. Rode over to town with the letters. Letter from home—Minnie.

27th. In the morning Rob went over to town with his Charlie. I believe he has said that he would prefer to give up a hope in Heaven rather than the horse. In the afternoon I took my boots over to town to get them repaired. Went for them in the evening.

28th. Spent the day in camp as usual. Read May *Ballou.* Some good things and some silly. In the evening felt quite aguey.

29th. Felt quite feverish in the morning. Afternoon, light attack of ague. Felt miserable all day. Got badly beaten at chess in the morning by Chester. Spent a very restless night. Sore, headache and uneasy every way. Thede very kindly did my work. Col. Kautz went out with 450 men. Aggravating.

30th. Rained last night. Eleven prisoners came in at 9 A. M. Pickets captured. Soon after 22 others. Kautz went to the forks before halting. Crossed at 2 A. M. and hastened towards Monticello, sending Detachments to the different fords to capture pickets. "E" and "C" covered the retreat. Skirmished a good deal. 20 to 40 rounds. I feel about the same, quite feverish and chilly at times.

31st. Felt better and got up to breakfast. Cleaned up and rode to water with Thede. Capt. N. has been quite sick for several days, bowel complaint principally. Thede called on him. C. G. came over. Walked a little. Wrote a few lines to Fred. Read the *Congregationalist.* Chaplain preached in the evening. Frequent thunder showers.

JUNE, 1863

Monday, 1st. Ration day. After breakfast and morning work, we went at it. Hereafter to have fresh beef every day. Pontoon train arrived in P. M. indicating a forward move. Talk of pay; order reducing of baggage to 30 lb. Capt. Nettleton sick. Commenced a letter to Fannie.

2nd. Saw the Capt. again and got permission to write to Melissa. Wrote short letter, did not feel very well myself. Sent letters to Melissa, Fannie and Sarah Felton. I believe 9th Army Regts. marched in the night. Destination supposed to be Vicksburg.

3rd. Day passed much as usual. Played a little chess with Thede and Johnny. Called on the Capt. Found him about the same. Stomach much out of order and some fever. Called for bread at Widow Vickery's. Permission to borrow some books.

4th. After usual work, read some in paper. In the afternoon, went for some strawberries for Brother A. B. and ourselves. Had a nice meal of them, 25 cents per quart. Enjoyed them much. Mailed a letter to Melissa from A. B. Offered to write myself.

5th. Big scuffle with Rob yesterday. Makes me somewhat sore. Played a game of chess with John. Read the *Atlantic* which A. B. lent me. Called on him. Rather better than for some time. Up most all day. Called at Mrs. Vickery's and got Shakespeare and some other books. Very pleasant.

6th. After breakfast and morning work issued rations—beef— at daylight. Felt rather tired after the work. Cleaned a carbine I had used for some time. Rather hard job. Another dry sultry day. Thede feels under the weather. Both have the diarrhoea. Boys went for strawberries, but could not get any. Paymaster here.

7th. After breakfast and morning work, went up to the bluff and enjoyed a good bath. A small stream of water enters the ground and runs for half a mile underground and comes out clear and cool from the rocks, beneath a high bluff. Runs through a big trough, falling several feet. Read the *Independent* and wrote home and to Fannie. Talk of a raid soon.

8th. Issued beef in the morning. Rob and I went out and got some strawberries and milk. Some for Capt. N., getting some better. In the P. M. orders for Kautz brigade to be ready to march at 4 P. M. Thede, Drake and I went together. Forded the river at Stigall's Ferry and encamped three miles on. Pulled grass. Bed at 11 P. M. Two days' rations. Tod and we boys got some tea. Very little sleep.

9th. Awakened at three A. M. Got coffee for breakfast, baked potatoes, but didn't get done in time. Marched on at daylight. Met the 2nd Tenn. at Capt. West's,[1] they had crossed and captured 7 or 8 pickets on Mills Springs road. Co. H in advance. Soon came upon the pickets and kept skirmishing for two or three miles. Drake, Thede and I followed Co. H. Soon body of rebs was seen to the left. Fences thrown down and boys went into the field. Georgia Regt. gave L Co. a volley with no effect and soon fell back. As we were advancing, a regt. 10th Confederate from Georgia, Florida and Alabama came out into a field on the hill with flying colors and gave battle. D and I were near K Co. in a little valley, but bullets whistled lively—horse and man wounded near by. Soon howitzers came up and before long started these. Rebels made several stands before reaching Monticello. Fought well. Several killed and wounded, Corp. Laundon. Last stand near town behind a wall, determined. Aggravating to see their colors. Charged after them through town. Quaker gun in courthouse window. Went out without carbine. Got but one good shot with revolver. Picked up a musket and carried it. Advance ordered back. 45th and 7th with section of howitzers went on and drove the Rebs

[1]In the official records this fight near Capt. West's is called Rocky Gap, Ky.

through the gorge. Went along. Soon drove them and turned back. Rested awhile in town. Destroyed arms and ammunition, then commenced the retreat—H, two companies of 45th, two of 7th rear guard. Went on and saw the wounded. Interesting conversation, intelligent prisoners from Georgia. One man killed whose father worth several millions of property. At Capt. West's, halted awhile, made tea, drank, when firing was heard. Col. Kautz heard enemy or force were following and overpowering the rear guard. All troops gone by but two companies of the 45th. Col. turned back with them. We went with him. Got to the woods and rear guard came up hurriedly, some boys running away. Dismounted the men and got into the woods in time to give the rebels a telling round as they charged up the road with a yell. Several of them killed and wounded. Rebs stood and gave fierce volleys. Very near a panic. Finally efforts succeeded. Kept up firing and drove Rebs a mile through the woods. Lt. Case severely wounded and other H Co. boys before. H boys did splendidly. Noble fellows. Few exceptions. Just at edge of woods rebs got behind stone wall and poured murderous volleys into the woods. All troops ordered up, and howitzers. Failed to come for half an hour. Boys had to stand and take it and be unable to do harm in return. Brush and woods too thick to see ahead far, and stone wall. Col. had good plans and had the Battery come up and everything gone off as he expected, we would have won a splendid victory. Our own boys fired some at one another—sad to see. Finally Howitzers came up and silenced the rebs and started them. Dark and too late to follow—also report that rebs were flanking us. Retreated to three miles up river. Command six miles. Brought off all wounded but Case and Chapman. Dr. Smith remained, John Devlin missing.

Wed., 10th. Up at three A. M. and on to the river. Forded and found rations for men and horses. Remained till noon. Talk of recrossing. Fresh troops on hand. Finally went back to camp. Took a nap and got rested—pretty tired.

Thursday, 11th. In the morning issued beef and rations for 5 days. Pontoons gone to the river. Dr. Smith returned and reported John Devlin found in the morning, wounded in bowels and died at 3 P. M. yesterday. Chapman also died. Uncertain in regard to Case. Badly wounded, brave fellow. He told me to tell the Capt. that he fell at the head of his company. Rebs came in with flag of truce to care for wounded. Made fair bargain not to parole our men, if would let theirs alone. Evidently considered themselves whipped and we still near. Afterwards claimed a victory. Took a good nap. Saw C. G. in evening. Letter from home. A. B. much better.

12th. Henry Drake quite bad with abscess on his knee. Rob and I sat up with him. Wrote a line home and to Fannie.

13th. Another hot sultry day. Flies swarm about the commissary by thousands—a continual fight to keep them off. Got some lemons for Henry and some candy. *Independent* and *Con-*

gregationalist came. Good sermon by Beecher. Both Thede and I are bothered with diarrhoea.

Sunday, 14th. No services during the day. Mr. Brown said he had an appointment to preach at 10:30, but no one went to hear him. I took a bath, changed my clothes and read in *Independent*. Stayed awhile with Drake.

15th. Passed the day much as the other hot days, doing little or nothing. Read some and lay around some. Tried to get some peaches for Henry. Found none, got candy and nuts. Had a very good nap. Sent out letters. The Col. got rations over from town and we issued in double quick time. Small rations of potatoes. Byerley was over to see us, so was Marx Kraus, the boy who worked at Mr. Clough's with me.

17th. A very hot, sultry, uncomfortable day. Suffered much from the extreme heat. Passed part of the day with Henry. Finished Emma Bartlett or "Prejudice and Fanaticism", a book borrowed from Mrs. Vickery. Treats some of slavery, both sides, very good.

18th. Orders to draw ten days' rations and be ready to march at a minute's notice. Drew and issued ten days' rations. Hospital boys sent back to Hickman. Brigade quite inquisitive as to where we are going. In the evening concert. Wrote to Will Hudson. Letter from Sarah Felton.

19th. Felt miserable in the morning. Hospital moved to the brick church. Col. Dod and Bob worked at the old wagon. Thede and Mike went for cherries for a cherry pie tomorrow. Byerley came over. Read some in "Barnaby Rudge." In the evening got a letter from Lucy Randall. Wrote a letter to Fannie.

20th. Awakened at 4 A. M. and ordered to take 3 days' rations, forage and provisions on horse and 3 in wagon. Marched at 6. Thede and I went together. Passed the 103rd at the river. Followed us to Monticello. Took the Albany road. Went five miles and camped. Cool day for marching. Saw Lt. Case at Capt. West's, doing well. Got dinner there, some coffee, green oats.

21st. Breakfasted and were off at 6. Rained a little. Crossed over to the Jamestown road. Found the roads over the mountain very rough indeed. Hills very steep and rugged. Several hills capped with high pinnacles of rocks. Rested at a house on the creek. One intelligent girl, but secesh. Reached Traversville at 4 P. M. Several houses but no occupants. Grazed our horses, camped. Scouting party went near Jamestown. Bathed in creek.

22nd. Last night was quite cold, suffered a little. Rash troubles me. Up at sunrise, breakfast of ham, potatoes and coffee. At 6 commenced falling back. No rebels near by. Seem to have gone to Knoxville. Reached Monticello at about 4 P. M., where found rations for ourselves and horses. Took care of Rowena and made our beds. Passed through a miserable country—poor country and people.

23rd. All astir again early. Soon after breakfast teams pulled out. Thede and I went ahead. Got a drink of milk at West's. Case not so well. Crossed the river and reached camp at 3 P. M. Found good letters from home and Fannie. Have had nice cool weather for marching all the time. Felt like having ague.

24th. A rainy, unpleasant day, such as they say Englishmen commit suicide in. Melancholy. Kept pretty close to the tent. Read *Independent* of May 28th, and some in "Barnaby Rudge." In the evening wrote part of a letter to Fannie. Am about free of diarrhoea. Feel encouraged.

25th. Answered home letter and wrote a little to F. Kept raining most of the day. Had to keep pretty close to tent. In the evening Rob and I rode to town. Got some figs and called at the hospital. Henry prospering nicely, so are the remainder of the boys wounded. Mr. Wright in the hospital. Gave some figs to the boys.

26th. Wounded boys all happy with the promise of going home on furlough. Rebs reported at the river again. Invitation to dinner at Mrs. Vickery's. Col. and his men. Stayed in camp. Bought some cakes, pies and bread from bakery. Still continues to rain. Makes camp life seem rather dull.

27th. Thunder shower during the day. Passed the day reading and resting. At 5 P. M. commenced marching towards Jamestown. 7th and 2nd Ohio. Rained very hard. Fishing Creek too high to ford. Bivouacked on the bank. Cleared off, so slept very well, save wet clothes. Thede and I went together. Three days' rations. A. B. along, first for two months.

28th. Up for breakfast at daylight. Fed and cleaned our horses and saddled. Creek quite high, current strong. One fellow got a good ducking. Rained considerable during the day. Passed through a thickly wooded, rough and barren country. Reached Jamestown about 4 P. M. Got a lunch of cakes and cheese. 112th Ill. there. Went back a mile and camped. Grass, had a few oats. Onions for supper.

29th. After breakfast and grazing, moved through Jamestown and on to Jackman's Bottom. Had a guide to get corn. Followed a long high ridge through the wood, then went by a rugged path to the flat for corn. Hard work. Some firing on both sides. At Jackman's Bottom ferry Bugler Co. B wounded in the leg. Went to main road and camped at Mr. Glenes. Thede and I occupied a shed. Husks for a bed.

30th. Saddled up about 8 and went towards Creelsboro. Went by another ridge, as yesterday, only a little path. Command stopped back behind the hills. Advance guard, Col. and we boys, L. and I went to town. Several rebs had just passed. Advance went up the river and we down to ferry. Ladies just over report the rebels all gone down the river. Stopped at a house during a thunder storm. Got dinner and returned by Jackman's Bottom to Hilms. Thence to town in the afternoon. T. and I got under an old house. Pleasant to get rest again.

JULY, 1863.

1st. Went to the 1st Ky. and borrowed a day's rations. A very hot sultry day. Everyone trying to find cool shade, almost impossible. The rash broken out on me makes me a great deal of trouble. Keeps me awake nights and gives me very little rest. Got some blackberries.

2nd. Borrowed one day's rations of the 12th R. I. Expecting a train for ourselves. Boys very accommodating. Regt. to be mustered out of service on the 13th. All very happy. It makes me almost homesick and still I am glad my time is not out. I could not be satisfied at home with this cruel war going on. Many will re-enlist. Boys went for forage.

3rd. Mail came in afternoon. Merely a paper and note through Lu. The Proclamation also by Ampt. Shows a mean spirit, considerable wit. In the evening orders came to be saddled. Stood all night. Two detachments went out. One under Seward and another under a Ky. officer. Co. B in quite an engagement at Columbia. Lt. Bills slightly wounded, one man wounded in hip, another missing and one killed. Morgan across at Burksville with 4000, advancing seemingly towards Lebanon. Expecting orders. (This was the start of Gen. John Morgan's ill-fated raid through Ky., Ind. and Ohio.)

4th. All aroused by the booming of cannon, Law's Battery. We understood it. 12th R. I. got out under arms. At 4 A. M. marched to town and got breakfast preparatory to a fight. Returned to camp. Went to the 12th and drew 3 days' rations; returned some to 1st Ky. Train came in—our boys. A very heavy thunder shower, wet through. At 5 P. M. orders came to march with 3 days' rations. Drew one more and issued three. Got off at 8 P. M. Thede waits till morning on account of his horse. Marched 10 miles and camped at 2 A. M. Morgan has succeeded in getting into Ky. and now the drama is to see if he can get out or whether he is to succeed in his raid. We are all anxious to overtake him and if possible to capture or annihilate him. Letter from Minnie.

5th. Aroused at daylight. Marched very soon, roads quite muddy. Crossed Green River about 7:30 and camped one mile out. Fed and breakfasted. Got a good meal at a large white house. Passed through a now almost wilderness till reaching the Green River. Some day this will be a rich country, good pine timber. Several little showers. Moved on to Dan Tucker's, 22 miles from Lebanon. Got supper and ordered to unsaddle ready to start again at daylight. Rained and all got wet through. Great time getting supper.

6th. Aroused early and breakfasted. Marched two or three miles and got forage. Our brigade in advance. Passed through several villages. A beautiful country for farming, good residences.

Reached Lebanon at 3 P. M. 20th Ky. 350, surrendered here to Morgan, but not till punishing him. Out a mile, fed and got supper. Passed through Springfield, 9 miles and camped on Pike, 8 miles.

7th. Morgan still 20 hours ahead of us. Out at 2 A. M. Passed through Fredericksburg. Forded Rolling Fork and through Bardstown. Got breakfast 2 miles farther on. Rested an hour. Reached Bardstown Junction (Kentucky) near dark. Got supper and fed. Train came in from Louisville, 36 miles with rations, bacon and bread. Issued them before midnight. Slept till morning, a very hot day.

8th. Breakfasted and moved out about sunrise. Boys found amusement reading our brother soldiers' letters which Morgan had feasted upon. Morgan reported near Elizabethtown. Find he turned off towards Brandenburg on the Ohio Road, over the hills. Reached Garnettsville before dark. Some fun with a girl who thought I looked like her former sweetheart—now dead. Three miles from Ohio. Morgan across the river. Captured several steamboats. Lay in the road till morn.

9th. On at daylight. Advance reached Brandenburg on south bank of Ohio River, just as the last boat of rebels crossed the river. He set the Alice Dean on fire. Burned to the water's edge. One propeller came down at 1 P. M. and commenced ferrying. Fed corn and looked about town. Before dark, 12 to 14 boats, steam, gun and packets. 'Twas a fine sight. Got over in the evening and camped on the hill—all over. Several boats ferried us. Two mills burned near river.

10th. Moved out at 4 A. M., our brigade in advance. Reached Corydon, 17 miles, before noon. Passed the barricade where the militia fought. Made of logs and rails, very good. Made little resistance, afraid of cannon. 350 taken prisoners. Many home guards went on with us. All the men, women, girls and children out to see us, water and grub. Did us all good to meet friends.

11th. Started at daylight. Thede, Steve and I went ahead to town. Several met us with "Have you been to breakfast?" "Come with us." We accepted an invitation of a gentleman, but a Mr. Lyon insisted on Thede and me going with him. Very pleasant people. Wanted to do everything for us. A girl, Emma, Ella or Anna Lyons, beautiful girl, 16 or 17 years. She went up town and we had a good visit here. Brought me some paper. Wrote home and to Fannie. Depot and bridges burned. Stores gutted. Levies made upon the people. A good many pretty girls—one Miss Reed. Oh it cheered our hearts to meet with such kindness and friends. Passed through Lexington and camped at 12 P. M. Morgan 25 miles.

12th. Moved out at 3 A. M. 10 miles from Paris. Reached Paris in time for breakfast at Mr. Dixon's, and little Lizzie Dixon attracted my attention, resembles, etc. Morgan served the town as others. Moved towards Vernon. Morgan turned off to Dupont, bridges and depot burned. Some Ohio people, Charlie Mc-Kane's mother. Very hearty reception, bread, beef and pies. Went to Versailles and camped at 11 P. M. in a meadow. Only 25 miles from Ohio line. Think Morgan will go to Ohio.

13th.   Breakfasted in town about 5 A. M., at Mrs. Harper's, very kind and hospitable people. Mrs. Derban's husband Q. M. in Grant's Army. Two little girls sang "Down With the Traitor." Passed through several German towns, very patriotic. Passed through Lawrenceburgh. Reached the Whitewater at dusk. T. and I stopped at a German's for supper and napped till 2 A. M. Rebels burned the bridge, compelling us to ford the river.

14th.   Entered Harrison on state line at 2 A. M. Napped and breakfasted. Seemed good to be in Ohio again, and see faces of Ohio people. Passed through New Baltimore, New Springfield, Sharon, Montgomery, Miamiville, in sight of Camp Dennison and camped 5 miles. Morgan has today burned 48 cars, captured 300 militia, etc. People very hospitable.

15th.   Moved out at 2 A. M. Mistake in road and went several miles out of way. Morgan 8 hours ahead. Passed through several little towns near Cincinnati. People out with provisions. very warm. Dinner at Batavia. Passed through Williamsburgh and camped at Sardinia. People out with baskets and loads of provisions. Bridge burning continues.

16th.   2nd Ohio in advance. Rations came and delayed us a little. Drew none. Breakfasted at Winchester. Our brigade ordered to the front and to act independently. Moved over a rough road by Jacktown and Locust Grove. A high mountain to climb. Stout work. Morgan but a few miles in advance. Bridge over the Scioto burned. Bridge and mill at Jasper burned. Bivouacked two hours. Could not ford the stream. Built a temporary bridge. One Union man shot because he would not take the oath. Put him in skiff.

17th.   Up at sunrise. Crossed after some trouble and breakfasted at Piketon. Morgan well in advance. A Miss Lou C. Bailey wanted my photograph. None along. Rather pretty girl. Newton, old Oberlin student, along. Reached Jackson a little after dark and found an abundance of good things for our craving appetites. Horse mired. Camped near the fair grounds, nice village.

18th.   Moved at 3 A. M. Up at 1:30 awakening officers, etc. Reached some large iron furnace where we fed our horses and got breakfast. Morgan stripped Rutland of most everything. Rested an hour and fed. Some old Vermonters. Reached Chester at midnight. Hour's rest. Got a lunch. People much frightened. "A" 31 bivouacked one mile in rear of Morgan. Awful roads through woods.

19th.   Moved at daylight. Soon came upon rebel pickets and fired. Skirmishing. Dismounted 2 and 7 and went forward. One man wounded soon. Mich. Battery came up and one piece fired shell. Almost simultaneously Gen. Judah and gunboats opened.

We heard musketry 10 minutes before ours. Before 10 minutes the rebels broke in a perfect rout, most complete, left wagons, cannon and any amount of plunder. I soon changed clothes, light clothes. Went with skirmishers, got several shots. Rested till 4 P. M. Marched up the river near Tupper's Plains, and then bivouacked. Rather hungry—all of us.

20th. Went on to Tupper's Plains. Rebs got around and made for 8 Miles Island near the shore. Moved rapidly. At Harrisonville and Rutland the hungry boys were satisfied. Little rain. About dusk the report came back that the rebs, 1800, had surrendered. Duke, Col. Morgan, Ward and other field officers. Had quite a visit with some. Seemed queer to see our Ky. boys hunting our brothers and cousins. Marched to Cheshire and camped. Rained during the night.

21st. About noon the Scioto came up with rations. Drew one day. Went to a kind old gentleman's for dinner. Thede and I went up and saw the prisoners. Boys went out and got good apples. Volunteers, 1000, went on with Shackleford and Woodford after Morgan. Would go but for horse.

22nd. Another chat with some rebels. Some intelligent, but impudent. Makes the boys mad that they are not deprived of their plunder. Drew and issued three days' rations. Managed to get a saddle. Day passed very quietly. Waiting for transports, they say.

23rd. Thede got on order a secesh saddle. Gave up my mare to Dr. Smith. Gave me an old plug. Traded her for a pretty brown mare, $25 to boot. Jeff gave us a shave all round. Apples. Cleaned revolvers. Traded and gave $5 for a silver mounted one. Ordered to march tomorrow with Com. horses to Cinn.

24th. After breakfast drew 5 days' rations. Regt. moved about 9 A. M. with horses. Got permission from Major to be absent from Regt. for 5 days. Going around with S. R. Nettleton. Thede goes across too. Shall send my mare home. Passed through Pomeroy, Rutland and Athens. Fed and rested.

Saturday, 25th. Breakfasted at a farmer's. Off at 7, towards Lancaster, 45 miles. At Chancey got some horses shod. Rained considerably. Road lay along the canal. Two miles out of Lancaster, rested and remained till after dinner. A very pleasant family by the name of McLeary.

Columbus, Ohio.

26th. At noon moved on. Passed through Groveport and reached Columbus a little before dark. Passed Camp Thomas and reached Camp Worthington about 11. Had hardly fed the horses when a squad of men came for us. Kept us under guard. Whole town and Militia near Columbus turned out. Morgan's advance reported at Worthington. Ludicrous.

27th. Guards and team came for us soon after breakfast and gave us a ride to Columbus. Provo. Marshal examined us and sent us to guard house, supposed to be implicated in stealing horses.

Thede and I do not feel worried at all, for we know we are in the right. The Sergt. Major of the 18th Regulars was the man who caused us the trouble—a Dutch upstart with little brains—was all in a tremor and frightened.

28th. Passed the night very quietly in guard house. Deserters and drunken men filled the room. Novel place. Before noon went down to Provost and saw Mrs. Mills. At 3 P. M. we took the train under guard to Cincinnati. Lawyer Hall came with S. R. N. Pleasant ride down. Reached the city and after marching half an hour took quarters on fifth floor of Military Prison. Felt sorry for S. R. and friends. Felt jolly enough myself. Floor filthy and no blankets.

29th. About 9 A. M. some coffee. Bought some cakes. Major A. B. N. called early and assured S. R. that all was right. Seemed good to see him. At noon went with A. B. and Mr. Hall to dinner at Gibson House. Got shaved and went at 3 to report to Gen. Cox. Released, without examination. Telegraphed to Columbus and received reply that I had been commissioned, 2nd Lt. Got me a suit of clothes. Went round with Thede. Took a bath at the Burnett house. Purington, Kautz and others laughed at me—for the scrape. Regiment came in and camped. Received some congratulations.

30th. After some shopping and looking around went on street cars to Regt. Met it and came back. Found everything all right. Went around with Tod. Many boys congratulated me, did me good. Received two good letters from Fannie and one from home. What a contrast between today and yesterday. In the afternoon helped some about filling furloughs for boys. Applied for leave of absence for ten days. Boys on tiptoe. Saw Bushnell and Shorty who was in Oberlin the Sen. Prep. year. Good men. Went to Wood's theatre to hear Minstrels. Went for ice cream with Maj. Nettleton.

31st. Didn't arise until nearly eight. Passed rather a restless night on account of rash. Went over to Covington and made arrangements for barracks for 2nd O. V. C. Only 30 allowed to go home now. Some disappointed. Called on A. B. in P. M. Took me to ice cream saloon and did the fair thing. Got leave of absence. Rained some. Off at 10 P. M. Jolly boys.

AUGUST, 1863

Aug. 1st. Reached Columbus about 3 A. M. Went to Niel House and rested two or three hours and breakfasted. Did business. Receipted for property. Left horse and equipments at Q. M. Burrs. All very pleasant. Left C. at 3:40. Took dinner at Mrs. Crarey's. Pleasant time. From Wellington rode across in carriage. Colored man company. Oberlin about 10:30. Happy boys. Saw Minnie and John.

2nd. Didn't rise till quite late. Thede went to Sabbath School. I remained at home, resting and visiting with Ma. Minnie came down after S. School. Good visit with Ma and the girls. Thede and I went to the Second Church in the evening. Saw Delos. John's after meeting.

3rd. Spent the forenoon at home and doing chores. Spent a little time reading. After dinner called on Fannie. Found her the same lovely creature as of old. One may well feel rich in the possession of such a friend. I do. In the evening attended Young People's Meeting. Did me good.

4th. Right after breakfast got a livery team and Thede and I were on our way to Amherst. Called at Helen's (Helen Rood), then Grandpa's. He seemed affected to see us. Growing old or rather young again (in mind). Stopped at Mr. Lysell's for dinner. Uncle Milo there. Stayed at Elyria three hours. Good visits with Floy, and Mr. and Mrs. Williams. Back, and in evening at Mr. Haynes'—good time.

5th. Went to Cleveland in morning on train. Did some shopping and then went to Uncle's. Mrs. Col. Webb, cousin of Ma's, there. Had a splendid visit with her. Very plain but rich and intelligent. Went home on the P. M. train. Attended Young Ladies' Literary. Miss Everson did well, natural. In the evening had pleasant visit at Fannie's.

6th. Engaged a carriage for the afternoon for a ride with Fannie. Went to meeting with Minnie and Ellie. Pres. Finney preached admirably. Was off with Fannie at 1:30 P. M. Drove by Boynton's S. Amherst to Lake. Enjoyed an hour's stroll on the shore and ate nuts in the grove. Then home again, calling at Mary's (Aunt Mary Hitchcock) to see the little boy. Home at 8 o'clock.

7th. Spent the morning reading and doing chores. In the afternoon made an hour's call on Fannie. Engaged Mr. Turner's horse and rode from 7:30 till 9 with Thede and Minnie. Very pleasant time. Went to George Fairchild's room and read class letters. Borrowed one from Burrell.

8th. Read some during the morning. At 11 went to Daguerrian Gallery and had likeness taken. New coat. Met Mr. Austin and wife, Miss Smith formerly. Helen and Aunt came. Charlie Fairchild treated boys to ice cream, lemonade, etc. Sorry can not stay in O. till after Com. too. In the evening went to N. P. St. and, shame to me, remained till nearly 11. But these farewell calls are excusable, if long, hard to say goodbye. Promised to meet the boys, but all abed. Reconsecrated my life and all to Jesus.

Sunday, 9th. Thede and I went to S. S. together. Visited the infant school. So pleasant. Enjoyed being back again. Bless God for these occasional home visits. Heard Mr. Finney in the morning. Good but queer sermon. Sat in gallery. P. M. heard Prof. Morgan, very warm. Girls and John at home. Evening Ed Williams gave an account of S. Carolina life. Very interesting indeed.

10th. Went to Minnie's at 7 and saw the folks off for the lake. Ed., Frankie, Phoebe, M., E. J. and Terrell's people. At 9:30 called on Fannie. Supposed I had gone. Interchanged sentiment, and agreeably. Happiest day of my life. Most fortunate boy. God grant it may cause no regret to either of us. Oh for grace to nobly do my part of life. Off at 2. Hard to leave again. Reached Columbus at 9:30 with Ampt. Supper at Exchange.

11th. Went to Capt. Burr's office and stable. Found my horse almost blind. Did some trading and did errand with Gov. Tod for Dr. Johnson. Over the State House with Ampt. Thunder shower. Took the freight train at 9:45. Got into a caboose and rested nicely. A Mo. Captain aboard. One fright. Brakes whistled down—all startled.

Wednesday, 12th. Took breakfast at Loveland. Reached Cincinnati at 9:30. Went to Gibson House. Room with Eggleston. Got my horse. Rode to Gen. Cox's and hospital, Covington, to see about Homer Johnson. Successful, I guess. Supper at Gibson. Saw Al Bushnell. Forgot letter from Ellen. Evening wrote to Dr. Johnson and Fannie.

13th. After breakfast and reading morning papers went over to City Library and read some in Quarterlies and Magazines. Mr. Brown came in. Saw Barnitz. After dinner took a stroll about the city in search of a lovely, honest, satisfied countenance, a person who seemed perfectly happy with self, world and God. A few happy children, but most of them even seemed marred, scarred and marked by contact with this world.

(Kentucky)

14th. Boys came down and got saddles, etc., and at the depot in time for the 6:30 o'clock train. Horses remained behind. Reached Nicholasville at noon. Tried to find rations, failed. Found a private house to board at, Mrs. Fletcher's. Plenty of negroes to wait on you. Wrote a letter home, read a little. Husband in our army, but all Southern sympathizers.

15th. After morning duties went with wagon and three men to Camp Nelson for rations. Had returned to within half a mile of the place when we met the boys in wagons. Turned back again. Camped near the 86th Ohio. Saw Capt. Lindsley and Lieut. Steele of our old regiment. Drew some horses. Had the blue sky for our covering, the first time for a long while.

16th. After a breakfast of boiled corn, bread and bacon, boys went after horses and I, in company with Eggleston, started for Stanford. Several thunder showers. Stopped at a farmer's for dinner. Reached camp near 4 P. M. Stopped at my old stand, the Commissary. Saw Nettleton and other officers. Made application for discharge from the army.

Monday, 17th. Reveille at daylight. Division moved to Crab Orchard at 8 A. M. I was left in charge of men behind with baggage. Stopped with A. B. Good time. R. M. Haskell's Division of Infantry came in, also three Batteries of Artillery, 19th Shield's, 2nd Ill. and 1st R. I. Went over and saw Ed. Byerley. He came over. Saw Capt. Shields and Mark Crais. Wrote to Fannie and sent home letter.

18th. Teams returned during night. Early in the morning, breakfasted and packed up the wagons. Off at 9. Went over to the 19th and saw Byerley and Ed. Cobb. Reached Crab Orchard at noon and got dinner at a private house. Ordered to report to Co. C for duty. Went over to roll call but stopped at the Commissary. Burnside and Shackleford, our Brigade Commander, came in. 2nd E. Tenn., 9th Mich., 2nd and 7th Ohio.

19th. Orders came to march at 8. Got my mare shod and prepared for the march, never moved more slowly, kept stopping to rest. Reached Mt. Vernon at 4 P. M. Have enjoyed the day first rate. Began to feel at home. Boys have treated me very respectfully and I like them. Hope to succeed well and through God's grace do some good. Oh may I behave myself seemly every day.

Thursday, 20th. After breakfast, went out for forage with the company. Found some hay out three miles over a rough stony hill. Got some corn for roasting. During the day read some in "Barnaby Rudge." Had a quiet visit with Henry Drake. In the evening went down to the brook and had a good bath. Hired a first rate boy last night—George. (Colored servant.)

21st. Soon after breakfast mail came. Letter for me from home. In the afternoon wrote home. Studied some in "Clerk and Tactics," then read in "Barnaby Rudge." In the afternoon marched, our regt. in the advance. Went 12 miles and camped, no grass or forage. Bunked with Spencer.

22nd. Reveille at daylight and orders to march at 6 A. M. Rear guard. Hastened breakfast and led out. Went down to the road to an orchard and dismounted. Remained there till noon, idling, joking and eating apples. Read *Independent*. How thankful I am that I can have something to read. Loitered along the road, getting to London at 9 P. M. 3 miles. Camped in a poor, nasty place. Slept well.

23rd. Boys got started for forage, but orders came to march. Reached London at 9 A. M. Went into camp and boys went for forage. I stayed in. Got some corn and had good dinner. Boys got oats and fed till 5 P. M., then moved on as far as the Laurel River. Camped about 10. Lay down near the road and was bothered by troops passing.

24th. Aroused at 4. Got breakfast and off between 5 and 6. Good many boys didn't wake in time to get their breakfast finished. Quite a time with 2nd Tenn.—passing and repassing. Moved along at very good pace. Crossed the Cumberland about 9 and camped near Williamsburg. Went out for forage. Rained some. Chilly. Wrote to Fannie.

25th. Was aroused at midnight to draw rations. Abbey away. Went to town and was told to come next morning. Rained slowly during night. Many out with no blankets. Train blocked. Wrote Sarah Felton and F. D. Allen. Still a chilly rain falls. Saddled at two and waited till five for rations. Marched three miles and camped at the foot of the mountains. Helped issue rations. Fannie graduates today. Great day in Oberlin. Would I were there.

26th. Crossed Jellico Mountain. Quite steep and long. Cool and very pleasant marching. Marched 10 miles over hilly road and camped for dinner. Ate with Chamberlain. Homeliest girls—least intelligent looking I ever saw. Went on to Chitwoods and camped. Cold night. Thought much of home and friends this commencement day. At 5:35 P. M. crossed the Tenn. line. Gen. Burnside passed us while at dinner.

27th. Breakfasted and moved out at 7. Passed the 44th, 104th, 103rd, 57th and 12th Ky. Watered and went into camp. Forage party detailed and started and then ordered back. Roads still among the hills, through woods. Pioneer corps finds work. Went on 1½ miles and camped with orders to muster. Boys returned with little forage. Read some in "Barnaby." Ate dinner at Commissary.

28th. Was mustered soon after breakfast (as 2nd Lieutenant). Ordered to march. Boys got in about 5, then started. Saddled several hours in the rain. Moved half a mile, teams fast. Stopped till 10 P. M., unsaddled and got lunch, just asleep. Wrote to Lucy Randall. Spencer ordered back to Camp Nelson, leaving me in command. Awful roads and hills, many wagons mired. Camped about 2 A. M. in woods. Had the pleasure of answering several inquiries from Gen. Burnside. Met 50 prisoners.

29th. Aroused at daylight. Saddled and waited two hours for "forward." Hornets' nest by road. Bees after Gen. Shackleford and others, occasioned considerable fun. Moved 5 miles and stopped for breakfast and to feed horses. More big hills. Air cool and bracing. Nice day for marching. 30 miles from Montgomery, where we camp. Four companies left with wagons. Ours at head of Batt. Rode some with Major Nettleton and Robertson. Camped about dark. Found hay and corn. In the woods.

30th. Reveille at 2:45. Moved out at 4. Made the best march for several days. Advance of Brigade. Came up with teams and had a slow time getting by. Gave way for Burnside, Carter and Shackleford. Reached Montgomery at 3 P. M. Occupied the ground of Rebels. Drew rations and forage. Infantry came up by Somerset. Big army. Enemy reported at Kingston—Forrest. Great report.

31st. Up at 3 and off at 4, rear of our brigade. Wagons in the way again. 8 hours going 10 miles. Camped on ground of Major Ellis' fathers. Went out with forage detail. Got plenty of hay and then let the boys go for oats. Got some peaches. Report that 20,000 rebels are at K. Rebs left here this morning.

SEPTEMBER, 1863

1st. Reveille at early daylight. "Boots and Saddles" at 6:30. Marched out on the Kingston road and halted till nearly noon. Gen. B. passed us. Infantry up and massed in a big field. Looks like business. Moved on London road, more big hills. Numerous reports about Rebs. Three taken at ford of Clinch River. Report that Rebs have left London. Camped after crossing river. Got corn.

2nd. Aroused at 2 A. M., in readiness for a fight. Got breakfast, fed and moved at 6 o'clock. General order from Burnside saying that any man guilty of stealing, robbing or pillaging should be stripped of clothes, flogged, head shaved, branded with letter T. and drummed out of service. Marched to Lenoir. Then artillery opened up at London and we took the trot for 5 miles. 2nd Tenn. attacked rebels. They burned the bridge and retreated. We too late. An order to scout. Alarm that rebels were crossing. Went swimming in Tenn. River. Half a mile wide. Current swift and water clear. Went to London bridge. Found 45th Ohio there. Took the company up there and showed the breastworks, good fortifications. Rifle pits and acres of trees cut down. Discovered nothing unusual.

3rd. After breakfast and feeding, moved to Lenoir. Stopped two hours in the shade near the big springs. Several Union men from over the river, Blount County, anxious for us to cross over. Camped in the woods on a high bank of river. Many girls out to see us. Several came up and took coffee with the boys, highly pleased. People all seem to be loyal. Lenoir old rebel. Confiscated corn, sugar, etc. Splendid crops along the river. Uneducated, homely girls and women.

4th. Boys got ready to go for forage, when orders came to report to H quarters immediately, lightly equipped. E, G. H and C went under Capt. Stewart over the river to Morgantown. A "coffee" girl brought us some peaches. Ate dinner with Rebs. $200 for a pan of flour. Lady said she paid $3,000 for 35 lbs. Take nothing but rebel money. Took two or three prisoners, citizens. E Co. let one get away. Camped at Mr. Griffith's near Unitia. Union people, gave us a good supper. Slept in a wheat stack.

Saturday, 5th. Awakened at 4. Breakfasted at 5. Kind people, intelligent woman. Most intelligent and pretty girls in Tenn., two. Had some music last night. Marched at 6. Rear guard. Passed through Unitia, all Union. Illuminated houses last night. All fared first rate, good time. Two meetings today and tomorrow. Forded the river. Reached camp at 10 A. M. Ben got an early dinner. Did some business and took a nap. Had a good bath and change of clothes. Some flour baked. Gave Ben $10 to pay for it! Thought it $1 and got 50 cents back.

East Tennessee

6th. Up early and on the march at 6:30 towards Knoxville. Passed through a very pretty country along the railroad. Passed Dr. Baker's, killed by Trescott, Co. C on raid, bushwhacker. Many rich people, many well dressed darkies. Reached K. at 3 and lay in dust for two hours. Major Seward—disgusted—marched us through town when Col. P. overtook us and ordered us back through town and to camp north of river. Very pretty town, 6,000 or 7,000 inhabitants once, many vacant houses now. Hartsuff's Headquarters. Depots, cars and barracks. Boys showed me old fighting ground.

7th. About 3 o'clock Thede came and awakened me. I was so glad to see him. Hardly seemed possible, the good boy. Wish he were entirely well. Gave me some letters, wanted more. Walked most of the way—two weeks on way. Drew rations and marched at 6. East of K. near Mossy Creek, and then towards Cumberland Gap. Fed twice. Rode in rear of Co. to keep closed up. Boys did nobly. Can't be beat by any company on the ground. Camped at 9 P. M. near a little stream. Some hills—one awful one. Road along the bed of a little stream, very stony. 2,000 rebs at the Gap and our men each side. A little skirmish yesterday.

8th. Reveille at 3 and off at 5. Marched near Tazewell and fed and got coffee. Saddled and marched half a mile and halted in shade most of the afternoon by order of Burnside, coming up with Infantry. Rode through town and got supper. Camped in a secesh widow's orchard, two sons in rebel army, Jones. Found plenty of peaches, apples and oats. Rest of the regiment remained saddled in the streets. Moved on at sundown, Burnside having arrived. Marched to within three miles of the Gap and camped on Powell river.

9th. Moved on at daylight without breakfasting. Reached Mr. Patterson's where the brigade was camped and fed and got breakfast. Col. P. and Major went to gap with flag of truce. Still refuse to surrender. Drew and issued rations. Burnside arrived, and we at noon received orders to proceed to Baptist Gap and clear the blockade. 8 miles we marched and then dismounted and climbed the high and rough mountain, cutting out the timber as we went. It was a hard job for me, came near bleeding. Thought at first we were to have a fight. Gap surrendered at 4 P. M. Camped at foot of the mountain.

10th. We were notified of the surrender of the Gap and 2500 prisoners and 12 pieces of artillery. Encouraged. Had been talk that we were to storm the works. 32 pounders to be brought by Baptist Gap. Had some chopping before getting to the main road. Saw a good many Ohio boys on the other side. Oh such strong works as those at the Gap—natural fortifications. High bluffs on all sides. Plenty of water. Many rifle pits, and intrenchments. Batteries well planted. Glad we went round. Two N. Carolina regts. One Ga. One Tenn. 5 days' rations on hand. Gen. Frazier afraid boys wouldn't fight. Camped near Mr. Patterson's. Drake ate supper with me. Chose Buell and Barber to go home for conscripts.

11th. Awakened at daylight and moved at sunrise. In advance. Gen. Shackleford now commands 4th Div. and Col. Carter the Brigade. Gen. Carter Prov. Mar. Gen. of Tenn. Reached Clinch River at sundown, and camped. Receipted for oats, plenty of eggs, chickens and potatoes. Camp near a little stream on Union man's place. Bosworth sick today and in ambulance. Chicken and potatoes for supper. Apples and peaches enough today.

12th. All ready to move at "To Horse" but had to wait for whole Brigade to move, being in the rear. Stopped about noon and fed, also got coffee. Passed through Maynardsville and Graveston. Went into camp a little after dark. Good deal of dust. Thunder storm came up too quickly for supper. To bed immediately.

Sunday, 13th. Most of the boys wet, and orders to move before breakfast. Then stopped at noon and hurried off before boys had time to swallow coffee. Straggling. Things don't seem to have been managed well for two days. Into and through Knoxville, then through again to our old camp north of town. C. G. F. back. Brought me letters from home and Fannie. Did me good. Can appreciate letters now—her vignette.

FANNIE ANDREWS
AT NINETEEN

14th. Talk about marching but no orders. During day studied some and wrote two letters. Finished "Barnaby Rudge." Gave a good many boys passes to go to town. Last night reprimanded Sergt. Beers for staying behind when we went to C. Gap. Glad to get a little rest. Went to town in evening. Provost arrested several of us. Managed to get released. Orders to march at 5 A. M. Tuesday. Wrote to Fannie and Sarah Felton.

15th. Reveille early and all ready to march at 5 but no orders. After remaining saddled two or three hours "Recall" blew. Ordered to be ready at noon. At 4:30 orders came and we saddled and went to town and witnessed the drumming out of a thief—whole Div.—sad sight. Pitied the man. Drunk and stole a horse. After dark marched out on Strawberry Plains road. Camped at 2 A. M. Quite tired and sleepy.

16th. Up before sunrise and had breakfast. Report that Longstreet and Ewell were at or near Jonesboro on Va. line. A very dusty day. Passed S. Plains and Newmarket and camped at Mossy Creek. Boy's master Dick came for them. I threatened him and he left. Expected an exciting time in night or next morning.

Had things arranged. Union man. Boys were working for rebel man when taken. Beautiful Mossy Creek.

17th. Made arrangements to get the boys away if possible. Had boys posted all night. No demonstration to our surprise. Passed through Morristown and Whiteville and camped at Bull's Gap or the junction on railroad. Went to a Doctor's and purchased some bacon and sweet potatoes and tomatoes. Good many citizens out to see us. The Doctor claimed to be loyal. Gave receipt. Boys fare pretty well, Co. "C." Many ladies along the road to see us. Morristown secesh, Newmarket loyal.

18th. Moved out between 2 and 3 A. M. Got on the wrong road and lost some time. Marched to within 5 miles of Greenville and got breakfast and dinner at 11:30 A. M. Bought a chicken and turkey. Good dinner. Drake ate with me, about sick, looks miserable. Moved on to Greenville and saw some of the 103rd Ohio. Very pretty town. Prettiest have seen in Tenn. Home of Andy Johnson. Woman said, "Noble and brave Union boys, God grant you may all return home safely, our country at peace." Camped with Brigade, 5 miles on. 18 miles to Jonesboro. Sent out squad for provisions.

Saturday, 19th. Remained in camp till 1 P. M. Orders came to report to Corps Hdqrs. at Knoxville. Supposed to go to Rosencrans. Drew flour and beef and made ready for the march. Marched at 1 P. M. Passed through Greenville and camped at Blue Springs, 8 miles from G. A very cold night. Boys jolly. Heavy frost and cold. Many reports as to where we were to go.

20th. Ground white with frost. Quite jolly at Hdqrs. talking over old Ky. times. Moved out at 7. Passed Bull Gap and got nearly to Russelville and received orders to return to Jonesboro. Battle expected. Stopped for supper and to cook beef and then moved on. Reached our old camp 5 miles north of Greenfield at 2 A. M. Sleepy time in the night.

21st. Got up reasonably early, breakfasted and then moved on. Reached Jonesboro near night. Quite a town and many secesh. Girls sang "Bonny Blue Flag." Marched 6 miles and camped on a Rebel's place. The prettiest and most refined girl I have seen in Tenn. Got some butter and biscuit. Abbey and Thede are messing with me. Our Brigade expecting a fight all the time, skirmish yesterday and fight today. Foster retreated.

22nd. Awakened at 1 A. M. Co. G and E made a mistake and didn't march out till daylight. Moved to Johnston's Station and got breakfast with regiment, then moved on to within a mile and a half of Carter's Station. Got in line and remained there overnight. Support of Battery. Some cannonading on both sides. 7,000 to 10,000 rebels. 2nd Brigade came up in evening, also Burnside. Rebs throwing up breastworks. Slept at heads of horses ready to mount.

23rd. Big smoke on Rebel side. Party went down and discovered bridge on fire, rebels all gone. Put out fire, only 20 ft.

burned.   Soon 2nd in advance and 7th O. moved on across the Watauga and followed Rebs.   Co. C in advance, came upon pickets, saw them one and a half miles and came back having learned that they had crossed the river, all but 60.   One of C got a prisoner and one shot a horse.   Was platooned as flankers, men in reconnoissance. Went back and camped in old rebel camp.   Chicken for supper.   Exciting day.   Hillhouse had few men as extreme advance.   None hurt.

24th.   2nd Tennessee and 9th Mich. made a reconnoissance towards Zollicoffer's Brigade.   Maj. Nettleton went along as guide. Found the rebel pickets on the same ground as yesterday.   After some skirmishing the boys returned.   Forage parties recalled on account of some exciting reports that a citizen brought in.   Nothing unusual.   Moved camp.   Most of forces retreated.   Report that Rosencrans had been whipped by Bragg.   Flag of truce.

25th.   Quite a cold day.   More exciting stories about flank movements by the enemy.   Several scouting parties sent out.   Saddled up all night.   Maj. N. and Dr. S. went with body of Reb. Lieut. under flag of truce to rebel lines.   Many reports.   Raising new regiment of Tenn.

26th.   Unsaddled after roll call.   Pretty early orders came to fall back at noon.   Cos. C and E with Col. Purington, Majs. Seward and Nettleton went over the river and burned block houses and bridges.   Co. C had charge of firing two large blockhouses.   Built large piles of light trash inside and out.   At the word all set fire. Maj. remained with reserve.   Marched 8 miles and camped.   2nd rear guard.   About 500 recruits went back with us.   East Tennessee encouraging.

Sunday, 27th.   Sent out foraging party.   Moved at 8 o'clock. Passed through Jonesboro about noon.   Camped four and a half miles from town.   Co. C detailed as picket.   Post northwest of camp on Kinsport road.   Two rebel families near by.   Made a levy of bacon and potatoes and chickens.   Gave receipt Bowman and Matthews.   In the evening Major N. came and told me he was going home.   Sent Buell and Baker into camp.   Gave notes to Case for $80.00 and A. B. for $40.00.   Wrote home and to Fannie Andrews. Boys all jolly.   Warden officer of the day.   (A. B. N. ordered to Cleveland on recruiting service.)

28th.   Went into camp soon after breakfast to see the Conscript messengers mustered.   Mail came, nothing for poor me— somewhat disappointed.   Boys all happy.   Firing on pickets in front.   Two men and 7 horses of 7th Ohio taken from Reserve. Whole command turned out.   Force sent out and met by Rebels with Artillery.   Train sent back in a hurry.   Fall back about noon, Carter's orders being not to risk engagement—from Burnside. People all sad to have us leave.   Reached Henderson a little after dark.   Boys hate falling back, pleases rebs too well.

29th.   Sent out forage detail and provision detail.   Train came up and got things out.   Issued rations to finish the month.   Plenty of everything save hard bread. Read some in "Harold." At 3 P. M. ordered out, scouting party reporting that enemy in column was moving this way. Was left temporarily in command of Battalion —three companies—in line on side hill two miles from camp; relieved by Lt. Bills. Remained saddled at night.

30th. At 3 A. M. whole Brigade fell back, 2nd Ohio in the rear. Arrived at Greenville and found that troops had all fallen back. People in town seem to feel very sad. All houses closed and hardly a person to be seen. Some few ladies in tears. Oh it seemed very sad indeed. Brigade moved on. 2nd Ohio camped two miles west of Greenville.

OCTOBER, 1863

1st. Train all gone to Bull's Gap. A drizzling rain all day. Had just got in with forage and provisions when several pickets were taken and camp alarmed. Fell back by companies for several miles to prevent a flank movement—reported. Co. C occupied a barn. Rained all night, very fortunate. My birthday anniversary (twenty-two). Would I could see my friends tonight.

2nd. After breakfast mounted and reported to Col. Purington, a mile ahead. Co. H had been to Greenville and discovered nothing but reports. Co. C, 23 men, ordered to go till we found whether the rebels were camped at Henderson, 6 miles east of Greenville. Things looked suspicious as we went along but nothing very strange. Found the pickets near Henderson. Ran them in and skirmished with the Reserve, then fell back leaving platoons and vedettes occasionally at favorable places. Squad tried to flank us a mile from Greenville, column of rebels charged upon our rear and took two prisoners. Messenger Bruce had just reported that he could not get through town, full of rebels. Had just told the boys when they charged with a yell, firing. Couldn't hold the column. Formed line at town. Came up with drawn sabres. Reason for thankfulness none of us were hurt. Rebels reported on all sides. Seems that rebels came from woods into town after we passed and waited for us.

3rd. Col. blamed none but himself yesterday; said he had misgivings immediately and thought fortunate that all were not taken. Moved before midnight. Camped at 2 A. M. near a creek, "Muddy," called, I believe. Five miles from Bull's Gap. In P. M. alarm, and 2nd and 7th took positions and had some skirmishing. One man, Co. "A," killed. Went back to camp and 7th Ohio relieved us. Camped a mile farther on. Got forage and settled down.

4th. Did very litle in the forenoon. Robertson and Ritter ate with us. In P. M. detailed with 20 Co. B as picket. Relieved Co. L and Lt. Hillhouse. House robbed by old relief. Went out and posted the pickets. Then went into camp and learned if we were right in instructions. Thede with me. Built good fires. Patrol every hour. Lay down and rested well. No alarm.

5th. Went over to the house and learned the damage. Very pleasant people. How these people are suffering and will suffer during the year. Whole Brigade and 103rd made heavy reconnoissance. Several killed, wounded and prisoners. Seven of the 103rd missing. Relieved after dark by Lt. Lough, Co. A and M. All in camp supposed Co. C committed the outrage. Boys told differently.

6th. In morning was called again to answer some charges against picket. Boys cleared everything up. Made me feel bad that so much should be charged against us when innocent. Sent boys out after provisions. Commenced work on Quarterly Returns. Mason down to settle.

7th. A rainy unpleasant day. Wagons up. Tent fly lost. Got one of Lt. Pedrick who had three. Also got hospital fly for the boys. Wrote to friends of Samuel Barnes—said a word in regard to the demise of his brother William. Co. felt sad that no notice had been taken before.

8th. Sergt. Beers worked on Quarterly Returns. Corp. Wood went out with detail and got potatoes and honey. Thede went for some apples, and took my washing. Orders came to make report or history of companies, all the details since their formation. A tedious duty with all books away. Wrote part of letter to Fannie. Rich prize. Captured Rebel train. Troops continually arriving. Forward movement soon.

9th. Sent out with "C" and "E" companies for forage. An attack on train anticipated. Went where Co. I had scare the other day. Was touched by the mourning of a lady over the devastation the army was causing. I feel thankful that my best friends are far from the presence of war. Finished letters to Fannie and home.

10th. Before breakfast was over, "Boots and Saddles" sounded. Packed up and moved to Blue Springs. Burnside up. Ordered to various parts of the field but always recalled till near night when the 9th A. corps charged and drove the enemy. Result of day's fighting, 60 wounded and 8 killed. Bivouacked where night found us. Troops moving up and taking positions. Big fight expected tomorrow.

Sunday, 11th. Enemy found to have gone. Infantry pursue. Pass them before reaching Greenville. Hear of the enemy at Henderson and Rheatown, and Foster heading them. Trotted and loped much. Could hear artillery from Henderson to R. Then dismounted and part of regiment went in. Enemy break, then again pursue. Keep the advance till sundown. Then camp where night found us. Plenty of forage and good night's rest.

12th. Up at an early hour, breakfast and then move on. Again took the advance. Reached Jonesboro. Rebels passed last night in great hurry. 2nd Batt. passed through Jonesboro and went on scout to Johnson's Station. Rebels left three hours before. One rebel deserter, W. S. Davenport, thinks of joining Co. A. Smart fellow from N. C. Reached J. about dark and went into camp.

13th. Got the desk out and papers to vote. Mail came. Seven letters for me. Fannie, Ella, Fred, Will and home. Never felt as today, an epoch in my life. Felt sad all day. Ordered forward. Moved out on Blountville road, damp day and somewhat rainy. Read considerable in the *Independent*. Letters seem so acceptable once more. Camped 5 miles from B. Hardly been myself today. Camped after dark.

14th. Up and breakfasted before sunrise. Skirmishing commenced before fairly on the road. 2nd called to the front, Co. C as skirmishers on left of the road in open field. Ordered to gain a piece. Deployed and advanced. When 10 rods from the woods, opened upon us. Boys dropped behind apple trees and fence and replied, waiting for skirmishers on the right. Bullets whistled close, when Battery on right opened a way to our rear and fired near us. Fell back behind the fence till they came up, then advanced into the woods. Could hear their train and sent word twice, but the right didn't advance soon enough. Had several good shots. Sergt. Bail wounded in the thigh. Good boy. Soon mounted and advanced within two miles of B. Dismounted and doublequicked two miles, to take a battery. Got out of the way. Spit blood. Played out. Camped four miles back. Rest was sweet.

15th. Breakfasted and moved through Blountville towards Bristol. Rested at B. till noon, waiting for reports from Foster's Brigade—gone to Bristol and 7th Ohio gone to Zollicoffer. Bristol very enterprising little town—thoroughly secesh. Girls all pouting. Sullivan County all rebel. Got a late rebel paper. Little news from Rosencrans. Not very encouraging. Passed through and camped at 8 miles, near Abington. Rained at 8 P. M. Aroused at 9 and returned to Bristol in Egyptian darkness.

16th. Kept watch over Davenport. About midnight scout went out. Got a tent from warehouse. Boys got plenty of tobacco from warehouse. Many stores and private buildings were broken into and plundered. Soon after daylight the Col. becoming disgusted moved out three miles for breakfast. Ordered back about noon. Burned 15 cars, three engines and building stored with salt. Any amount of salt stored here left undisturbed. Burned three bridges and tore up two miles of track above Bristol. Rained all the afternoon. Camped about two miles from Blountville—good place. Had charge of Batt.—quite honored. Heard Lewis Jones.

17th. Early breakfast and then moved. Took the Zollicoffer road, whole Brigade. Co. H went on with Shackleford. Stopped and tore up two miles of track and burned the bridges. Still in charge of Batt. Capt. Stewart sick and Lt. Bills under arrest. About 5 P. M. report came that enemy were coming. To horse. Such a run. 8th Tenn. pickets fired upon and several captured. Moved towards Jonesboro. Camped on byroad to Carter. Good camp but far from water.

18th. Moved on after breakfast. Passed through Jonesboro. Stopped and saw Dick Bail and Bishop. Both doing well. Camped about two miles west of town. The Batt. gave three cheers for Brough, 65,000 majority. At 3 P. M. Col. P., Lts. Hamlin, Houghton, Eggleston, McBride and self and 8 men started for Knoxville. Stopped three miles from Rheatown at good Union man's house, tolerable supper and bed.

19th. Breakfasted and got under way about nine. People very afraid that we were going to fall back again. Passed through Rheatown, Greenville and reached Bull's Gap about dark. Got supper with Lt. Pearson. Stopped to see Darling—away visiting. Getting along well. Stopped to make inquiries about the chase. Killed one man, wounded one and killed a horse. Others reported wounded at Greenville. Whole regiment followed us. 150 tried to flank us. 60 or 70 in town from 11 A. M. till 1 P. M.

20th. Cleaned up and started for Knoxville at 8 A. M. Came near being left. Hired a horse and hurried on. Davenport with us. Went about K. some with him in search of friends. Went up and saw Charlie. Supped and stayed with him over night. Had some barbering done. Went to hospital and saw the sick boys. All getting along slowly. Anxious to get back to regiment. Saw Sergt. Bosworth and squad at Morristown. Ordered them back to regt.

21st. A rainy unpleasant day. Col. saw Burnside and got order (?) for us to be mustered. Sergt. Munson did the business. All right. Saw Pike and Co. D boys. Wrote a letter to Fannie. How anxious I am to know the future. It looks dark enough to me now. C. G. and other boys doing well—100 and 125 dollars per month. Tully and Allie home on furlough.

22nd. After breakfast went to hospital. Did some chores. Got horse for Davenport, who has enlisted with C Co. and took the cars at 9. Crowded. Mason coming back to regiment. Proposals for re-enlistment talked of. Co. D about concluded. Reached Greenville about dark. Stopped with the boys. Very comfortable time. Boys rather discouraged at war news, shortage of rations, etc.

23rd. Cloudy, started out at 8. Commenced raining. Slippery and nasty roads. Passed the train. When 6 miles from Jonesboro stopped at a big house for dinner and feed. Old rebel wanted Confederate money for pay. Let the boys stay over night. Went on and found all regiment but stragglers gone to Watauga River. Two letters from home, seemed good.

24th. Another unpleasant day. Boys drew some boots. Brought in big pile of butter, bacon, potatoes and oats. Receipted to Union man and Confed. money to Reb. Seems good to have the boys back again. In the evening wrote home and to Ella Clark. Feel ashamed of my carelessness. Ordered up with train. After forage remained over night. All glad.

25th. Morning work over, set out for regt. Stopped in town and saw wounded boys. Glad to see the boys so long absent. Reached Watauga about noon. Found most of Co. C absent on a scout. Came in about dark. Grand jubilee. Proposed to re-enlist as regiment. All would like to go home this winter but some don't want to be bound again till time's out.

26th. Got out desk and Co. property to work. Trains reloaded and sent to the rear. Fear of an attack. Proposed to the boys the order for re-enlistment. Read some in "B. House." Boys got some good apples and apple butter. Cloudy and quite cold. Contradictory news from the Army of the Potomac. Election news.

27th. In the morning, read some late newspapers—month old. Took Davenport over to be mustered. Found no difficulty in examination. Co. detailed for picket, also myself. Took 50 men to Vaul's Ford on Blountville and J. road. Awkward place for picket, 7 miles from camp. Long ride posting pickets. Two letters from home. Good. No alarm.

28th. At 2:30 relieved and ordered to Jonesboro, 11 miles. Cold ride. Reached there at sunrise, reported to Shackleford. Sent on G. road half a mile, dismounted and fed. Whole army retreating. Went mile east of town where Regt. in line. Stayed and waited for Capt. Case to come from the river. Got chestnuts. Sent for provisions. Fed below Leesburg, then marched to old camp at Henderson Station.

29th. Boys went out for forage, every man for himself, horses having stood hungry all night. Lay and slept considerably during the forenoon. Boys got some apples. Saw the boys play poker some. Am glad I have not the habit of playing. Col. sent for wagons to come up. Mail sent for. Bosworth went. Getting uneasy.

30th. Train and sutler came up. Got Co. property. Mail came. Letter from home, expected more. Had inspection and charged boys with ordnance and ordnance stores. Quite a time. Appointed L. H. Thomas Corporal. Busy on muster rolls and Quarterly Returns. Hugh is busy enough. Wrote a letter home. Ordered to march at daylight. Rain poured during night. Uneasy night.

31st. Immediately after breakfast commenced muster. Co. "C" was first on hand. Teams and 9th Mich. went for forage. Considerable trouble drawing enough. At 2:30 P. M. companies went out and fired revolvers and rifles. I made several good shots with the carbine. Good many boys under the influence of liquor. Helped some about ordnance papers.

NOVEMBER, 1863

Sunday, Nov. 1st. Took a bath before breakfast. A beautiful Sabbath day. Wish I could spend it quietly at home. May the time soon come when we may all be at home in peace, but contentment we should ask for. I find myself uneasy nowadays. Mr. Brown preached at 2 from Ecclesiastes 12, 1. Very good. Read some in Burns and several chapters in the Bible. Good visit with several boys.

2nd. Wrote a letter home. Helped make our ordnance returns —about square in everything. Was kept busy till quite late. Ordered to be ready to march tomorrow at daylight. Plenty of rumors. Col. Kautz came to inspect the cavalry—all wished he would come to stay.

3rd. In the morning went up and saw Provost Marshal about Hayes, also saw him. Fear he will be caused some trouble before getting away. Inspection at 1 P. M. Horses, men and arms. Co. C did itself up in array. Col. P. loaned me "Lillian." Finished up Quartermaster and clothing, camp and garrison equipage.

4th. Aroused before daylight. Struck tents and loaded wagons. About 8 A. M. again pitched tents and sent out forage detail. Voted on re-enlistment question. Co. C, 21. Well done for it. Felt proud, better than most companies. Had good visit with many of the boys. Finished "Lillian." Thede got some apples. Pleasant day.

5th. Up at 4 A. M. Co. "C" ordered to go with Capt. Easton on scout. Got on wrong road, being dark. Trotted two or three miles, returned and fell in with the regt. Moved to near Rheatown and waited for 5th Ind. to come down from Leesburg. Rainy and unpleasant. 14th Ill. to front. Returned near old camp. During night rained heavily. Boys got very wet. Slept well and dry.

6th. After breakfast sent out forage and provision detail. About 8 heavy firing in the direction of Rogersville. Ordered to be ready to march as soon as detail sent for comes in. Got in. Just got supper ready and had to move out. Rested an hour in field—disgusting. A very tedious night ride, heavy frost, boys without coats and half naked. A great number of stragglers—getting warm. Clear. Thousand fires.

7th. Halted near the gap till daylight. Moved on to Russelville where we got forage and halted for dinner. Unsaddled and remained over night. Great reports about the Rogersville affair. 7th Ohio passed by, rather thin. Several 2nd Tenn. prisoners came in, having escaped from the rebels.

8th. Before noon detailed for picket with the company and part of Co. E. Went on Rogersville road, relieving Co. "B." Got forage and some provisions. Posted pickets. About 7 P. M. Lieut. Newton came out and relieved me. Found at H. Quarters an order to report to Col. Garrard for duty.

9th. Up before sunrise. Got breakfast and was off before sunrise. Reached Morristown by 7 A. M. Reported for duty as Commissary. Saw Lt. S., then went back to Russelville and got rations for 2nd and 7th of Lt. Leavitt, Div. Com'ry. 2nd and 7th went into camp north of town in the woods. Cold and chilly night.

10th. Had little or nothing to do. Went up to see Commissary on business. Absent. Went out to Mr. Lynch's to see a horse. Learned he had sold it and returned to camp. Left detail for Thede, June, Lewis Emmons and Dan Coats. Night before received letter from Lucy Randall—married.

11th, Sent out June for cattle. Brought in several nice ones. About noon drew rations and issued them to the 2nd and 7th Ohio. Did the work myself with the help of Mose. The detail for the boys was received. They reported. Mail came. Nothing for me. Oh!

12th. Late in the morning sent June and squad out for more cattle. Killed three beeves for 2nd Ohio. Went to town and saw Div. coming. Lot of clothing came. Got some horse shoes. George very bad face. Powder exploded and burned his face badly. Letter from Fannie. How anxious I have been and still am. Oh the future—dark.

13th. Drew flour for the brigade. Set the butchers to killing hogs, 20. Some talk of moving. Wrote a short letter to the "blue eyed bonnie" I once called mine. No particular news. Wrote to Delos. Long time since I wrote to him. Weather pleasant. Got "Spike" shod. Oh my heart is sad and weary. Issued clothing.

14th. After breakfast bugle sounded and tents were struck, horses saddled and 2nd Ohio moved to St. Clair, 9 miles distant. Moved qrs. up near d rs. Rainy day, very during the night. Went down and saw the colored men dance jigs and reels. Quite a jolly time. Commenced messing with Com'ry detail. Good time. Heavy shower.

15th. After breakfast packed up. Went up town and got rations of coffee and sugar for ten days, and beef. 7th marched to St. Clair, also Col. Garrard. Drove the cattle. Found a comfortable room. An old stove for quartermasters and Commissary. Cleaned it out, and got stove and seemed comfortable. Little like Sunday. Thought often of home and home privileges.

16th. Before rising, was ordered to Garrard's quarters. Went over and received orders to go to McKinney's Mill and get 40 sacks of flour and then go to Bulls Gap where Hdqrs. had moved. Did my business and rode to the Gap after dusk. Cold ride. Learned that the Brigade was at the Lick Creek bridge. Pickets very exacting. Infantry moving.

Siege of Knoxville, Nov. 17 to Dec. 4

17th. Sent Lewis to Russelville to see about rations. June came with load of flour weighing 4,000. 2nd. N. Carolina and 23rd Ind. Batt. in our Brigade drew rations. Saw post Commissary. No rations. Things begin to look a little dubious. Considerable running about for one day. Rode from Gap to camp with Lt. Pearson.

18th. Aroused early and notified that a general evacuation is to take place. Saddled, and so till noon. Train ordered to Rice's Lower Ford. Rode over hastily to St. Clair and notified Pearson when to cross. Got two teams to go to Kirkpatrick's mill. Some fast and hard riding. 2nd O. V. C. train ferried but the rest crossed at Cobb's Ford and trudged on towards Bean Station. Some mud. Good joke on 11th Mich. Batt. Sergt.

19th. About two stopped at a house and warmed. Got into a bed for two hours. Pitied some poor people. Gave a woman $22 scrip. Wolf and I went to a Mr. Tate's (rebel off the road) for breakfast. One very affected rebel girl with curls, perfectly disgusting. Train corralled near. One and one-half miles from Bean Station. Lay down and took a nap. Mack lost his horse last night, left him standing while he went to warm, walked 8 miles. Found him today. Pearson and men messing with us. Went with Mr. Berley to Div. Com. to sell him some beef and hogs. Boys came up before night. Sent Lewis back to see about flour and beef for Brigade. Moved about 8 P. M.—just settled for night's rest—to the foot of Clinch Mountain. Trains and troops crossing all night. Slept well in open air. Hired George

20th. Troops still passing. Various rumors as to the position of Burnside in Knoxville. Got breakfast. 2nd O. V. C. came along. Nearly 20 ate with us. Moved on at 9. Got over the mountain nicely. Two wagons broken. Long hill and rather steep but smooth road. Went down into the valley and fed. Made me sad to see 6 mountain stragglers passing, all half famished and worn out—poor fellows, no rations and no prospect for any. Left flour for Command and 6 beeves. Moved on to Tazewell in rain. Went to Mr. Epp's, Union man, and heard some music. After supper remembered hearing Maj. Nettleton speak of him. Good time. Camped at T. Rained steadily all night. Many poor, hungry and footsore soldiers and citizens today and tonight.

21st. Raining heavily. Issued flour and beef to 2nd O. V. C. Robertson came down. Moved north of town and pitched tents and sent for forage. Two boys, "Shorty" and another, sat by the light and played "Seven Up." Became pleasant before night. Left flour for the brigade with Powers. All wonder at our movements.

22nd. A bright pleasant morning and day. After breakfast went up to Col. Foster's. Telegraphed to Garrard whether to go to Command or remain at T. while the train went to the Gap. Ordered to report. Drew rations and moved to Sycamore. Saw the papers at the Col.'s Hdqrs. Talk of the paymaster coming. Burnside thought safe at K. Four men started for K.

23rd. Went to mills and put them to running as fast as possible. Capt. Rankin in charge of two mills. June and Dan went to town. No pay. Read papers. Alarm towards night. Pickets fired upon. Some arms lost in the river. Pleasant day. Very strong position here at this gap.

24th. Rob came before daylight and got flour for 2nd O. V. C. Hard up for rations seemingly. Another alarm and all saddled up before noon. Wagons moved to the rear and flour and meal collected. Letters from home and A. B. Moved to Tazewell. Wagons moved beyond. Couldn't find them. Slept at d rs. after rambling round awhile. Cold night.

25th. In the morning rode out and found the wagons 1½ miles from town. Had Dan and Lewis go with Lt. Leavitt 14 miles for flour and meal. Got back about midnight, clear and cold. One of the Drivers came down. No move today. Spent the day at the wagons mostly. Read some, pitched a fly and took our ease. Numerous reports as to Burnside.

26th. I shall be glad when the suspense shall end and we can move forward or back where we can find plenty to eat. Had some hogs driven up for 9th and 2nd. Bought 5 head of cattle. Drove up 7 from near Gap. Infantry Brigade, Wilcox's, came up, still half starved. Jackson so begged that we lent him 1,200 lb. of meal. Letter from Ella Clark. Answered it. Did me good. Hid a dispatch on a messenger.

27th. Lt. Byard started for home. People sick. Sent two letters, one home. Did some writing, business. Near night moved to Bay Springs. Foster's Brigade passed today on K. road. Crossed Clinch River. Sent Lu Emmons to the Gap to see if he could not get rations. Cattle came up. Gave hogs to the regiments.

28th. Have an old store for the Commissary, storehouse below and office above. Cleaned up and put up a stove. Looked about to get mills. Hear no word from B.—borrowed meal. Aggravating. Lewis not successful. Dan fixed up a very good desk from an old P. O. box. Read some in Burns. Settled some accounts.

29th. Started Theodore to find Leavitt and rations and to see Jackson. Also sent for salt. Read several chapters in Bible. Have neglected reading Bible too much since I have been in the army. Borrowed "English Orphans" and reviewed it. Good story. Mrs. Jones' Hdqrs. Two sons in rebel army.

30th. June came down looking better. No news of importance. Yesterday morning firing heard in the direction of Knoxville, very heavy. None since. Rebels thought to be leaving. Thede came back about dark with rations of sugar and coffee. Had a long jaunt of it. Went from T. to Walker's Ford.

DECEMBER, 1863

Tuesday, 1st. In the morning issued rations to the 9th Mich. Sent Coats to see Fisher. Promised to send to me or come himself. Rebels reported across the river. Scout sent out. Maj. Gen. Foster arrived last night. Guns fired in his honor. Telegram from Leavitt to know about rations.

2nd. Finished Burns yesterday. Pleased with him except that he tends too much to vulgarity. A good deal of wit. Firing all day in the direction of Walker's Ford. Infantry moved down. Cavalry obliged to fall back across the river. Commenced running mill at Big Springs. Fisher failed to return the meal. Teams sent back in evening. Put on my Regimentals.

3rd. During the day was quite busy getting wheat, etc., together. Ordered to be ready to march this P. M. Got all ready but failed to move. Issued meal and flour till Tuesday. Wrote in the evening. Had some apples to eat. Boys played checkers. Two poor stoves.

4th. Considerable movement among the troops. Beers and Woods up from the 2nd Ohio. Played considerably at checkers with the boys. Saw paper of the 27th. Several scouting parties sent out and appearances of rebs leaving Tennessee for W. Virginia. Sent letters yesterday home and to Fannie.

5th. A damp cloudy day. Sent out for meat and wheat. All failed save the butchers. Some talk of moving. Played checkers with Ordnance Sergt. Got badly beaten. Went to bed early with orders to be ready to march at 7 A. M. the next morning. All quiet.

6th. Up at daylight and breakfast in time to move at 7. Cloudy, cleared up in P. M. Moved down near Maynardsville road and halted. Sent for rations. Scare in 2nd Brigade. Some firing. Rebels left Knoxville and on way to Va. Cavalry here in valley. Graham's Brigade after them. Guess all will get away. Few captured this P. M. Glorious for E. Tenn. Ours forevermore.

7th. Awakened by firing over Clinch Mountain. Sent back details and teams for rations. Clear beautiful day. Moved at 9 A. M. up the valley. About 3 P. M. arrived at Bunch's Trail, a pass through Clinch Mountain. Rebel pickets here and drove them. Col. Acker dismounted 9th Mich. and dislodged them from the Gap. After dark fell back to same place started from in the morning. Very cold night, huddled down by fire with saddle blanket.

8th. Awoke considerably rested. Surprising how a tired man can sleep. Drew one day's ration of meal and two of H. Bread. Moved around Clinch Mountain to Blains Cross Roads. Boys killed a flock of sheep. Passed a division of the 9th Army Corps in camp. Stopped with boys at a house near road leading to Walker's Gap. Got coffee and then slept in good bed—secesh.

9th. Up early and breakfasted on mush. Supper last night the same. Infantry soon commenced passing. Left all boys but Thede and went on. Passed through Rutledge. Command moved on to Bean Station and camped—some skirmishing. Issued Hard Bread and beef! Boys came up. Bunked down by the fire and slept soundly. Cold night. Boys go for secesh badly on this trip.

10th. Soon after breakfast brigade ordered to Morristown on a reconnoissance. Sent June to see about rations and left the rest of the boys to go for cattle and pork. At the river encountered rebel pickets. Drove them back on Morristown and Cheek's Cross Roads. Drove the pickets steadily. 2nd O. V. C. on X roads, 9th Mich. and 7th O. V. C. and section of Artillery on M. road. Mile from M. found rebels posted in woods and cornfield behind a fence. Artillery brought up and men dismounted in front and 9th sent to the flank. Soon commenced in earnest. Our A. did badly, rebel artillery first rate. At dusk 9th made a charge and routed three regiments, 8, 21, 36th Va., from intrenchments. About 50 rebels killed. Our loss slight.

11th. Last night command marched across the river after caring for the wounded—building campfires. I rode on into camp and read home letters brought by Maj. Nettleton. He called this morning and took breakfast with us. Went down and got hard bread and a little sugar and coffee. Saw Corp. C. S., a little active fellow and

knows his business. Do not feel well today—hard cold and bad boil.
Read the news and *Cincinnati Commercial* of Dec. 1st. Nettleton
called in evening. Resolutions passed eulogizing Burnside and re-
gretting his loss.

12th. After breakfast rode to station and got bread. Went
down to the 2nd O. V. C. and saw Co. C boys. Seems good to mingle
with them occasionally. Brigade ordered out to scout. Gone before
I was aware of movement, but unable to go anyway. Went four
miles above Morristown, and ran against too large a force, and
obliged to fall back. Unpleasant rainy afternoon. Read a little in
"Scottish Chiefs." Pleased.

Sunday, 13th. Remained at quarters nearly all day. Rainy in
the morning. Read in the *Independent*. About noon ordered to
pack wagons ready to move. Struck tents and all ready. Troops
returned to camps and tents again pitched. Begin to worry about
Thede. A. B. thinks he had better be discharged. So do I.

Bean Station, Tenn.

Monday, 14th. Dark, cloudy and foggy. Hear Jacob Smal-
lered of "C" Co. was killed yesterday. At noon Col. Garrard came
along with the Brigade. Teams ordered to hitch up. Didn't feel
well but concluded to go out. June went with me to station. Artillery firing commenced. Found rebels near the station in position.
Forces were disposed of and work commenced. 2nd Ohio moved
from under fire. Ordered back again. Hot fire from 2 till dark,
awful firing. Heavy body of rebels on flanks and center.

15th. Last night I accompanied Col. Garrard, carrying his
orders. He is very cool under fire and indifferent as to the nearness
of shell, shot and musket ball, many of which gave him a close call.
Hugh White, Co. A. killed. Many narrow escapes. The scene after
dark was fine. I felt a wild enthusiasm at the work. Fell back 1½
miles and in line till morning. Moved back to some infantry who
made breastworks. Skirmishing all day. 250 lbs. of hardbread for
the Brigade. Fell back through Rutledge during the night.

16th. Long, Normaldorf and I went ahead and lay down by a
fire. Went back early to command and took breakfast on popcorn,
rather weak subsistence. Our brigade in rear. Remained two
hours after command left. Rebels soon commenced work and we
fell back and soon took positions. 7th O. V. C. in rear. Rebels
came out, skirmishers dismounted and reserve mounted in line of
battle. 7th fell back and the rebs charged. 2nd Ohio formed on a
hill in time to check rebs. Howitzer fired several shots. Continued
to fire back to two miles of cross roads and went into camp.

17th. Boys with no rations last night and none this morning.
Started details this afternoon. Issued meal in evening. Brigade
marched three miles, little northwest of cross roads.   d rs. at
Sawyer's, he away. Brigade ordered to the front. Cold night.
Beef killed but not issued. Col. permitted me to remain. Expect-
ing brigade back tomorrow night.

18th. Got 2nd O. and 7th O. details running mills. Bought some
beef cattle and settled some accounts. Various orders for the bri-

gade. Uncertain about its movements. McDowell paying off 2nd Brigade. Our Brigade to be paid off soon. A cold day. Water frozen. I am so anxious to hear from Fannie. I am miserable indeed.

19th. Up quite early in the morning and sent word to the details and to Leavitt. June came up with two wagons. Got 975 meal. 4th Army Corps camped near Cross roads. Saw Ed. Brice, orderly for Gen. Hazen, 41st near by. A good many troops here now. Sleep in a bed again tonight.

Sunday, 20th. June and I rode to cross roads, but got no rations,—discouraging and disgusting the way things run. Leavitt is no man. Returned to camp. McDowell paying off our brigade. Drew pay while Lieutenant—State Agent here. Sent $250 home and paid all my debts, including servants. A cold night, read some in "Scottish Chiefs." Still worry and feel uneasy as to the future. Wait I must.

21st. Remaining troops paid off. About noon went down to the 2nd Ohio and to my unspeakable joy found a letter from Fannie. How long I have suffered from anxiety and suspense. I love the dear child more than ever, if such a thing be possible. I answered it during the evening. Col. Purington got a leave of absence through Corps Hdqrs. Signed my "final statements." Henry Drake, Houghton, Parish and Anderson were singing "Annie Laurie," "One Vacant Chair," and other pleasing songs.

22nd. Sent out my letter early in the morning. Had some pork and soft bread to issue. Saw A. B. and talked about Thede. Concluded to have him start for home with Hillhouse and George also. Both talk of going to Knoxville tomorrow. Mark goes down to work for Chamberlain. Finished the first volume of "Scottish Chiefs." Much pleased with it. Thede and I had a good visit.

23rd. Hillhouse came around early. Hurried breakfast and wrote a few lines home and to Fannie, for Thede to take. Got George a saddle and Lewis govt. horse. How I dislike to have Thede leave me. I shall be homesick. Still it is best. Poor fellow. God grant he may get well soon. Command moved at 9 A. M. following Woolford's division. I waited till near dark. Lu (Emmons) and I went together. Awful ford over Holston. Found brigade at Newmarket. Took supper with Maj. Nettleton. Slept on floor.

24th. At 1:30 orders came to move immediately to the Chuckey for the purpose of capturing a rebel brigade. Campbell's brigade to attack in front and Garrard the rear, Garrard to have command. Col. Palmer, senior, of G.'s, had detachments from 11th Ohio, 75th Penn., 1st Tenn. When half a mile from road, rebels fired on our pickets and Palmer rushed out, bringing on an engagement. Rebels charged nearly to our horses, then we charged them for half a mile. Ordered back by Sturgess just as were making a flank movement. Rather heavy loss on each side. Saw Bennie Sears. Things looked rather scaly for awhile. Got out all right. In camp at 10 P. M. Supper.

25th. Cloudy and letter from home. How I should like to be at home today. God bless all the dear friends. Wonder where Thede is today. Gave two or three little Christmas gifts. Rachel Brazelton gave me a nice large apple as a Christmas gift. Took dinner with Maj. Nettleton. Had some apples to eat. In the evening wrote letters home and to Fannie. Sent Lu to Strawberry Plains.

26th. At midnight orders came to be ready to move an hour before daylight, not much sleep. Lewis not back. Col. Cook attacked the enemy near Mossy Creek. Capron and Garrard for support. Rained all the morning. Uncomfortable. Regts. in line all day. Some artillery and a little musketry firing. Foster sent his thanks for getting out well the other day. Our brigade rather light, 656. Camped near by. Made d rs. at Dr. Peck's, a rebel, clever, 6 ft. 4 in. in height. Gave me "The Autocrat of the Breakfast Table." Occupied a good room. Comfortable.

27th. A rainy unpleasant day. A negro came into the lines giving news, making an attack on the rebels expedient. Wrote a line more in F's letter. Were out all the P. M.—most of the fighting on horseback. Some artillery firing. Drove the rebs beyond "Talbot Station." Regiments lay in line saddled, our brigade in a piece of woods. Lay upon a couple of rails with saddle blanket comfortably. Rained some all night.

28th. Dried our clothes and got breakfast. Col. Purington came and reported under arrest for disrespectful language to Gen. Potter. Read a little in "Scottish Chiefs" and *Independent*. Good article on a visit to Oberlin. Lay about the fire until night. About 7 P. M. got an order to report to Col. Foster and then to Gen. Sturgiss. Awful muddy and dark. Got back to qrs. late and went to bed.

29th. At 2:30 A. M. got orders to march to Mossy Creek. Marched at 3. Waited at the creek till nearly daylight, quite cool. Went into a house and warmed. Woodford's and part of McCook's divisions went with Foster's to Dandridge. Found no enemy and returned to Mossy Creek. Stopped to feed. Heard cannonading and got orders to report to Newmarket and then to M. Creek. So far started that went around by road. Quite a heavy fight. At first our men fell back and then we drove in turn. 100 killed and wounded on our side and as many rebels. Saw two of our men, heads shot off. Went to old place to camp.

30th. Slept by a big fire last night—very comfortable. Regiments saddled ready for a fight. Sent Lewis back to S. Plains for rations. Had some beef driven up and killed. Boys would have suffered had they not been fortunate in getting from the country.

31st. Looked for rations all day. Read some in *Harper's*. In evening Lt. Baird and I rode to Mossy Creek in search of rations and to make an effort to procure a mill. Put up a tent fly in the P. M. Rained till 12 P. M. and then turned awfully cold and blew a hurricane. Fly came down. Wet and cold. Year comes in rathe˘ roughly.

JANUARY, 1864.

In East Tennessee.

1st. Happy New Year! Gay and festive. Frozen and just starving. Re-enlistment question presented to the boys. Three from the 2nd Ohio. Took dinner at hdqrs., at white house. Cabbage and beef and mutton. Had a chat with the people. All have suffered badly. Even underclothes taken during the late fights by rebs, also wheat and corn. First-rate visit with Col. Garrard and Allen. Review of campaign. Hard bread, flour and pork for the boys. Makes me happy. Don't ask more satisfaction than to get plenty of rations. Have been half crazy with anxiety for days. First command in line east of Mossy Creek. Rained last night. Turned cold about 12 P. M. and blew a hurricane. Awful tedious day. Boys must suffer very much. Col. and staff up and around fires early.

2nd. Still cold as Greenland. Spent most of the day at the white house. What a splendid day to attack the enemy were our infantry on hand. Wrote letters home. to Fannie and Ella.

3rd. Ordered to fall back to McCook at daylight in anticipation of a fight. Went to Dr. Peck's. Sent up beef and meal. Went to New Market in P. M. Got receipts and invoices. Let Spike go at 2:40 on a trot. Good chat with the boys around the fire.

4th. Enlistment question all the go. Maj. Nettleton gone to Knoxville with proposition and application.

5th. Last day for re-enlistment. Most of the boys in favor. N. telegraphs that proposition has been accepted and regt. will be ordered home within fifteen days. Boys all excitement.

6th. About quarters most of the day. Read in "Autocrat of the Breakfast Table." Cold. Evening Dan and I went to Regt. Good time. Lost sugar. Back late. Little "taffy" and to bed.

7th. Regt. passed by to Strawberry Plains to turn over horses and equipments. Saw Col. Garrard and got his photo. Bade him goodbye. Gave me a compliment. Got relieved. Saw Miner—full of bombast and gas.

8th. Lt. David relieved me. Went to company and returned. All busy at work. Got permission to remain at Dr. Peck's till Sunday. Rode back very fast.

9th. Busy on company papers. Helped Davis. Still very cold. Got June to take Jennie to Maj. N. Rode my Spike. No trouble.

Note—The "Jennie" referred to was Jennie Green, a bright and comely mulatto slave girl of fifteen, who was owned by Dr. Peck who lived near Knoxville, Tenn., and who begged Major Tenney to rescue her from slavery. Accordingly he arranged with one of his assistants, Ed. June, the night of the Regiment's departure for the North, to take the Major's extra horse, "Spike," and bring her to A. B. N.'s headquarters. This was skilfully done, and Jennie was safely brought to Ohio. She was given schooling, and thereafter lived with the Nettleton family until she was married in 1876. She was in all respects an admirable character.—(A. B. N., June, 1911.)

10th. Packed up and moved to regt. Boys got their things ready to turn over. Hines inspected property.

11th. Several boys not inclined to go home. Assigned to 7th O. V. C. Thomas, Peck, Kearn, Beach, Montgomery, Bentley, Rutzel. Good boys, sorry. Relieved Hamlin. Went to Knoxville to fix papers. Slept with Avery on floor at Charley's.

12th. Went to Hospitals with Dr. Smith to see sick. 2nd O. V. C. hospitals in wretched condition. Saw Joshua—sick—and fixed papers. Part of regt. came down.

13th. Rations of flour. Up early. Many officers at Chamberlain's. Off on the cars at 9:30. Gen. Foster on board—don't like his style. Loudon at 2 P. M. Went to barracks. (30 days' "veteran furlough" for those of the 2nd O. V. C. who re-enlisted.)

14th. Little to do. No boat. Marched at 2 P. M. for Kingston—6 miles—and camped. Dr. Noble and I bunked together.

15th. On soon after daylight. Meal and coffee for breakfast. Raised a little blood. Hard work. Meat and salt. No prospect of boat. I am played out.

16th. Went down with Smith and Bob for dinner. Failed. Good supper at the hotel. Started down the river at dark—in pontoon. Smith, Sheldon, Stopper, Rol. Morgan, Ab Cole, Nash, Geo. Hart, etc. Went down three miles and put up at log barn—fire.

17th. Found a dugout at noon. Rol and I went ahead and engaged dinner. Pulled on in P. M. Ab and I in canoe. Stayed over night at a Union man's. Courtship scene. None of Tenn., her women, institutions and privileges for me.

18th. Rainy. Passed White Creek Shoals in the morning as Regt. came up. Let several boys in flatboat. Many boys on the river. Gay times. Stopped at Mr. Brown's—rebel. Good accommodations. Snow.

19th. Early start. Water rough. Gave up canoe. Stopped for dinner. Put up 12 miles from Hiawasse. Mr. Georges, poor man, but rebel. Rebel girl. Member of church, chews, smokes and dips and drinks poor whiskey.

20th. Off early. Every morning and noon have to wait for somebody. Considerable sport. Took dinner after passing the Hiawasse, where they had a rail-mauling, quilting and dance last night. Most of the country turned out. Good deal of smallpox scattered through the country. People alarmed. Put up with some poor Union people. Slept in room with whole family.

21st. It is astonishing how much the people of E. Tenn. have put up with, and how ignorant and coarse they are. Have seen but one young lady in Tenn. whose clothes have fitted her and who has acted the lady. 27 miles from Chattanooga. Great time at dinner at one Shoemakers—rebel. Guard there—impudent. Got into Chattanooga at 4 P. M. Good time with the Co. Rough night. Routed twice.

22nd. Aroused at four to march at 5. Failed to get off. Saw Hy Smith, Goodsell and Walker, Charley Brooks and Milo Cravath —Chaplain 100th O. Climbed Lookout Mt. with Hugh, Smith and Lu Emmons. Difficult job, but well paid. Scenery grand. In camp at 11. Coffee and went to bed. Scarcity of blankets. Much noise.

23rd. At 5 filled box cars. Rode outside. Cold and frosty. Very crooked road winding among the mountains south of Tenn. River. 7th on at Bridgeport, Alabama. Saw Oberlin boys. Three months more only. Lay at Stevenson till dark. Read, ate, lounged and napped. Made the most of a crowded car for sleep. Would have liked to pass Murfreesboro and Tullahoma in the daytime.

24th. At Nashville, 9 A. M. quartered at Seminary Barracks. H. Drake and I went to dinner at a restaurant. Saw colored troops drilled and inspected. Went about town. Some splendid residences. Randall quite sick with pleurisy.

25th. Breakfast with Drake, Maj. Seward and nephew. Dinner with Capt. Case. Turned over arms. Lt. Pedrick wounded accidentally in foot. Cars at 5 P. M. Crowded and slow. Private Extell died.

26th. Found Extell under seats dead, poor boy. Has suffered much, not been alive for months. Procured coffin. Started from Bowling Green before noon. Slow work. At Louisville at 10:30 P. M. Went to Barracks in city, coffee and bread, poor and nasty barracks.

27th. Concluded to bury Extell's remains in city. Went to Galt House for breakfast. Bought a pair of boots. Evening saw Corsican Brothers, went with company.

28th. Took Burs, Thomas, Wood and Bosworth to Galt House for breakfast. Wrote a line to John's parents. Crossed the river at 2:30 P. M. Charge of I Co. too, stopped at Seymour till 9 P. M. Changed cars. Rode in passenger car during night. Some sleep.

29th. Passed through Cincinnati before daylight. Left for Columbus at 7:30. Stopped opposite Camp Chase and walked over. Got supper at boarding house. Boys poor accommodations.

30th. Barracks fitted up as comfortable as possible. "I" and "C" officers together. Wrote a line home and to Fannie. Paroled. Moved.

31st. The day in camp. Read in *Atlantic* and wrote a letter home. Mr. Brown and a friend made a formal Sunday call. Disgusting—his preaching and practice.

FEBRUARY, 1864.

February, 1st. Worked on the rolls. Read the papers and a little in *Atlantic*.

2nd. Cold, disagreeable day. Letters from home and Fannie, 1st of Jan. Both happy and sad. Made a fool of myself talking to old Brown at d rs. Wrote to Fannie.

3rd.   Hugh and I went to town in evening and heard the Swiss Bell Ringers. Good time. Zettler House.

4th.   Went down to the stable with the boys to see the horses. Went to clothing store—vest and hat—measured for pants. Camp in time for dinner. Wrote some.

5th.   Stayed in camp. Board of Survey. Read in "Tales and Sketches."

6th.   In evening went to town to see about assignment. Went to Atheneum. "Hidden Hand," Miss Sallie St. Clair played her part well—pretty actress.

7th.   Made arrangements for 13 men. Went to camp again after making diligent inquiries, and partial agreement.

8th.   Saw several committees in C. About 11 made arrangements for rest of company in Polk Township, Cranford County. $100 bounty. Several of us went to town and to theatre. Restaurant first for supper.

9th, 10th, 11th, 12th, 13th and 14th spent getting mustered and rolls completed. 8th boys paid off and furloughed Saturday. Most of the regt. already in city. Work on company papers.

15th.   Packed away C and G equipage and blankets. Boys went to town early. Tom, Smith and I went after dinner. Saw the washerwoman. Pity her but disgusted at her freedom and fondness. Went to Zettler House. Good many of C Co. there. Houses all full. Randall down again. Got my horses out. Am uneasy to get away. Oh dear!

16th.   Cold. Did my business. Got transportation for boys and by permission at 3 P. M. left for home. Had to stay over at Grafton. Cold day.

17th.   Went on my way rejoicing at 9 o'clock. Found open arms at home. How good to be here again. I couldn't realize it down in Tenn. I am happy—one thing short! Treasure Carrie! God be praised for the blessing of home and friends.

18-20th.   Remained quietly at home resting and reading and playing chess till Sat. P. M. went to C. In evening called on Fannie. Happy time—same creature. (She spent the winter of 1864 in Cleveland at the home of her sister, Helen Cobb.)

21st.   Attended Plymouth Church in the morning. In the P. M. went over to Uncle Jones'. In the evening heard Fred Douglass. Much interested.

22nd.   Went over to Bazaar with Roxena. Saw Fannies Hudson and Henderson. Saw R. to cars at noon. Heard Garfield with Fannie. Saw Will H. and Hub Terrell. Not much changed. In the evening called and walked with F. Good visit, then went to Bazaar.

23rd.   Morning and dinner at Mr. Cobb's. Think much of Mrs. C. P. M. at Bazaar. Evening with the fairy belle. Had a splendid visit. Feel benefited. Future and prospects.

24th.   Up and took cars at 7:30 for home. Thede back from Swift's. Somewhat tired.

25th. Folks went down to Cleveland even to Carrie. Floy came. She, Agnes and I kept house. Good time. Commenced letter to F. Attended meeting.

26th. The day at home. In evening called at Ella's. Had a pleasant visit and a good game of chess—Prof. Clarke.

27th. Folks returned from Cleveland. Called at Mrs. Hudson's. F. not at home. Visited a little while at Tutor Fairchild's. Read Charlie's last letter. Good time.

28th. Thede and I attended church together. Heard Prof. Finney in the morning. Prof. Morgan in P. M. Good sermons. Heard Mr. Fairfield in evening. "Repent, lest we grieve the spirit of God." Thede went forward. I feel determined through God's grace to do, work and live for Jesus hereafter, less for self.

29th. Thede went to Pittsfield and around to see if he couldn't find a recruit. Melissa and I went to Minnie's. Came home for Thede but he had gone away. Took Floy over. Waffles and sugar for supper. Floy and I went to Young People's meeting. Interesting. M. caught cold.

MARCH, 1864.

1st. Spent the day at home. Commenced the "Dutch Republic." Much interested. In the evening Thede and I went to meeting. Prof. Peck. "If I am thy Father, where then is mine honor."

2nd. Maj. Nettleton returned from Sandusky and started for Washington at 2 P. M. Thede and I rode horseback to Amherst. Saw Mary, Grandma's and Helen's folks. Called at Mr. Kline's. Spent the evening at home. Uneasy for some reason. Am looking for a letter but it doesn't come.

3rd. Spent the morning at home. In evening called upon Fannie Henderson. To my joy a letter from F. came this P. M.

4th. Read and visited during the morning. Floy, Thede and I went to Cleveland on the P. M. train. Went to the various halls at Fair (Sanitary Commission) and to Uncle's to tea. Mrs. D. so hoarse as to be unable to speak. Floy and Thede went to Minstrels. I called at Mr. Cobb's. Spent a very pleasant evening with F. and Mrs. Cobb. Saw Floy off on morning train.

5th. Rain and snow. After dinner Fannie and I went to Fine Arts Hall. Very pleasant time. Called at Mrs. Cobb's. Went to Uncle Jones' to tea. Company, Mr. Kingsley, Chas. Spencer and Mrs. Turner. Passable evening.

6th. Sunday. Thede and I attended Prof. Thome's church with the friends. Communion. Season of rich feasting. Benefited. P. M. went to S. S. Bible class. Adah sang S. S. hymns. Of course nearly went up. Evening heard Mr. Thome. Quiet visit with Adah.

7th. At 10 A. M. went to the east side with Roxena. Fine Arts Hall and then for bath. P. M. called at Mr. Barnitz', Bys', Mrs.

Cobb's and Cous. Brougham's. Fannie and I rode out—E. Cleveland, etc. Enjoyed myself hugely. We also went to hear Anna Dickinson. "Words for the Hour." After lecture, walked and talked over our love affairs, and discussed our relations and feelings. Had it not been for a few hindrances and contingencies, I think we would have engaged ourselves. Under the circumstances I could and would not entertain the thought. I love the girl and hope she loves me. God forbid that we should ever be married to be unhappy, if ever done must be mutual self-sacrifice from choice. God help and bless both of us.

8th. Came home on morning train. An hour too early at the depot. Chester called and played three games of chess. Victor. Minnie at home in evening. Played authors. Saw her home. Am quite uneasy yet as to the result of F's decision. Anyway I will try to be happy myself and to make others happy, be good and do good. God help me.

9th. Wednesday spent the day at home. Somewhat rainy. Played chess with Thede and read in "Dutch Republic." What is more trying to be borne than suspense.

10th. Major Nettleton returned. Told M. this morning in regard to F. and myself. She thinks as I do, that if the girl really loves me she ought to know it. If not, we ought to stop our intimacy. So shall I act. Received letter, unable to decide, does not know her own heart. Answered, after a crying spell, and consulting with Ma and M. We all think alike. Feel as if I were doing my duty anyway. Finished the letter and went to Friday prayer meeting. Spoke. Did me good. Determined through the grace of God to make my trial a blessing. Will be a man and a Christian. Called at Fannie Hudson's. Meeting in the evening.

12th. Wrote to Alf Webber and Hugh. Read some in Dio Lewis' "Weak Lungs, and How to Make Them Strong"—much interested. Called yesterday to see Jamie Johnson. Walked home from town with Ella and challenged for a game of chess. Went down and played in the evening—the champion. Letter from Fannie asking me to come down.

13th. Felt so unwell and uneasy, concluded not to go to church. Lay down part of the day. Read "Bitter Sweet," by Holland. Much interested.

14th. Ma, Thede and I went down and looked at the Bushnell place. Concluded to take it. Went to Cleveland on P. M. train. Considerable snow last night and yesterday. Pleasant overhead but bad underneath. Almost concluded not to go out today on account of feeling so miserably weak and nervous. Went immediately to Mr. Cobb's. Helen came to the door. I fairly shook. Oh, could I see Fannie. I went in. Helen brought me a letter from Fannie. Soon F. came. The letter told her sorrow at the trouble, reviewed our friendship, told her doubt and how she had hid it and smothered it and not allowed herself to think she hadn't true love for me. She said "With my child-love, I loved you Luman. Why I do not now, I do not know." Again, "I never would admit that I did not love you, I can not say now that I do not." Helen came. She pitied both of us. 'Twas a sad misfortune, but it was probably for our good. She felt from her conversation with F. and questions that she did not love me as she should. She thought we had better part friends and await the will of God. F. said once, "Oh it seems as though I could throw my arms around your neck and take it all back." Helen was very kind to me and wished me to write to her. How sad the necessity of such a course. F. had been crying. She undoubtedly sympathizes with me in my sore trial. She prayed and hoped it would be different some day. If the change did come, she would fly to me. Her sympathy, if that it is, is deep. I can not realize that she does not love me. How can I have been mistaken these years—since she was seventeen. I can forgive all, for she suffered herself to please me. How strange our parting was—solemn, but as of old. Oh it all seems but a mere dream to me. Can it be reality? It seems cruel, but a wise God will make it a blessing, I hope. I pray God that he will sustain and bless us and bring us together here below, if he can consistently, if not, grant us both a rich inheritance in Heaven. This meeting and parting, can I ever forget it? No, never. Can it be that we have parted to be mere friends forever? It can not seem so to me. It always has seemed to me during these years that we were fated to be and dwell together, bearing each the other's burdens and each other's joys, most of all happy in each other's love. Time will disclose all of its secrets and eternity, all till then remaining mysterious. I'll await the result as trustfully and patiently as possible. God's will, not ours be done. I must use every exertion not to allow this to ruin or seriously injure me. It will not do for me to think much of the matter.

Went home on the night freight. Home after 10. Showed Ma my letter and told her the result of interview.

15th. All the young folks were invited to Dea. Turner's to tea. I remained at home. Played chess with Thede. Read some— attending preaching in the evening. Prof. Fairchild made a good discourse. Got out my letters from Fannie, reviewed them and burned them. It seemed hard and sad to do so, but I knew it was best. Could not discover any change in the style of her letters in the spring of 1861. They seemed full as warm and affectionate then as ever during the whole year.

16th. Melissa wrote a letter to F. I enclosed a note speaking of my burning the letters and asking F. to do the same way with mine and also my pictures. Melissa took my letters around to Minnie's. Thede and I walked around before supper.

17th. Stormy day. Played a little chess and read some. In the P. M. went to Thursday lecture. A stranger, an old graduate, occupied the pulpit—from a tent on Tappan Square. Columbian's concert in the evening. Remained at home with Ma and baby Carrie.

Friday, 18th. Spent most of the day in the house. So interested in a game of chess that I forgot the church prayer meeting till too late. Attended preaching in the evening.

19th. Spent the day getting things ready for leaving. Saw Prof. Peck. Called at Maria's (Jewell) in the evening, then at Minnie's. Game of authors. Melissa, Flora and I at M.'s. Nettleton came in on the night freight. Regt. received marching orders, Mt. Sterling, Ky.

Sunday, 20th. Went to S. S. in the morning. Mr. Fitch spoke splendidly. Pres. Finney preached, the old and new heart, righteous and wicked man. Minnie and John came over in P. M. Called at Mrs. Holtsander's. Went home with Minnie to tea. Then to preaching by Mr. Fairfield. Neglect of so great salvation. This has been a happy day to me and withal a sad one. Oh it seems very hard to leave home again. Would that I could go with affairs in a little different state.

21st. Packed up in the morning. Went to Cleveland on the P. M. train. George went to the depot with me. Thede rode the horses. Saw Will, took supper with him. Went to the depot and around somewhat, expecting Fred. Good visit with Delos. Put up at Forest City Hotel. Saw most of the Co. Boys. Half of 2nd O. V. C. on a drunk.

Tuesday, 22nd. Went with Thede over to Uncle Jones'. Stayed till after dinner. Visited with boys. Saw Will and Terrell play billiards. Introduced to Mrs. Case. Col. Purington asked me in to see his wife. In the evening officers presented Mrs. P. with a silver tea service. $3.00 per man. Wine, etc. Didn't indulge. Saw the Arabs perform—great feats.

23rd. Boys on hand to start. Didn't get off. Tomorrow at 10 we now expect to leave. Most of the regt. has got along. Thede and I went over to Uncle Jones' to tea and remained till 8:30 P. M. Then went to depot and welcomed Fred. Delos and Will there too. We four "B. F.s" spent several hours very pleasantly. Made me both happy and sad. Seemed good for so many to be together again.

Thursday, 24th. After breakfast went to town. Forgot my belt. Had to go by Mr. Cobb's three times. Felt sad as I breathed a goodbye. Sad sad, sad! Will times ever change? I am glad none of my friends can know the feelings of my heart. Fred and Will and Terrell went to the depot with me. Boys feeling well. Got off at 10. Reached Columbus at 7 P. M. Left at 10 P. M.

Friday, 25th. Reached Cincinnati a little before daylight. Marched in the rain to barracks up town. Got breakfast at a restaurant. Telegram came ordering us to Annapolis. Boys received the news with huzzas. Rejoiced that we were not obliged to go to Knoxville. Dismounted and encamped as we had orders to do. Took the cars again at 8 P. M.

26th. Reached Columbus at 10 A. M. Took the Central Ohio. Never passed through the country before. Pleased with Newark and Zanesville. Country rough east.

Sunday, 27th.   Reached Bellaire at 2:30 A. M. and were ferried across the river.   Took the Baltimore and Ohio road before daylight.   In box cars—plenty of straw.   Very rough country. Fairmount, Grafton most important town today, junction of the two branches.   Road ran along the Monongahela for a time, then the Cheat River. . Passed through several tunnels, one nearly a mile long.   Some very heavy grades—117 ft. per mile for 17 miles..

Monday, 28th.   Passed through Martinsburg and Harper's Ferry.   Saw John Brown's engine house, a very strong position indeed.   Great amount of work on the road, 13 trains passed us this morning going west.   Road along the Potomac many miles. Passed Relay House about 9 A. M.   Annapolis Junction at 10 P. M. Tried to get the landlord up to get some supper.   Great time.   After rattling away at doors and windows, got up on roof to window where there was a light.   People nearly frightened to death.   One woman about eight months gone—man feared for her.   Officers went to saloon and then back to cars.

29th.   Reached paroled camp at Annapolis before daylight. Passed the day in camp.   No stores and no wood.   Good time chatting, laughing and fooling.   In evening played a game of chess with Major Nettleton.   Slept with him at Post Quartermaster's, Maj. Carpenter from Akron.   Camp very pleasant.   Barber shop, reading room, chapel, news depot, neat buildings and good soil.

30th.   A rainy unpleasant day.   Detailed to act as R. Q. M. vice Bills, who thinks of resigning on account of matters at home. Played some at chess.   Boys seem to regret my leaving the com‧ pany.   I know I do.   I do desire to do my duty well, faithfully and honestly.   In the evening took the non-commissioned officers over for oysters.   Went to chapel to prayer meeting—interesting.

31st.   Went to town to the Q. M. with Bill.   A rainy unpleasant day.   Slept with Brother N. at Q. M. Carpenter's.

APRIL, 1864.

April 1st.   Moved camp over the railroad, three-quarters of a mile.   Went to town and got camp and G. equipage, and hay and wood.

2nd.   Got up some straw and forage.   A rainy day. Slept with Bill in Q. M. Dept.

April 3rd.   Sunday.   Went to town and receipted for clothing.   A rainy unpleasant day.

4th.   Went to town with Tom Wood.   Worked all day and finally succeeded in getting two loads of clothing.   Very rainy and unpleasant.   Teams got lost.   Worried Tom—misunderstanding.

5th.   Burge and Tom went to town.   Found the teams and got the rest of the clothing.   Still unpleasant and chilly.   Boys all catching cold.

6th.   Issued clothing to the companies.   Short on several articles.   Had Thede detailed.   Barber commenced cooking.

7th. Thursday. Letters from home yesterday. Read the "Life of Capt. Hurley Vicars" in the morning. Tom and Thede went to town to see Dan. P. M. went out to see companies drill. Would like to drill right well. Dreamed of Fannie last night.

8th-19th. Generally went to town once during the day on business and to see Dan. The boy has seen trouble and I fear that it will be too much for him. He had been intimate with and for some time engaged to a young lady of wealthy family. The father opposed the intimacy and engagement and ordered all attentions discontinued. Burned Dan's letters and her letters, taking them from the office privily. She remained true, but her father compelled her to marry another, she all the time protesting. I know how to sympathize with Dan, poor boy.

Twenty-six officers and non-commissioned officers ordered into Penn. to buy horses for the regt. to be gone five days or thereabouts. Gen. Burnside came to see us one day. Another day, Burnside, Grant and Washburn reviewed us. Have read "Sutherland," author unknown, not much liked because it has a pro-slavery tendency. "Red Tape and Pigeon Hole Generals." Telling criticisms on Fitz-John Porter, Butterfield, McClellan and Regulars generally. Written in a spicy and entertaining style and withal quite interesting and I guess, truthful.

Reported that Burnside's expedition will leave on the 24th. Fear that we will be left in the lurch. Dread to be. Have played chess somewhat with A. B. N. Ma has moved to Minnie's, Minnie very sick. Written home twice and heard twice.

20th. Received orders to turn in A Tents and draw shelter tents in readiness to go to Washington for outfit. Went to town late on bus. Drake received commission and Brown acceptance of resignation, good all around. Gave an oyster supper. Was not present.

21st. Went to town half a dozen times. No train comes yet. Struck tents and moved out to camp. Parole before dark. Turned over property. Slept in open air.

22nd. Cars ready and off at 10 A. M. Got to Washington at 4 P. M. Rode to 6th St. wharf and made arrangements for transportation to Giesboro. Rather disappointed in the city of which I have read so much, where so many great men have congregated, where so much treason has been plotted, inhuman laws made. Penn. Ave. is a moderately pretty street, but otherwise the city seems the poorest I was ever in. The capitol is grand, massive, grounds beautiful.

23rd. Went to the White House and went through the East Room and two or three reception rooms. Eight very large mirrors in the East room, velvet and gilt papering, heavy brussels carpet, elegant sofas. Reception room surpasses anything I ever saw. Waited at Soldier's Rest from 9 till 1 P. M. for Major Seward. Then got teams for baggage. Went to depot to have boats ready. Weather as mild and warm as in June. Streets very, very dusty. Wil-

lard's and Metropolitan fine hotels.   Passed Treasury Building.
Moved at 4 P. M. to Camp Stoneman, via Giesboro Point by boat.
Drew tents.

24th-29th.   Busy at work supplying the regt. with horses,
etc. 29 officers, on extra duty, returned to regt. Orders to march
as soon as possible. Papers from home. Busy exchanging horses.
Got 33 good ones in Washington.

30th.   F.'s birthday—alas! alas! Busy all day getting Q. M.
stores and fixing up for the march. Wrote home and to George.
Didn't get to bed till nearly one. Have had hard work for several
days.

MAY, 1864.

May 1st.   Busy getting ordnance boxes returned to Dept. till
10 o'clock. Regt. marched at 11. Train off at about 1 P. M.—12
wagons. Thede and I stayed behind to get receipts for property.
Left Washington between 5 and 6 o'clock. Capt. and A. D. C.
on Maj. Gen. Auger's staff disliked to give me a pass for fear we
would be gobbled! Caught up just as the regt. camped 9 or 10
miles from Washington. Supper and to bed at 10 P. M. Slept well,
beautiful day.

2nd.   Reveille at 4. Off at 7. Pike road still. Passed through
Fairfax C. H. a place of only half a dozen scattered buildings. No
fences along the road and very few houses, and those abandoned,
hilly country and considerably woody. Camped near Bristol Station. 22nd and 24th N. Y. and 3rd N. J. near us. Commenced raining before we got our tents pitched. Cold, wet night. Slept very
well.

Monday, 3rd.   Moved on at 8 o'clock having waited for tents
to dry off. Passed Catlett Station and reached Warrenton Junction at noon. Burnside's d rs. here. One Div. here. Passed one
at Manassas, at Ferrero and one at Bristol. Drew hay for our
feed, also oats for three days. Also 7 wagons. Kept quite busy.
Didn't get much sleep; ordered to march at 2 A. M. Cold—Tea—8
days of commissaries and 5 of forage.

4th.   Got off before 4 o'clock. Came up with one div. of infantry at Bealeton Station. Beautiful morning. Went on to Brandy
Station, unsaddled and got dinner and finally remained overnight.
Drew hay and picked up some oats. Fight at Chancellorsville. Did
some business.

5th.   Orders to march at 4 o'clock. Got up in time for breakfast. Today our forces seem to abandon Brandy Station, and the
railroad. Most of the army across the Rapidan and Germania Ford.
Reached the ford with 300 cattle at 10. Four companies reported
to Gen. Wilcox. Infantry crossing all day, 9th Corps. A very
warm day. Dusty roads, faces all crisped. Rapidan a narrow
rocky bottom, high banks, rapid stream. Rappahannock narrow
and less rapid. Went into camp about a mile from the river, rode

out Pike to our pickets. Rebel pickets in sight. Very heavy firing on the left in the 6th Sedgwicks Corps. Quite heavy loss. Rumor that Butler was in Petersburg and Thomas fighting at Dalton. (Beginning of Grant's attack on Lee and the Campaign of the Wilderness.)

6th. Regt. saddled and moved out into position at 2 o'clock. After breakfast went out to Regt. awhile. Very hot. Firing commenced at daylight. Heaviest again in Sedgwick's Corps. Burnside over near Chancellorsville. Just about dark firing was very heavy. Various reports in regard to loss. Dreamed last night of Fannie.

7th. At 1 o'clock, received orders to pull out. Followed some 3rd Div. trains. Went down near Chancellorsville and breakfasted. Firing commenced early. Very hot and sultry. Regt. still back at the Ford. Moved to Chancellorsville (the walls of a brick house mark the spot) and remained over night. A good many fortifications remaining of those thrown up a year ago. Firing has been incessant all day. Troops passing towards Spottsylvania all night.

8th. During the day moved to Todd's Tavern. A large open space. All the trains of the army parked here. An ocean of teams. Pulled out a short distance after dark. General order saying that our armies had been victorious at Spottsylvania during the day. Parked near Gen. Burnside's Hdqrs. Saw Gen. Stevenson, Patten and Patrick. Maj. Nettleton stayed with us. Considerable encouraging news in regard to Butler and Thomas.

9th. Moved half a mile in the afternoon and then divided my forage to last till Sunday. Many of the teams on quarter rations. Hard fighting, all day.

10th. During the day went to the regt. Some beef, 16½ cents per pound. Thomas and I went to the front. Arrived there at nearly sundown just as a charge was to be made. Gen. Grant, Meade and several lesser generals with staffs out. We fell in. Col. Upton's Brigade charged and took the enemy's works with a brigade of rebs under Dough. Grant had one of his never-ending stubs in his mouth, and puffed freely. Both Grant and Meade looked serious and thoughtful till the news of success came. Then they seemed pleased. Grant said "That looks like desperation, surrendering without firing a gun." But they had held their ground stubbornly during the day. Grant said "A brigade today, will try a corps tomorrow." Never felt more animated. I felt such a relief from the suspense and anxiety which had been upon me for several days. I presume nearly the whole of the army and country are as uneasy and anxious as I. I awake frequently during the night. "H." moved half a mile last night towards Fredericksburg. Rained most all day. Heavy fighting all day, with little success. Several charges made, but rebs repulsed them.

12th. Orders early to move. Sent 10 teams yesterday after forage. Sent two today for rations. Went with Pike and Ed. Livingston to the front, raining quite hard. Last night Gen.

Hancock moved from right to left and this morning captured a division of Rebs under Johnson—Bushrod, I hear. Several charges made to little purpose. Ed and I visited our breastworks and one battery of 15 guns, Napoleon 12 and Rifled guns. Artillery firing very heavy all along the lines. Train pulled out about 2 o'clock and moved to within 3 miles of Fredericksburg. Cut off several miles of bad roads. Camped a little after dark. Rainy night. Firing still continues.

13th. Comparatively quiet today. Christ's brigade, Pa. and Mich. 9th Corps badly cut up in a charge. Com. killed beef and took to the command. Saw a paper of the 11th. Forage train arrived.

14th. Sent forage to the Regt. Maj. Seward came with four companies from Belle Plains. Gave several some dinner. Maj. Seward remained with us, unable to ride further. Regt. near Todd's Tavern. No news from the army. Report that it is swinging round to the left. Some fighting in Burnside's Corps.

Sunday, 15th. Trains passing to the rear all night and today. Started teams for forage. Rainy night and cloudy today. Several from the Regt. down, Col. P.—Regt. under Maj. Nettleton had a fight with a brigade of rebs. Lost 15 or 20 horses, and four men were wounded. Rebs fell back as soon as the "dark cloud" made its appearance. Big reports came to the rear. Guess Dutton showed little pluck.

16th. Moved down to the valley near Fredericksburg. Went into town twice and looked at the fortifications and city. It must have been beautiful before the war. Scenery along the river splendid. Went around with Nettleton and Seward. Town full of wounded.

17th. Lay in camp all day. Played whist with Seward and Abbey.

18th. Read *Independents* and "Night and Morning," by Charles Leper. Hard fighting today at Spottsylvania, nearly a drawn game. Ours if either.

19th. Went down with Thede to Spottsylvania. Visited all the fortifications. Went to the picket line. Could see the rebs very distinctly in rifle pits and works. Our fortifications only 1200 yds. apart. Train captured and recaptured.

20th. Birge got in last night with oats. Went out to Regt. Considerable excitement on account of report that Ewell had flanked our army and was about to attack Fredericksburg.

21st. Regt. back at F. All trains leaving on Bowling Green. Got off at dark. 4 miles during the night.

2nd. Got into Guiney Station at noon. Stayed till the next day:

23rd. Aroused at 1:30 A. M. Got off at 3:30. I went back to the regt. and remained till 3 P. M. Reached the train at Milford Station, 3 miles below Bowling Green. A beautiful little village. A splendid rolling country. Rows of trees along the road each side. A good night's rest.

24th. Read in "Villette." Saw Lt. Bennett, 44th N. Y. Heavy firing in the distance nearly all day. Train moved out in the evening. Crossed the Mattapony. Went one and one-half miles and camped at 1:30 A. M.

25th. Troops crossed the North Anna. Regt. camped near the train. Read in "Villette" and played a little at cards.

26th. A rainy unpleasant day. Went down to the Regt. Regt. moved in the evening to Milford and on towards the "White House." Trains commenced passing to the rear by another road to the white house.

27th. Orders to hitch up about 11 A. M. Moved about 3 P. M. Read one volume of "Marble Faun." Marched all night.

28th. Saw Col. P. Train moved on to Newtown and camped. Regt. ordered to the cavalry corp. Made preparations to remain with the Regt.—Thede, Hank, Barb and I. Regt. captured nine reb wagons yesterday. Plenty of corn and bacon. Glee Club gave some music at F. F. V., reb family.

29th. Sunday. Reached the 3rd Div. C. C. little before midnight. 1st Brigade Col. McIntosh. Camped near Hanovertown on the Pamunkey. Crossed the Mattapony today and passed through Dunkirk. Like to remain with the Regt.

30th. Remained in camp till 5 P. M. when we were ordered to march. Went out one mile and dismounted. Soon received orders to return to camp. Artillery firing commenced early in the morning and continued all day—terrific towards evening. A continuous roar. What suspense. God grant that we may be successful. May He give wisdom and grace to our leaders, strength and nerve to our men and victory to our cause. We must be successful, for it must be that the right is on our side. I would give anything to know and witness how goes the battle. A very warm day.

31st. Saddled up and moved at 3 A. M. Crossed the Pamunkey and took Hanover Court House. About two miles from town began skirmishing. At noon 2nd made a charge, driving the enemy and capturing some prisoners, skirmishing till about sundown, when the brigade formed and charged the rebel position about the court house. I was on the left. Rode my horse. Firing very hot indeed. Rebels held a fence along a sunken road and several houses. 2nd charged this position. The number of dead (rebs) left upon the field told plainly the work we did. Rebels gave way. Came near capturing two pieces of artillery which played upon us till the last minute. Our regiment lost 25 in killed and wounded. Remained in position during night. In the morning moved on towards Ashland.

JUNE, 1864.

June 1st. Skirmishing all the way to Ashland under McIntosh. 5th N. Y. in advance. Soon after reaching Ashland rear was attacked. Then commenced a fight lasting till near sundown, when we left up the R. R. track by order of Gen. Wilson, who was on the telegraph road with the remainder of Div. Reached Hanover C. H. about 11 P. M., the object of the movement being accomplished, viz.: bridges over the North Anna were destroyed. Again the 2nd O. V. V. C. did splendidly—probably saving the Brigade.

June 2nd. Lay in camp near Hanover C. H. at Dr. Price's till dark when we moved towards White House. Went into camp about 2 A. M.

3rd. Reinforcements coming in rapidly via W. H. and also Fredericksburg. 13th O. C. arrived. Saw paper of the 31st. News very encouraging. Reported move of rebel infantry around and to rear of Burnside's right. Guess old Grant has fixed it so as to give them a warm reception.. Rained yesterday and last night. Our troops in good spirits. 2nd Brigade in our advance. Fought over the ground near Salem Church where our Cavalry Corps had a severe fight with rebel infantry the day they crossed the Pamunkey. Col. Prescott, 1st Vermont, killed and Lt. Col. 1st Conn. wounded in the thigh. Rebs retreated beyond our fortifications. 1st Brigade Battery fired a little. Moved up to the outer works and remained till night. 2nd Brigade formed over to the left nearly at right angles to Burnside's line. Three Divisions of rebel infantry, Heths of Ewell's Corps, Rhodes of Hill's, and one of Longstreet's charged the flank of Burnside. Rebs were repulsed with great slaughter. 2nd Brigade did splendidly. The cross fire of artillery and musketry just mowed down the rebels. 1st Brigade moved back and formed where we formed in the morning. Slept till morning. Letter from home, May 15.

4th. Soon after daybreak Regt. moved up. Packs ordered up and breakfast got near the church. Regt. dismounted and put into the breastworks. Rebel cavalry charged and drove our boys from the first line of works, by flanking them. Soon column came up and rebs ran back. Had one killed and two or three wounded in their scrape. Tom came up in the evening, going back to the company, would like to go myself. About sundown the firing on Burnside's right was the most terrific I ever heard and continued for nearly half an hour. It must have been an assault. Am anxious to hear the result. Gen. Torbert's division of cavalry arrived. Regt. nearly all on duty.

Sunday, 5th. Rainy and cool this morning. Would that I could see some of the dear home friends. A letter from Minnie Friday did us much good. Hear the glad result of the fighting last night. Rebels charged our center from five to eight times and every time were repulsed. Passed the day mostly under the fly, visiting with the boys, reading my testament and thinking over old times, troubles, joys, blessings, etc. The phantom form still haunts me day and night. Cleared off before sundown. All the commissary corps here now. Gen. Wilson remarked today to Gen. Sheridan that the 2nd Ohio was the best regiment in the Div., that the 5th N. Y. was formerly but it had to yield to the 2nd now.

6th. During the morning the corps fell back to "Old Church Tavern," near Newcastle on the Pamunkey to rest men and recruit horses. I went on to the train to see about forage, etc. Took supper with the boys. Like Capt. Viall very much. A very pleasant man but of little principle, I guess. Tom came back with me. He returned to company.

7th. Our wagons came up. Went down again to train. Took four mules to draw forge. Q. M. away, so failed. Have worked pretty faithfully for a forge but yet without success. Saw Col. of 2nd N. Y. this morning and borrowed a forge—temporarily. Got some clothing and shoeing tools.

8th. Got an order from Col. Hammond and procured a forge of the 5th N. Y., an old one, shoes and nails. 2nd O. V. C. went out on picket. Relieved 1st Conn. Firing still continues at intervals along the line. Grant is getting siege guns up to the front. Everything looks encouraging. Railroad in progress.

9th. Read in "Queen Mab," by Julia Kavanagh. Shoeing horses as rapidly as possible. A very sultry, oppressive day. A few drops of rain. Turned in to Capt. Viall 3 contraband mules temporarily. Hired David Brooks.

10th. Friday. Cloudy this morning and a cool refreshing breeze stirring. Wrote a letter home. Would we could see the dear friends. Regt. relieved from picket. I feel happy and contented today. Would that these uneasy, dark, gloomy moments would never come again. Night of the 4th dreamed of a lost friend.

11. Wrote to Fred Allen, and Watson Jones. Big mail came. Whole month. Big feast.

12th. Wrote a letter of apology to Mr. Brown, our former chaplain. Would my temper, etc., never got the upper hand of me. Read *Independents*. Afternoon ordered to move in evening. Sent off train. Our Regt. in rear till midnight.

13th. In the morning our regiment left at White House road on picket and rear guard. Several prisoners. Whole army moved. Rear guard until we crossed the Chickahominy, a narrow, swampy, insignificant stream. Remained near the river—south bank—till dark. Moved on towards Charles City C. H.—camping from 2 A. M. till daylight.

14th. Moved on to Charles City, and drew one-half day's rations of provisions. Remained saddled till 3 P. M. when we moved back on the Richmond road to the junction of Richmond and Harrison Landing roads. Remained saddled at some church till morning. Hasty breakfast.

15th. Moved out on Richmond road, and Malvern Hill road till we encountered the enemy. Six companies of our regiment on extreme left skirmish line—rest in reserve, till the 18 P. V. were driven back in a little disorder; then the six companies were ordered in. So much confusion on part of 18th that we were into the rebs or they into us before we knew it. Then came confusion of orders. Our boys saw rebel infantry. Did them some damage.

By order fell back a few rods and then held our line. One of Co.
A killed and one of Co. M wounded. After one-half hour ordered
to fall back. Nettleton's Batt. holding the rebs—mounted—2 men
wounded and 3 horses killed. Awfulest place for a fight we were
ever in. Very thick pine brush and few trees. Woods on fire and
smoke almost intolerable. Got out well. Fell back to junction
of roads. I dismounted to fight. 2nd Ohio on picket. Co. M. ordered back to Smith's store where we had fought. Rebs came in
rear. Killed Sergt. Edson. One missing. Quiet till morning. Deep
sleep. Rations issued. We failed to get any. Oh this is the most
fatiguing work we ever did.

16th. Engineer Corps came out and made fortifications. 2nd
had strong works. Co. D left in a fort thing built by Co. in evening
over night. Just at dusk before regt. fell back, rebels came out to
open place and we gave them a volley. Co. D withdrew to works
soon after daylight—rebs appearing in force. Great deal of sport.
Rebs came down to mill. Our boys would fire and they would aim
to kill. Dropped one horse and probably one man. Withdrew at
dark to Charles City Landing, arriving at 3 A. M., horses having
remained under the saddle 108 hours with no feed and little grazing, horses very weak. Report that Petersburg had been captured
—false.

17th. Moved soon after daylight across the James River on
pontoon bridges. River full of boats, splendid river. Camped
till 3 P. M. Drew rations and forage. Moved to 4 miles of Petersburg, other brigade too. Camped at 10 P. M. till morning.

18th. At 4 A. M. moved out on Sussex C. H. road and camped
8 miles from Petersburg. In evening drew rations and forage. In
P. M. awful connonading and musketry, the most terrific we have
yet heard. Already last night we held all but the inner line of
works. Captured 22 guns and many prisoners. Report that the
blacks captured one fort with 4 guns, and killed all the garrison.
Yesterday was almost sick, am better today, but weak. Awful bad
water for a few days. Oh the anxiety to know the result of the
fighting today. God grant us success.

19th. Sunday. Bathed and washed shirt and drawers. Read
some in the Acts of the Apostles. Went to headquarters with
Purington.

20th. Moved camp into the woods to the left of the old camp
in the open field. Major Nettleton attacked with dysentery. Letter
last night from George, the night before, from home. Both welcome. Drew two days' forage.

21st. Tuesday. Wrote home and to George's people in Tenn.
Saw Gen. Kautz. He came over to pay us a visit. It seemed good
to shake his hand and talk with him once more. Hope that we can
be transferred to his command. He encouraged us. Preparations
for a big move tomorrow by the cavalry. May success attend us.
Kautz thinks that Richmond is a certain capture. Very hot day.
Maj. N. goes to hospital, best man in our Regt., brave, upright,

modest, dignified and sound in principles and morals. Would the same could be said of more of our officers.

22nd. Up last night till midnight issuing oats, etc., and drawing clothing. Regt. up at 1 A. M. and moved at 2. Moved through byroads around to the Jerusalem Plank road across to Reams' Station on the Weldon and Petersburg R. R. having crossed the Norfolk R. R. Burned the station and water tanks and a quantity of wood. Moved off to Dinwiddie C. H. and then across the country to the Petersburg and Lynchburg R. R. Destroyed several miles of track, tearing up much and burning fence rails on the rest. Don't think this did much good. Kautz captured two trains of cars loaded with furniture, etc., from Petersburg. Went into camp at 11 and remained till 1:30 A. M. (This began the famous and rather disastrous "Wilson's Raid.")

23rd. Moved on the R. R. destroying as we went till noon, when we got dinner. 12 miles from Burkesville a rebel force under W. H. Lee as reported of about 2000 cavalry got between Kautz and Wilson. Fight commenced immediately and lasted till dark— our brigade in rear. Drove the rebs at dark in a charge—our regt. on picket and in support of a battery. Got a good night's rest. Pickets firing all the time.

24th. At 3 A. M. breakfasted. Column moved out on Meherrin road—our Regt. the rear guard. Reached the station at 4 P. M. On picket. Troops destroyed the track as they advanced. Road made of stringers and bar iron spiked on. Destruction almost complete. Disturbed but little on picket.

25th. Up early and moved at 4 A. M. 2nd Brigade in rear. Passed through Keysville at 5 A. M. Took a detail of 20 men away from column for horses and mules. A great many men dismounted in the heat of yesterday. Went 6 or 7 miles to the right of the R. R. Passed through a very rich and beautiful country. Never saw more splendid crops. Went to Charlotte C. H. (Charlotte (Co.) C. H. is given as Marysville on war maps, and in Century Atlas as Smithville.) Detachment of 2nd N. Y. broke open stores, released two civil prisoners and did many things out of the way. Our boys did not indulge in one thing disgraceful to my knowledge. People complimented us very highly. Seemed very thankful that we were so kind to them. They seemed perfectly surprised that we did not burn and rob. What a shame that Southern papers should deceive the country so in regard to our army. Got dinner at Mrs. Smith's, very pleasant and kind. Wanted my name, for she should always remember me with a feeling of kindness and obligation. Son in Wise's brigade. Rejoined the column near Mossing Ford with about 25 mules and horses. All the stock and carriages had been run farther off. Many pretty girls in town, some refugees from Fredericksburg. Most of them had been north and had dear friends there. Dressed neatly, pleasant and educated. Pleased with the trip. Halted one mile from the Staunton river. Artillery firing. Rode up to the front with Col. Purington. Rebels fortified on west bank of the river. Heavy fort on one side of the R. R. and a battery on the other. Entrenchments right on the bank of the river. Our boys on the east bank without protection. Our batteries in prominent position commanding bridge and reb works. Quite a duel. Our boys suffered from grape and canister. Reb force supposed to be about 1000 militia and 300 regulars. At 11 moved by our batteries in easy range of reb batteries up the river R. R. crossing covered with hay to muffle the sound. Depot buildings full of wounded. Moved on to Wylliesburg, arriving at daylight.

26th. Kautz left the Staunton just before daylight. Passed through Christianville, getting a good supply of corn and oats. Crossed the south fork of the Meherrin river and camped. All quiet.

27th. Moved out early in the morning. Encountered rebs about noon. Encamped an hour. 2nd Ohio on picket. Moved nearly all night. Stopped from 1:30 till 3. 8 miles from Lawrenceville.

28th. D. and L. companies extremes. 2nd Ohio in advance. Stopped at one rich plantation thoroughly secesh. Col. said to the lady of the house, "We are out foraging today and are coming down here to live soon." She said, "I guess Gen. Lee will have something to say about that." Crossed the Nottoway at the double bridge. After crossing Stony Creek encountered rebels in force. 2nd soon in. Charged—drove rebs. Rebs charged back again and drove us. Brigade dismounted and went into the woods and soon into the open fields and drove the rebs back some distance. 2nd Batt. in picket. After firing moved up to a house and lane and formed. Advanced. Soon close and heavy work. Night came on. Boys hastily built breastworks of rails 50 yds from rebs. Soon our Regt. was reduced to 50 or 60 men who lay upon their faces till midnight, when the line withdrew a little. I was mounted for some time in the lane and behind the house, firing and carrying orders till the line advanced when I dismounted and led forward with the line. Awful hot. Horse got away once. Before midnight my lungs began to bleed so badly that I mounted and went back to Artillery and then to a fire. Several very heavy volleys by the rebs—said to be infantry.

29th. By daylight, all our force save three Regts. and brigade for rear guard had moved out towards Ream's Station. Heavy firing in rear. Soon heard that rebs had got between horses and men and captured nearly all. Reached Ream's Station about noon. Rebels in heavy force, cavalry and infantry. Longstreet's Corps being along the railroad to Weldon. Kautz went on in morning to take position. Sent back word that the command could not get through. Wilson said we must. Soon organized to charge through. Then this was given up. 5th N. Y. partly dismounted and part in reserve. Same with 2nd Ohio. Then mounted as reserve. Wilson got ready to leave by the road we came—burned the wagons and moved on. Soon rebs came on dismounted in our rear. Very heavy force. Moved off regularly towards the battery, which opened with grape and canister. Moved up to Kautz' division through the woods. Col. absent—don't know why. Kautz said the orders were to get out the best way possible. Columns moved near together. Moved to the southwest to near Stony Creek Station and crossed the R. R. Advance charged the rebs. Kautz had considerable fighting at first. Soon after crossing the R. R. rebs came upon our rear and we had a run of several miles—5th Penn. and Detachments of several regts.—Col. West in command. No advance or rear guard. Had I been a line officer, I should have organized a force rear guard. Did propose the thing to Capt. Easton, but he couldn't see it. Held up and walked determined if there were any more firing to fall out and call upon 2nd Ohio and wait. Tom Wood, brave and true boy, fell out with several others and formed rear guard when almost within our lines. Rebs in ambush fired upon them and killed Tom. Poor fellow. How sorry I am for his young wife. Camped soon after passing our picket.

30th. Moved on to the 2nd Corps inside of the entrenchments. 6th Corps moved out too late yesterday to relieve us. Tore up several miles of the Welden R. R. We are satisfied with our work. Several miles on the south side R. R. and 25 or 30 miles of the Danville R. R. Sorry that we could not get out without so much loss. Blame Wilson. No grain and no day's rations.

JULY, 1864.

July 1st. Got a light ration of forage. Lay in the dirt all day. Bought some rations and got some sanitary stores. Got along well. Ordered to move in the morning at 6.

2nd. Rations of forage and commissary. Marched about 8. Went by the 9th Corps. Maj. Seward, Meeks, Thede and I rode over to Wilcox's Div. and saw Reeve Spencer. Went up to the line and saw the 60th Ohio. Got popped at twice by sharpshooters, and were careful too. Took dinner with Reeve. Our works strong but rebel works full as strong and occupying more commanding ground and much of the ground in rear of our 1st line. Sharpshooters doing much damage. About 20 hit each day in the Div. Interested in the heavy works taken by the 18th Corps and by the Darkies. Saw quite an artillery duel between a heavy battery on our side and reb battery on the other side of Appomattox. Petersburg in plain view. Splendid time. Rode down to City Point and thence to Light House Point where we found our corps, about 200 2nd O. V. V. C. quite encouraging. The Detachments came down behind us.

3rd. Went to City Point with Kelly. Had a real good visit with Brother John. Seemed splendid to see him. Got back to the corps about dusk. Visited the Sanitary. Big thing. (Prof. John M. Ellis was serving on the Christian Commission at City Point.)

4th. Spent the day very quietly in camp. Have been great rumors as to today's proceedings, but nothing has occurred as we hear.

5th. Marsh came down and stayed to dinner. Moved camp a mile. A very hot day indeed. Good visit with Marsh. Better camp.

6th. Passed the day quietly in camp. Spencer here today. Very warm. In a shady place. Nice bower and shade trees in afternoon.

7th. Got clothing and issued. Not very well today. Have had several good games of chess with Major. Wrote to Roxena yesterday.

8th. Barber was sick so Bob and Thede got dinner. Very warm day. Did very little. Read some.

9th. Finished a letter to Uncle Albert. Not as neat and concise as I wish it were. I am too apt to hurry my work of all kinds—I must be more guarded. Thede went down to see John.

10th. Took the inspected horses to Quartermaster Stone and turned them in—79 to be receipted for by Lt. Spangler. Had a good bath. Read several articles in the *Atlantic*. My eyes are occasioning me considerable trouble. Have thought of home a good deal today. Many of the officers are thinking of going home when their three years' term expires. Of course it would be pleasant to go home as soon as possible, but many officers promised their men that they would remain with them. I don't know what I shall do. I could not go to Oberlin to stay and I have no desire to go elsewhere and I think for the present every man able should bear arms.

11th. Was busy in the morning. Went to Q. M.'s and C. S.'s. Thought some of going to see John, but gave up the idea. Wrote home. Thede wrote too. Read some in *Atlantic*. Played game of "Seven Up" with Lukins.

12th. Drew and issued clothing. Very sultry day. Sprinkled this morning and tonight. Wrote to Tom Wood's wife. Nettleton went to Point. Good many rumors about our going away North, and others.

13th. Wrote home and to Hugh Beer's wife. More clothing.

14th. Papers of the 13th. Grand panic in Baltimore and Washington.

15th. Extra men moved near d rs. John came down and remained over night. Splendid time. Brought stores for Regt.

16th. Rode to City Point with John. Visited the hospitals of 5th Corps with him. Good time. Enjoyed it much. Saw Hamilton. Surg. N. Y. Regt. Eyes quite sore.

17th. Spent the day very quietly in camp, over *Independents* and other papers. Wrote home and to Lucy Randall Campbell.

18th. Relieved the 1st N. H. on picket near Cox's Mills. Major Nettleton, while relieving pickets, had horse shot. Lt. 1st N. H. killed by his side. Guerrilas in ambush. Hdqrs. in a pleasant shady yard.

19th. Played some at chess and read a little in Shakespeare. Eyes quite weak. Letters from home and Floy. Quiet. Heavy firing in direction of Petersburg. Rained almost all day.

20th. All quiet with the pickets. Played some at chess. Read papers and "Othello." Wrote to Ella Clark.

21st. 2nd N. Y. and 1st Conn. came out early and relieved us. Beat Col. P. a game of chess. Camped in the woods near our old camp. We have a nice place.

22nd. Transferred forge to 3rd Jersey. Thede and I rode to City Point. Bigelow and we took dinner with John. Pleasant time. Visited Capt. Dorsey. Enjoyed the ride.

23rd. Saturday. Nettleton went to the Point yesterday so he did not go down this evening for John.

24th. Sunday. A. M. went to the Point for John. He came out and preached for us at 4 P. M. Goodly number out. Excellent remarks. A. B. and I rode back with him and remained over night on account of rain. Horse fell upon my leg going down. No serious harm. Came near breaking it. Good visit with John. Saw Dorsey.

25th. Monday. Waited till 10 o'clock and saw John off. Started for home. We envy him. Would we could go too. Got home about noon. In the evening marched to left of the army and relieved a brigade of the 2nd Div. on picket. Our regiment on the right of the brigade.

26th. Day spent improving the picket line, etc. Word came in P. M. that rebs were preparing for a movement on the left. Caution ordered. No demonstration.

27th. In morning accompanied Col. P. and Maj. N. on a tour to visit our line, and brigade of infantry. Rebs in plain view. No firing in front of infantry for two weeks.

28th. Boys exchanged papers with Johnnies. Got one of the 27th. No news. Have played chess considerably for a week or two. Have not been victor for a few days.

29th. Friday. The Major went down to see friends in the 18th Corps, a failure. I thought of accompanying him but through a blunder didn't go. My eyes have occasioned me much trouble of late. At 10 P. M. Thede and I made our way to 9th Corps d rs. to see affair reported to come off in morning.

30th. Got a sightly position in front of the 18th Corps where all points of interest were in view. Lay till sunrise upon one of the leveled forts, a cannon ball visiting the vicinity frequently. Just at sunrise a cloud of dust and dirt rising suddenly into the air, followed by a distant rumble, gave us warning that the work had commenced. The dust had hardly reached its height when 200 guns opened. The scene was wonderfully grand. We watched for two hours. We couldn't see the maneuvering of troops. As the fort went up, the 9th Corps went in with a yell, and took the works where the opening was made. The colored troops charged on against the next line and were repulsed with great slaughter. Many regard the whole thing as a failure. Returned to camp. (This refers to one of the most spectacular and unsuccessful events of the war—Burnside's explosion of a mine under Mahone's rebel division and forts in front of Petersburg. This "crater" is still a "show" place. 1911. A. B. N.).

31st. Sunday. Relieved from picket and marched to Brigade d rs. Camped in woods. Fixed a bower. A very hot day, yesterday too. Report that the portion of the enemy's works occupied after mine explosion was abandoned today by order of Gen Grant. Received letters from Mr. Brown and my good Sarah Felton, also notes from Ed and Otto.

August 1st. Monday. Commenced a letter to Sarah. Wrote home. Regt. remained saddled some time in the morning in anticipation of an attack. Went on picket in evening.

AUGUST, 1864.

2nd. Finished a letter to Sarah. My eyes are so weak that I can use them but very little.

3rd. Received papers of 1st claiming a grand victory here—all bosh—sorry. Some one is much at fault that the grand plan of July 30, 1864, failed. Grant seems to have used the best strategy and skill. Who is at fault will soon be determined. Visited the picket line. Saw the Johnnies. Many amusing incidents occur daily. As our line fell back July 30 the rebel line advanced. When we went back Johnnies occupied one of our posts. Had saluted the sergeant and asked if we intended establishing our old line and carelessly fell back. Today Johnnies and our men gather apples from the same trees. Boys trade tobacco, coffee and many things.

4th. Thursday. Letters received from Mr. Charles Wood and Mrs. Beers. Regt. relieved in the night.

5th. Friday. Brigade marched at sunrise. Relieved by 2nd Div. Reached City Point before noon. 18th P. V. embarked for Washington. 2nd Ohio went to Landing. On board and anchored off the Point. Took a bath before leaving wharf. While hastily looking for Col. P. for detail to load oats, I accidentally walked off into the river. Had my revolver on and coat and pants in my arms. Soon found a board nailed upon a pile and hung on till helped out. Lost my hat. God is kind. I owe him gratitude for saving me. (This was the beginning of Sheridan's Shenandoah Valley campaign in which the 2nd Ohio was prominent.)

6th. Saturday. A very pleasant ride down the James. Rounded Lighthouse Point. Soon passed Harrison's Landing, then Fort Powhatan and Wilcox's Landing. Here danger from reb guns ceased. The old Jamestown site on left bank, a few chimneys still standing. Newport near where the Merrimac fight came off, Cumberland and Congress sunk. Sewall's Point across, eight miles down Fortress Monroe. Went ashore. Everything carried on in the finest style. Splendid fort, having an armament of over 200 guns and "The Union" monster gun which fired a shot from Fort Monroe to Sewall's Point, 8 miles. Ripraps still progressing. A splendid fort built in center of stream on the shoals, Gov't prisoners at work on it. Through Hampton Roads into the Chesapeake and Atlantic. Passing Old Point Comfort, the bay is very wide. Saw an American and English frigate and a French gunboat. An English cutter manned by 8 or 10 fellows in white came ashore. Reached Point Lookout about sundown, the ironclad Roanoke lying off the point. Up the river, 12 miles, and anchored for the night. A most pleasant trip. Stormed enough to roughen the bay a little. Good fare upon the boat. Pass hundreds of boats, most of them making their way to City Point, I suppose. Phosphorus.

7th. Sunday. Moved up the Potomac. Had a good view of Mt. Vernon. A beautiful location. Passed Fort Washington. Reached Giesboro about noon. Moved up to the woods between Camp Stoneman and Washington. Got forage and settled down.

8th. Put in an estimate for clothing and drew forage.

9th. Tuesday. Thede sold his horse. Went over to town and procured some clothing.

10th. Wednesday. Had charge of the dock and disembarking of troops at the wharf. Rode to town near evening.

11th. Retained my order for duty but was allowed to go to town. Tried to find Mr. Mills' and Mr. Holtslander's but A. B. gave me the wrong directions. Filled up my requisition and went to Washington and drew clothing. Visited the Capitol.

12th. Friday. Drew and issued more clothing during the day. At 5 P. M. division moved. A. B., Thede and I went ahead. Had two dishes of ice cream at expense of George Palmer. Went to the depot and saw 150 O. N. G. starting home. It makes us almost homesick and yet we do not envy them much. Called at Mr. Holtslander's—away. Then at Mr. Mills'. Much pleased with the family—pretty children—Flint, Leof and Lyra. Marched 15 miles. Crossed the river at Chain Bridge. Went into camp about midnight.

13th. Saturday. Awfully warm. Lay in camp till 4 P. M. Had charge of brigade train. Rained.

14th. Sunday. Got into camp at noon. Lay all day near Dranesville.

15th. Monday. Brigade commenced pulling out before daylight. 1st Brigade in rear. Passed through Leesburg about 3 P. M. Once a very wealthy little town apparently, now old and rusty. Very noted for rebel sympathy. Saw several pretty ladies. Camped near Purcellville. In P. M. near Leesburg one wagon got behind and two rebels jumped out upon the road, stripped a sergeant of his arms and clothes and took four mules. Rear guard was too far behind.

16th. Tuesday. Marched at daylight. Passed through Berryville, where Moseby burned 40 wagons for the 19th Corps a few days since. Div. Q. M. Cole went to Harper's Ferry with empty wagons for supplies, leaving the Div. train, etc., under my charge. Moved on the road to Front Royal. Camped about midnight.

17th. We moved out at daylight. Passed White Post and turned towards Winchester, which we reached about noon. Train passed through and camped on Berryville road. Major Seward reported to escort the train. Moved at 5 P. M. 1st Cav. Div. and 3rd and one brigade of infantry in line south of town. Skirmishing till dark, when rebs charged on skirmish line on left and captured a good many prisoners. Major Nettleton acted as rear guard through town. Lost one killed, Johnson, and 8 wounded. Command got through town in haste. Col. Purington and Dutton again skedaddled, guess they will hear from it this time. Moved to Summit Point, 16 miles from Harper's Ferry. Rained during the night.

18th. Thursday. Division came up. Moved east of town to give it opportunity to take position. Unharnessed most of the day. Visited some with Major Nettleton. Had a good night's rest.

19th. Friday. Have settled several claims during yesterday and today. Two girls just came with a hay account. If we remain here it will be pleasant to call there. Harnessed before noon. Our pickets driven. Read "Roue" by Bulwer.

20th. Saturday. Spent the day quietly in camp. A little skirmishing between pickets. Rebels reported moving on Martinsburg. Some talk about officers in regt. Rained.

21st. Sunday. Pickets driven in early. 2nd sent to support the 3rd N. J. Suffered some. Train ordered back one mile. Went back. Found rebels in possession of Charlestown road, one mile further. Sent out a picket from an escort with ambulance train, and made a little reconnoissance, discovering a small rebel force. Soon two regiments in charge of half a dozen aides came back to guard the train through. Laughable time. Passed through Charlestown and by order of Gen. Torbert, went on to Bolivar Heights, near Harper's Ferry. Major N. sick and along with us. Got a supper in town.

22nd. Monday. Breakfast at a house near camp. Went over and saw Lt. Cole, a division Q. M. Went to the Ferry, drew forage for animals. 2nd Ohio was on picket last night, deployed as skirmishers, 2 miles west of Charlestown. At daylight attacked by the rebels. Capt. Denning, the brave man, and Henry Drake, the noble and true soldier, mortally wounded, poor men. All forces fell back. Went out with forage in P. M. I feel it almost a duty to return to some of the dangers of the officers of the line.

23rd. Tuesday. Lu went back to the regt. Remained with the brigade all night. Returned to train in time for breakfast. Moved train over to Cole's. Went with Bob to barbershop. Sent Barber to his company yesterday. Ficklin has taken his place and is doing splendidly. War news seems favorable. Reports that the enemy are retreating down the valley, also that he has turned towards Washington, former probably true. Lee cannot spare so many men. Cavalry force, 2nd Ohio a part, sent out light on reconnoissance.

24th. Wednesday. A beautiful day, a little hazy. Forage issued. Boys sent to Frederick to look up brigade train. Fears of its capture. Train arrived. Boys came down to shoe horses.

25th. Intended to join the regiment, but heard that it had gone out early on a reconnoissance. Eggleston remained with me. Maj. N. came up after dark tired out. Train pulled out in night and Div. crossed the river.

26th. Moved out at daylight. Overtook the command before it reached Boonsboro. Called on Bayard and Babcock. Was up on Maryland Heights day before yesterday. Camped at Boonsboro.

27th. Rained last night. Thunder heavy. Moved through Sharpsburg and over the Antietam battle ground. Turned towards Williamsport and camped three miles from Sharpsburg.

28th. Sunday. Reveille at 2 A. M. Breakfasted and were on the road at daylight. Our Brig. in advance. Passed through S. Rebels in retreat. Overtook the infantry on Jamestown road. Camped at C.

29th. Up early but did not march. Considerable firing in direction of Smithfield. No reports. Good news in papers.

30th. Marched at 12:30. Received letter from Mrs. T. Wood. Camped at Berryville.

31st. At daylight went on a reconnoissance towards Winchester. Found rebs and drove them to their main body on the Opequon. No one hurt. Very spirited little affair.

SEPTEMBER, 1864

1st. Lay in camp all day. In evening relieved 3rd Jersey on picket. Busy most all night drawing oats.

2nd. Friday. At daylight fell back. Left the main road. Passed through Kabletown and reached the fortified position 3 miles from C. On picket two miles toward B. Nicely settled down, when ordered to march. Reached B. about midnight. 5th N. Y. had skirmish with pickets.

3rd. Saturday. Soon after daylight moved out. Passed through Millwood and White Post, two miles, and returned to M. and camped. Rained. Moseby has gathered up quite a number of our men within a few days.

4th. Sunday. Moved back by road. Rebs at Berryville and in our rear. 2nd Ohio train guard. Custer's brigade suffered some. Train moved to Rippon. Parked.

5th. Monday. Moved back to B. last night. Rained. Drivers and dead-beats got scared and pulled out very quickly before we moved. In line on left of infantry. Skirmishing soon after daylight. News of fall of Atlanta. All jubilant. Lay in camp till P. M. then went on picket. Rainy and very unpleasant. Boys suffered. Sat upon their horses and at the foot of trees all night.

6th. Tuesday. Relieved at dark. Spent the day getting papers signed. Letter from home. Oats and rations. Not in camp till after dark. Pleasant place.

7th. Wednesday. Division moved out at 4:30. Our regiment in rear, reconnoissance. Went within two miles of Winchester, found the enemy and returned—sharp firing. In camp at dark.

8th. Thursday. Rainy and cool. Lay still all day. Read "Charles Vivasseur." Wagons came up, oats and rations. Wrote home and to Mrs. Wood.

9th. Friday. Moved camp, beautiful place on left and rear of infantry. Busy. Regiment not to be consolidated.

10th. Saturday. Busy over monthly papers. Letter from home. Fixed up my commissary returns.[1]

11th. Sunday. Spent the day quietly in camp. Read papers and "Lady of the Lake."

12th. Monday. Regt. went out on a scout to Millwood. Remained in camp. Read some and worked. Considerable rain for two or three days. Cold nights.

13th. Beautiful, clear morning. Brigade on a scout. Took in a S. Carolina regt. The 2nd Ohio charged them (Infantry) driving them into a little piece of woods and surrounding them. Whole line of battle in sight. The Col. and 145 men surrendered, our loss slight. In good spirits.

14th. Wednesday. Regt. was on picket near Berryville. Went to Harper's Ferry with forges.

15th. Thursday. Returned to Berryville. Rode rapidly without company most of the way.

16th. Remained in camp. Read and wrote.

17th. Saturday. Got officers to sign papers. Forges get back loaded.

18th. Sent regt. wagons loaded to Ferry. Preparations to move. 2nd Ohio made a reconnoissance, driving rebs across the Opequon. All Q. M.s ordered to Ferry with wagons. Houghton told me there was business on hand and the General would like me for aide. Soon an order came for me to report. I was pleased. Moved out and then back into camp over night.

(Battle of Winchester)

19th. Monday. Moved at 2 A. M. Slept with Houghton. Reached the Opequon about daylight, 2nd N. Y. charging. After

---

[1] In my possession are a large number of these duplicate packages of "Monthly Returns of Quartermasters Stores," "Monthly Returns of Clothing, Camp and Garrison Equipage, Abstracts, Vouchers," etc., etc., all carefully assorted and securely fastened. (F. D. T.) The following is a copy of one of the vouchers: "I certify on honor that during the months of November and December, 1864, the following quartermasters' stores were necessarily expended under my direction in Co. C, 2nd Ohio Cav.: 113, one hundred and thirteen grain sacks (worn). During the greater portion of this time our Regiment has been continually moving and these sacks have been used for bedding, for horses and men.   Luman H. Tenney,
                                                    Capt. 2nd Ohio Cav.
Camp Russell, Va., December 30, 1864.   Com'd'g Co. C."

this, constant charging till we drove a rebel brigade of infantry from fortified position. Very hard fighting. Gen. McIntosh always in the van. When Gen. Sheridan came up he patted Mc. on shoulder and said, "You have done nobly." Moved to left. More charging on flank. Gen. Mc. and Chapman wounded. Purington in command. Just before dark whole rebel force was routed. Followed 8 miles and camped.

20th. Followed up, picking up stragglers. Halted near Front Royal.

21st. Wednesday. At daylight in fog crossed the river at a charge, driving Wickham's brigade. Came upon their force in strong position, 8 miles, reb battery.

22nd. Rebs at Milford, fortified. Whole Cav. corps up. Skirmishing all day. At night fell back. Great victory by infantry.

23rd. Friday. Withdrew to Buckton across the South Fork. Had we only gone in yesterday, what success. Moved back near Milford. Camp at 12 P. M.

24th. After breakfast moved on. 1st and 2nd in advance, rebel works strong. Crossed the South Fork and camped in Massanutten Gap. Passed Luray. Captured some prisoners.

25th. Went through the gap to New Market. Clothing and rations. Marched to Harrisonburg. Infantry here.

26th. Monday. Marched to Staunton, 3rd Div., Regular brigade 1st and 2nd Div. went to Port Republic.

27th. Tuesday. Burned R. R. and stores. Captured Com'y and Q. M. stores. Quite a time. Visited rebel hospital, Deaf and Dumb Asylum, and Insane Asylum. Marched to Waynesboro in eve.

28th. Wednesday. Tore up R. R. and iron bridge. Near dark rebs came up the valley and attacked. Reb infantry got on our flank. Had to run a gauntlet. 2nd Ohio and 3rd N. J. rear guard. Through Staunton.

29th. Thursday. Marched on back road to Bridgewater.

30th. Friday. Rainy day. Borrowed "Charles O'Malley."

OCTOBER, 1864

1st. Saturday. My birthday. Would I could see Ma and sisters. God bless them. Gen. W. relieved by Gen. Custer. Gen. W. ordered to Gen. Sherman, Chief of cavalry.

2nd. Sunday. Changed camp. Not unsaddled before enemy came up and charged pickets through town. 2nd N. Y. and 18th P. V. charged back, driving rebs over abutments into the river. Moved back near Dayton.

3rd. Saddled at 4 A. M. No demonstration.

4th and 5th. Paymaster paid off 1st Conn. Drew 8 months' pay. Lt. Meigs of Sheridan's staff killed by guerrillas.

6th. Moved back, burning every barn and stack on road. Followed closely. Camped near Brock's Gap. 5th N. Y. and 18th P. V. driven back. Considerable uneasiness during night.

7th. Friday. Daylight advanced the line of pickets. Saw reb. Division massed, 2nd Brigade in rear. Attacked and broken in the P. M. 1st Brigade checked the rebs, lost some forges and sheep and cattle. Col. Pennington took command today. Camped at Columbia Furnace.

8th. Saturday. Moved on at 6 A. M. 1st Brigade in rear. Rebs charged. 18th P. V., 2nd N. Y. charged back. Then Brigade formed for the regt. to come in. 18th lost some men, 15.

9th. Sunday. Ma's birthday. God bless her and grant her many years to live. 55. Packs and train ordered back. Moved back to fight rebs. Found them at Tom's Brook hill. 5th N. Y. in advance. 3rd N. J. support. Line soon formed and advance sounded, then charged. Went in with 2nd Ohio. Completely routed the Johnnies and ran them pell-mell several miles, capturing 6 pieces of artillery, 12 wagons, 14 ambulances, 154 prisoners. 1st Div. about the same success. 5 pieces of artillery.

10th. Monday. Lay in camp at Tom's Brook. Letter from Minnie. Wrote home. Captured property sent to Strasburg.

11th. Tuesday. In camp till 4 P. M. Moved to position on Cedar Creek, passing Fisher's Hill, via Pike and Strasburg. Camped near Middletown.

12th. Wednesday. In camp all day.
Report of Lee's Cav. Div. in Sept.:

1st Va. 171	}	
2nd " 183	} Wickham's Brigade.	
3rd " 160	}	
4th ' 245	}	
5th ' 183	}	
6th ' 318	}	
15th ' 110	} Lomax' Brigade.	
————		
1370	}	

W. H. F. Lee's Brigade, 9th Va., 10th Va. and 13th Va.
    Majors F. H. Furguson.
            George Frasier.
            Thomas Bower.
    Dr. A. C. Randolph.
    Capt. Chas. Cavendish.
    Lieut. Chas. Mummigerode.
    Lieut. Mason.

13th. Thursday. Lay in camp all day. Forage.

14th. Friday. Rebels made a reconnoissance along our whole line.

15th. Saturday. Moved out to Brigade d rs. in evening. Two boils. 2nd Ohio on picket.

16th. Sunday. Returned to regt. Ordered to escort Sheridan to Piedmont. Remained in camp. Read some.

17th. Monday. In the morning rebs attacked pickets. Captured Maj. Morey. 20 men.

18th. Tuesday. All quiet. 2nd Ohio returned.

19th. Wednesday. Firing again on picket. Turned out. At daylight heavy firing commenced on left with infantry. At 8 A. M. learned the infantry had fallen back in confusion, losing 24 pieces of artillery. 8th and 19th corps broken. 6th corps firm and in line. Cavalry went into position immediately and gave infantry time to form. Crossed the pike and formed again—under heavy fire all the time. Kept the position until Sheridan came up, then sent over to the right again. Charged rebel cavalry. Little before dusk whole line advanced—routing the rebs. Two regts. of 3rd Div. charged to the right, driving reb cavalry over Cedar Creek and the rest charging on right of 19th corps, 5th N. Y. in advance. Overtook the artillery and wagon trains, capturing it and many prisoners.

20th. Thursday. Pursued on back road 15 miles, picking up some prisoners. The victory complete. All worship Sheridan who turned a complete rout into the most complete victory of the war. Rebs panic stricken, not even forming at Fisher's Hill. Our loss in killed and wounded heavy. Gen. Ramseur mortally wounded. At our old camp.

21st. Friday. Moved camp. Wrote a line home. Beautiful day. Letter from home yesterday. Regt. went on picket.

22nd. Saturday. The Major started for home on leave of absence. Wrote a line and sent my money, $750.

Note—The modest entry under date of Oct. 19, 1864, refers to the historic battle of Cedar Creek, Va., when Sheridan made his famous ride on his black horse from Winchester, "twenty miles away," and saved the day. During Sheridan's temporary absence from his army, Gen. H. G. Wright, the next in command, permitted himself and the army to be totally surprised at three o'clock in the morning, by the recently defeated army of Gen. Jubal A. Early. The Union troops were nearly all sleeping in their tents when the enemy's cannon and musketry opened on them in a terrific onslaught at close range. The Union artillery was mainly captured, nearly 5,000 Union soldiers killed and captured, and our army, except the Cavalry and one Division of Infantry, started in panic and confused retreat towards Winchester in the rear—where Sheridan had spent the previous night. Up to that point the event had been one of the greatest Union disasters of the war. But about 10 o'clock in the morning Sheridan arrived on the field in the dramatic manner described in the poem, "Sheridan's Ride," and instantly all was reversed. Meanwhile the Cavalry, which had not been involved in the surprise and panic and slaughter, being encamped on the right and left flanks of the army out of the line of the attack of Early, had promptly been ordered to the center and front, where they held the Confederates back from further pursuit until Sheridan's arrival. Sheridan's presence promptly restored confidence. The retreating and disorganized troops quickly rallied, and by 3 P. M. a general charge was ordered all along the line occupying some four miles front. The Cavalry charge on this occasion was the finest performance and spectacle at any time witnessed by the writer during the war. The astonished and recently victorious Confederates broke in confusion, their retreat was a worse panic than that of the Union army in the early morning. All our artillery was retaken from the enemy and some thirty cannon captured in addition, besides great numbers of prisoners and the entire wagon train of Early. Early's army never made another serious rally.—A. B. N.

23rd. Sunday. Rode to Army Hdqrs. and to fortifications. Artillery parked near d rs. Read *Independents*. Splendid sermon by Rev. R. W. Hitchcock. "Blessed be the Lord who teacheth my hands to war and my fingers to fight."

24th. Monday. Rode to several Hdqrs. with Adj. Pike. **Watson** and Pearson mustered out. Read papers and letter from home.

25th. Tuesday. Teams came up. Seems good. Hurrying up Q. M. papers. Letter from Ella Clark.

26th. Wednesday. In camp. Regt. not picket. Cloudy. Paymaster came.

27th. Thursday. Regt. paid off. Drew pay for Sept. and Oct. On picket. Clothing drawn but not issued. Rainy.

28th. Friday. Regt. came in and drew clothing. Wrote to Will, Fred and C. G. and D. R. H. Letter from Will, one month on way.

29th. Saturday. Wrote to Grandpa and Watson Jones.

30th. Sunday. Received order relieving me from Q. M. duty and assigned to Co. C. McBride a Q. M. Desire to do God's will.

31st. Monday. Spent the day in camp. Wrote home. Read some in "Dombey & Son." A great deal of poker going on, commencing with Hdqrs.

NOVEMBER, 1864

1st. Went on picket in P. M. Board of survey in A. M. Beautiful day. Busy on returns.

2nd. Wednesday. All quiet. Relieved in P. M. Raw cold day. Dreamed of F. last night. Grief of soul.

3rd. Thursday. A rainy day. Read and wrote on papers. Was at Brig. Hdqrs.

4th. Friday. Went out with forage detail over in Little North Valley.

5th. Saturday. In camp all day. Straightened Q. M. accounts and turned over property to Lt. Dutton.

6th. Sunday. Inspection of division by Major Otis. Undress parade. Col. Purington took leave of the boys. Given three cheers. Ordered out on two days' scout. Went to forks of road, Cedar Creek and Strasburg over Little North and camped. Acted Adjt. Very laughable scene. A drunken citizen came in, bewildered and lost, almost frozen. He could find a demijohn of brandy if we could only tell him where he laid down.

7th. Monday. Went to Cold Spring Gap in Great North Mountains, then around to Russel's Mills and for forage and camp in old place.

8th. Tuesday. The decisive day of the nation. If the cause of the Union prevails today, liberty and union will be ours forever. God grant the right success. Ordered into camp. Moved back through Newtown. Rosser reported prowling about. Voted. **201** for Lincoln, 4 for McClellan. Glorious for the 2nd Ohio.

9th. Wednesday. After dinner moved to Mt. Zion church. Met the infantry marching back. Rainy day.

10th. Thursday. Pleasant morning. Clear and mild. Moved back 2½ miles into camp.

11th. Friday. On picket in P. M. Letter from home. Rebs around.

12th. Saturday. Gen. Rosser attacked 1st Conn. on reconnoissance. 2nd Ohio charged to help them. Both driven back after several charges, in some confusion. Brigade out and drove rebs back—at Shells—hand-to-hand encounter—charge after charge. Col. Hull killed. Drove rebs over the creek, four miles. Rebel brigade came in rear and picked up many stragglers. 2nd Ohio lost 20. Had my horse wounded. Early's whole army at Middletown.

13th. Sunday. Reconnoissance by all cavalry to Cedar Creek. No enemy. Very cold.

14th. Monday. Lay in camp. Wrote home, to Sarah and Ella Clark.

15th. Tuesday. In camp. Read some and did company business.

16th. Wednesday. On picket. Had charge of 2nd Batt. on outpost. Deserters came in. Quiet time. Guard mounting. *Harper* and *Atlantic*.

17th. Thursday. Relieved by 18th P. V. Got into camp a little before dark.

18th. Friday. Nettleton returned. Letters from home. God bless the good friends. Commissions for boys. 1st Lt. for me. Letter from Roxena.

19th. Saturday. Officer of the day. "C" Co. on picket in rear of camp. Wrote to Uncle Branch.

20th. Sunday. Rest of regt. on picket. Wrote to Lizzie Cobb. Drew rations and ammunition.

21st. Monday. Out before daylight and moved at 6 A. M., 2nd and 3rd Divisions. A rainy, cold, disagreeable day. Camped just beyond Woodstock.

22nd. Went on to Mt. Jackson and found the whole of Early's army posted two miles beyond. Quite lively skirmishing. 2nd Ohio in rear at the creek. Had charge of 3rd Battalion, broken as soon as rebs charged through town. Colors in front. Charged back several times. Infantry kept close on heels of the cavalry. Lyons, poor boy, is missing. Camped on old ground at Woodstock. A very cold night.

23rd. Wednesday. Resumed our backward march, the rebs following as far as Fisher's Hill. Very cold. Walked till sore footed. Went into old camp.

24th. Thursday. After breakfast went on picket on middle road, on reserve post. Very quiet but cold—little sleep. Many prayers have gone up today for the welfare of the soldiers and the salvation of the country. May God soon bring the rebs to their senses and bring an honorable peace with freedom to all men.

25th. Friday. Thanksgiving chickens for dinner. Wrote to Mrs. Beers. Forage caps issued. Considerable dissatisfaction among the boys. Band played some time.

26th. Saturday. Remained in camp. Read and wrote to Will.

27th. Sunday. Brigade inspection in the morning. Officers and men are becoming pretty thoroughly disgusted with Col. Pennington on account of his mean and inconsistent orders. Wrote home.

28th. Monday. In camp all day. Got mustered as 1st Lt. After supper, "General" and "Boots and Saddles" blew. Lay till twelve and then pulled out on back grade and Moorfield Pike.

29th. Tuesday. Crossed the Big North at Cold Springs Gap. Passed through Wardensville and got dinner and fed. Co. "C." eight men. Very disagreeable march last night. Beautiful day, mild and delightful. Am happy as a lark in the sunshine. Enemy reported at Moorfield. Went on after half an hour's rest. God grant us success if we meet him. May the right soon prevail and this cruel war end. Camped on the Shenandoah mountain top.

30th. Wednesday. Up at 4 and on the road at 5. The most beautiful sunrise from the vast height. A grand view of mountains stretching away for miles in all directions. 2nd Ohio in advance. Reached Moorfield at 10 A. M. Remained till 2 P. M. Returned via northwestern grade. Camped 13 miles from M. on an old gentleman's farm. I had quite a talk with him. He owned a farm, sterile and poor, of 200 acres in among the hills. He was 70 years of age. Moved there 34 years since when all was a wilderness. Had never owned a slave. Had cleaned up the farm, built a log house and made all the improvements with his own hands. It made him almost crazy to see all going to destruction in one night— all his fences, outbuildings, cattle, sheep and fowls. An only son at home, an invalid. Had always been true to the government. Only wished that God would now call him, that he might be with his many friends in the church yard—pointing to it near by—and this aspect of suffering and starvation be taken from him.

DECEMBER, 1864

1st. Thursday. 2nd Ohio in rear. Kept along down North river. Passed through "Hanging Rock" Gap. Scenery grand. Camped at Capron Bridge in Lost River valley, 18 miles below Wardensville. On picket. Easy post.

2nd. Friday. Went into our old camp at 2 P. M. Mail from home.

3rd. Saturday. Spent the day in camp. Was officer of the day. Wrote to Uncle Milo.

4th. Sunday. Wrote several letters and read. Heard a sermon at Brigade d rs.

5th. Monday. 2nd Ohio went out to Fisher's Hill on a scout. Got back in evening. Enemy reported in front by 2nd N. Y. Big fires.   Thought they heard bugles, etc.   Co. C in advance.   No enemy.

6th.   Tuesday.   In camp.   Bill Smith officer of the day.

7th.   Wednesday.   On picket.   Put up with Co. B.   Charge of 3rd Batt.   Pleasant time.   Cold night.   Excellent letters from Ella and Will.   Heard reports of promotion.

8th.   Thursday.   Relieved in good season.

9th.   Friday.   In camp.   Wrote to cousin Sarah in answer to letter received today.   Drilled 3rd Batt. in rear formation.

10th.   Saturday.   Cold day.   No drill.   Boys on picket.

11th.   Sunday.   Snowed all last night.   6 inches of snow this morning.   Wrote to Fred, C. G., Ella and home.

12th.   Monday.   Wrote letter for Fecklin and several in answer to letters for Co. "C" people.   Awfully cold.

13th.   Notice of appointment from Adj. Gen'l of Ohio as captain came.   Went over to muster.   No success.   Several promotions.

14th.   Went twice to mustering officer without success.   Finished "Dante" and "Dream Life" by Ike Marvel.   Beautiful pictures of life, beautiful because so real.   Good lessons.   Had good visits with Easton and McBride.   Clear.

15th.   Got horses shod.   Cloudy.   Saw F. again in my dreams. I wish I could be rid of this thought about such things.   Could never live at home.   Am better off here than I would be there.

16th.   Got news of Thomas' attack on Hood's flank.   Great rejoicing in infantry.

17th.   Saturday.   More good news from Thomas.   Brigade officer of the day.   Rode over to infantry.   Received a beautiful pair of shoulder straps as Christmas gift—with a note from A. B.

18th.   Sunday.   A good letter from Prof. Peck.   A beautiful picture of Melissa and the darling baby (Carrie Nettleton Thurber). Letter from home.   Wrote to the Prof.

From his letter to Prof. Peck.

Everybody in the 2nd Ohio is familiar with the name and services of Prof. Peck, of Oberlin, the man who has always done so much for the Ohio soldiers, both the sick and well, and who had an article in the paper a short time ago about the 2nd Ohio.

The boys are *delighted* with *your praise* of the Regiment.   I have told a good many what you wrote in regard to us.   All say, "Well, if *he* says that he does not know a regiment which has done better than ours, *we ought* to *feel proud*, for he is well acquainted with Ohio troops."

Our Regiment has been sadly depleted during the campaign.   It has not been recruited, but we hope to have it filled up, if another call for troops shall be made.   Perhaps a portion of the records of Company C, with which I am serving will interest you.   On the 1st day of May, 1864, the Company left Washington with forty-eight men, all told.   During the summer, seven recruits joined it, making a total of fifty-five.   From May 1st until this date, the losses foot up as follows: Five killed—all brave and good—thirty wounded and seventeen missing.   Today we number for duty, eleven enlisted men, every one good soldiers.

Theodore is robust and always ready for duty.   He is well-fashioned for a soldier, having a hardy constitution and a jolly temperament.   He was pleased to be remembered by you.

Yesterday I received a beautiful Christmas gift from my friends, Will Hudson, Fred Allen, Delos Haynes and Charley Fairchild, a pair of shoulder-straps. The Col. received a very cunning picture today of Sister Melissa, with her little treasure Carrie in her arms.

The glorious news from Gen'ls Thomas and Sherman has just been read to us. We gave three hearty cheers. We hope that the end is not far distant.

Yours truly,

Luman H. Tenney,

Capt. 2nd O. V. V. C.

MELISSA AND BABY CARRIE

19th. Wrote home. Orders to march in the morning at 6:30 A. M.

20th. Up at four. An early breakfast. 3rd Div. started up the valley, while 1st and 2nd went in another direction with 10 days' rations. Camped at Woodstock.

21st. Wednesday. Orders regarding success of Sherman and Thomas, read to us near Mt. Jackson. Camped 8 miles south of Newmarket. Rained.

22nd. Up at 4. Rain froze as it fell. Awfully cold. At 5:30 "To horse" sounded. Soon a yell went up near the 2nd Brig., then a few shots. We were ordered to mount immediately—did it. A line could be seen on a distant hill. A few men came up within a few rods of camp. We moved to the flank, came front into line, my Batt. 1st in advance. Threw out skirmishers. Firing commenced immediately and we advanced, firing. Rebs run. Captured two and killed two. The command proved to be Rosser's Div. which came in from the back road and from the flank. Charged the 2nd Brig. and drove it. Passed to the rear and captured several ambulance horses. Result was 30 men killed, wounded and missing on our side. 22 men captured from rebs and 10 killed. One of H Co. sabre cut, and one horse killed. Moved back and camped at Woodstock. 2nd on picket. Small force of the enemy followed. Skirmished till dark.

COLONEL ALVRED BAYARD NETTLETON
BREVETTED BRIGADIER GENERAL MARCH, 1865, ''FOR GALLANT AND MERITORIOUS
SERVICE.''

22nd. Marched at 5:30. The most uncomfortable day I ever passed. 45 2nd Ohio men with frozen feet. Much suffering throughout the division. Wind blew the snow right through us. Camped in rear of old infantry line, in awful place, with no wood. Boys went for fences about Hdqrs. Col. Pennington threatened to shoot some of the boys. ‘ Chet, Houghton, Eggleston and Smith captain's commissions.

23rd. Friday. Application made to send Sergt. Laundon and myself to Ohio. Have enjoyed looking over the papers. Everything looks very bright indeed. The new call and the late successes are glorious.

24th. Saturday. In the morning helped Hillhouse fix up his ordnance papers. P. M. whiskey issued. Boys pretty jolly.

25th. Sunday. A rather unpleasant day. Spent Christmas quietly. Ate dinner with Capt. Chester. Oysters. Wrote home.

26th. Monday. News of the fall of Savannah. Monthly inspection. Detailed for picket.

27th. Relieved from picket and ordered to appear as witness in case of U. S. versus Seth Combs for desertion. Did what I could for him.

28th. Moved camp upon a hill near by. Awfully muddy. Made a large fire.

29th. Field officer of the day. Moved over upon the Romney pike. Visited the picket line.

30th. Went to work cutting wood for quarters.

31st. Split logs and laid them up nearly high enough for comfort. Mustered. Very disagreeable morning. Pleasanter in the P. M. Cold night. Home letter.

Upon the fly-leaves of the little 1864 war diary book are the following quotations from Dante's *Divine Comedy*. The Cary translation was used. My references as to pages are to the edition of Oscar Kuhns, T. Y. Crowell & Co., New York and Boston.   (F.D.T.)

"With such a smile
As might have made one blest amid the flames," (p. 346).
"So shall delight make thee not feel thy toil," (page 360).
"Let not the people be too swift to judge;
As one who reckons on the blade in field,
Or e'er the crop be ripe. For I have seen
The thorn frown rudely all the winter long,
And bark, that all her way across the sea
Ran straight and speedy, perish at the last
E'en in the haven's mouth" (page 376).
"For one of these may rise, the other fall," (p. 376).
"These eyes are not thine only Paradise" (p. 395).
        "voice hath not uttered
Nor hath ink written, nor in fantasy
Was e'er conceived" (p. 399).
        "A man
Is born on Indus banks, and none is there
Who speaks of Christ, nor who doth read nor write;

And all his inclinations and his acts,
As far as human reason sees, are good;
And he offendeth not in word or deed:
But unbaptized he dies and void of faith.
Where is the justice that condemns him? Where
His blame, if he believeth not?" (p. 401).
                        "And ye,
Oh mortal men! be wary how ye judge;" (p. 407).
"The sword of heaven is not in haste to smite,
Nor yet doth linger;" (p. 412).
"Faith of things hoped is substance, and the proof
Of things not seen" (p. 422).
"With hope, that leads to blissful end;" "Hope," (said I,)
"Is of the joy to come a sure expectance;" (p. 426).
"Good, inasmuch as we perceive the good,
Kindles our love;" (p. 430).
"Keep the choicest of thy love for God." (p. 430).
"One universal smile it seemed of all things" (p. 433).
                        "Oh, mortal lust!
That canst not lift thy head above the waves
Which whelm and sink thee down." (p. 436).
                        "faith and innocence
Are met with but in babes;" (p. 437).
                        "The aim of all
Is how to shine: e'en they, whose office is
To preach the gospel, let the gospel sleep,
And pass their own inventions off instead" (p. 444).
"Here break we off, as the good workman doth,
That shapes the cloak according to the cloth." (p. 458).
                        "Oh, speech!
How feeble and how faint art thou, to give
Conception birth." (p. 461).

JANUARY, 1865

1st. Sunday. After roll call earned a breakfast by chopping wood. Made a good fire. Drew a load of bricks from the country. Many of the boys are suffering from poor boots and short rations. Have worked some today, but conscience clear.

2nd. Monday. Commenced building fireplace. Morrison worked for me. Very busy day. Tired out at night.

3rd. Finished the chimney and moved into the new house— little more than 8 ft. square.

4th. Wednesday. Charge of picket. This morning failed to get out at roll call. Did not hear the bugle. My first failure since I have been an officer in the 2nd Ohio. A very cold windy day. Reserve at a large stone barn.

5th. Thursday. Relieved late in the day.

6th. Friday. Worked on house some. Uncomfortable day.

7th. Saturday. Letter from home. Sarah Felton.

8th. Sunday. Bruce got me a door. Busy with fireplace.

9th. Monday. Put up picket poles and policed ground.

10th. Tuesday. Officer of the day. Brigade Hdqrs. A pleasant ride around the lines.

11th. Wednesday. Letters from Mrs. Wood. Watrous.

12th. Letter from Frank. Answered all my letters. Played some at chess.

13th. Friday. Drew some extra ordnance. Inspected by Corps Inspector. Complimented by him. Have very neat quarters and neat ground.

14th. Saturday. Drew clothing. Beat Col. at chess.

15th. Cleaned up and rested. Prospect of going home on recruiting service.

16th. Monday. Read some. Application for an officer and 8 sergeants made to go home on recruiting service. Officers' meeting. Determined to have a history of the 2nd Ohio. Newton, Houghton and Dr. McReynold as committee to get up a plan.

17th. Tuesday. Spent the day in camp. Grounds fixed up nicely—are complimented often. Boys take hold well. Non-commissioned officers' meeting.

18th. Wednesday. The glorious news of the fall of Fort Fisher on Sunday, the 15th. Another officers' meeting. Plan of history submitted—descriptive. The same committee continued for general supervision and compilation.

19th. Thursday. Quiet day in hut. Out to daily duties. Read *Atlantic*. Coates made Capt. in Colored Regt. yesterday. Snowing.

20th. Friday. On picket. Bill Smith on, too. Line visited by Col. Randall, Brig. Ins. and Capt. Houghton, and Officer of the Day.

21st. Saturday. Rainy and raw. Scouting party went out to Cedar Creek, through the Gap and around the mountain and came back by Fawcett's Gap. Awful day. A hunt for Imboden's men. No one seen.

22nd. Sunday. Storm continues. Some snow on the ground. Worked on shelters for horses out of pine brush. Bosworth and Robinson discharged. Ordered to write of East Tenn. campaign, one chapter in the history of the 2nd Ohio.

23rd. Monday. Dan left us. He has been a brave and faithful soldier. It seems hard to lose him. He will make a splendid officer. Still rain and hail fall.

24th. Tuesday. In camp. Played chess with A. B. Read "Two Gentlemen."

25th. Charge of picket. Bill Smith with me. Cold day. Very comfortable time.

26th. Thursday. Relieved by 1st Conn. Cold, some chess.

27th. Friday. Chess with Laundon. Cold night. Clear.

28th. Saturday. 50 men of the 2nd Ohio on a scout with sabres under Capt. Chester. Clear and cold.

29th. Sunday. Weather moderated. Scout came in at midnight. Wrote home. Captured 16 or 20 rebs on picket.

30th. Monday. Spent the day in camp. Fixed up sheds.

31st. Tuesday. Millard on picket. Read "Rob Roy," "Lucile," *Harper's*. Drilled.

FEBRUARY, 1865

1st. Wednesday. Grand Cavalry review. Raw day. Grand sight. Whole corps. Lady with Gen. Sheridan. Passed through Winchester.

2nd. Several furloughs came back. Boys happy. Am almost homesick, but put on as good a face as possible. Who knoweth the heart?

3rd. Friday. Brigade Officer of the Day. Rode around the line with A. B., Div. Officer of the Day. Stormy day. Deserters came in.

4th. Saturday. Made out my report and handed it in at Guard Mount. Learned that recruiting orders had gone by the board.

5th. Sunday. Spent the day in quarters reading *Independent, Testament* and a story. Windy.

6th. Monday. In camp. Officers' school.

7th. Great snow storm. Six or eight inches. Read in *Atlantic*. Letter from home. No school.

8th. Wednesday. Weather rather mild. Good sleighing. Wrote home. Shoveled the snow from the parade ground. Read in *National Magazine.* In evening attended school. Interesting time. Capt. Easton called to inquire into certain reports he had heard circulated by me. We had a plain talk. Sorry the thing came up.

9th. Cleared up the grounds during the day. Received a letter from Sarah Felton and Will Hudson in evening, with Sarah's picture. School in evening. Detailed for picket.

10th. On picket. Had a first class guard mount. Everything passed off splendidly. Made the rounds with the Brigade Officer of the Day in the deep snow.

11th. Relieved about 11. No excitement during my tour. Billy Smith on duty with me. In evening school. Made several ignorant blunders. It vexes me to make mistakes. I wish I knew more. I am so ignorant on all subjects.

12th. Snowing in morning. Blowing all day. Batt. inspection in A. M. Undress parade in P. M. Read sermon in *Independent* and considerable miscellaneous matter. Wrote home.

13th. Batt. drill in P. M. Read a general order in regard to the duties of sentinels and soldiers off duty. Read "St. Ronan's Well." Thede brought it up to me. Letter from home.

14th. Spent the day in camp. School in the evening. Had a very pleasant time. The more I have opportunity to learn and the more I am questioned, the more I realize my own ignorance and insignificance.

15th. A detail for picket. Bill on. Answered all my old letters. Will's excellent one. Fred's, Sarah's, C. G.'s and Dan Coate's. Spent most of the day thus. Read some.

16th. Cleared up the snow from the ground in the morning. Boys came in from picket. How bright the war prospect looks. Hope to see home by July 4th, '65·

17th. Friday. Class in evening. Good news of Sherman's march. Barnitz returned. Inspection in the morning by Capt. Lawder. The regt. looked splendidly. Talk with Nettleton about home.

18th. Saturday. Another stormy day. Snowed all the P. M. No mail or papers. Read and wrote. Class in evening. Am enjoying the discussions very much. Home Sweet Home—on the brain.

19th. Sunday. Battalion inspection in the morning. Had a good bath. Cleaned up grounds. In the evening Capt. Newton came in. Had a good visit. Talked Tenn. experiences. Traver and Barnitz in awhile.

20th. Officer of the Day. Beautiful day. Clear and mild. Went the rounds with Div. Officer of the Day and Sergt. Bail. Pleasant time. Lots of deserters coming in. One batch of 23. News of fall of Columbia, S. C. Glory! Read to troops. God be praised for the prospect. Chet back.

21st. Went down and saw Chester. Went home with Houghton and played chess. Beat him three games. Cold and chilly. In P. M. studied my lesson. No school in evening—very stormy. Signed and returned a Warranty Deed for a lot.

22nd. Spent the day in camp. Read Scott's "Heart of Midlothian." Much interested. Smith and I studied our lesson together. Capt. Barnitz in class. Got the bundle from home. Am pleased with the new clothes. Good friends.

23rd. Soon after breakfast received one wagon to each company to fix up stables with. Worked all day in rain. Great improvement in them. Macadamized them. Not done yet. Interesting school in evening.

24th. Wilmington ours! Went to Winchester to get some barbering done—Smith and I. Pleasant time. Beautiful day overhead. Roads bad. On board of administration with Barnitz and Easton to make appropriation of Regt's fund for colors. Regt. on picket. Felt most sick. Proposition to go home when A. B. returns with Lissa to Washington.

25th. Furloughs stopped and pontoon train came up today. The Col.'s leave failed. He was in great trouble, having promised his wife to come home and yet expecting to remain with regt. after leave. Muddy, but pleasant overhead.

EXTRACT FROM LETTER OF BREVET BRIGADIER GENERAL NETTLETON TO MRS. LUMAN H. TENNEY

Lakeside, Mich., June 20, 1911.

* * * Today in looking over war-time papers I came across the originals and copies of certain letters from General Custer. They relate so closely and importantly to the history, career, and military standing of the Second Ohio Cavalry that it occurs to me that you might like to file copies with the War Records which you are now collating and arranging.

Luman Tenney's admirable service, his high qualities as a disciplinarian, and as a commander of men in the battlefield, so largely contributed to the good record made by the regiment that that record is in one sense a part of his own. These letters from General Custer, the idolized commander of our Division, are exceptional in the history of Army experience.

Headquarters 3rd Cavalry Division, Mid. Mil. Division,
Feb. 24, 1865.

His Excellency Gov. Brough:

As Lt. Col. Nettleton of the Second Ohio Cavalry is about to proceed to his home in Ohio with the intention of procuring as many men as possible to fill his regiment, I desire to urge upon your Excellency the propriety of rendering Col. Nettleton all possible facilities for accomplishing this end.

The Second Ohio has been under my command for a considerable period, during which time they have been repeatedly engaged with the enemy. Upon all such occasions their conduct has been most gallant and deserving. I have known this regiment to hold positions against vastly superior forces of the enemy under circumstances which most regiments would have considered as warranting a retreat; and I take pleasure in assuring your Excellency that in my entire division, numbering twelve regiments from different states, I have none in which I repose greater confidence than in the 2nd Ohio. For these reasons I feel assured that the interests of the service would be greatly promoted by filling the regiment to the maximum number.

Your Excellency cannot find among the many gallant sons of Ohio a more gallant or deserving officer than Lt. Col. Nettleton.

Very Respectfully,
G. A. Custer, Bv't Major General.

Headquarters 3rd Cav. Div.
Feb. 24th, 1865.

Lt. Col. A. B. Nettleton,
Comdg 2nd Ohio Cav.,
Through 1st Brigade Headquarters.

Colonel:

The General comdg Divis. has directed me to express to you his great and entire satisfaction with the manner in which the pickets from your regiment were performing their duties today while he was inspecting the line. Not a man failed to understand and execute the orders issued from these and superior Headquarters, not a man but who did credit to himself and his regiment.

The General is much gratified to see that your men on the picket line are anxious, like true soldiers, to keep up the excellent reputation your regiment has won on the battle field.

Very respectfully yours, etc.,
L. Siebert, A. A. Genl.

The incident which called forth the above letter occurred the day before and while Sheridan's army was in winter quarters at Winchester, Va. Gen. Custer with his staff and escort galloping out the Romney Pike, came suddenly upon the sentinel at the picket post, who ordered "Halt" and demanded the countersign.

An attempt by the General to awe the sentinel, who was told that certainly he knew well who it was seeking to pass, made no difference; and the General proceeding to ride forward was again abruptly stopped before the sentinel's raised gun and the declaration that he would shoot anyone attempting to pass without first giving the countersign. Thereupon the General dismounted, advanced, gave the countersign and was permitted to pass.

26th. Every preparation made to move. Ordnance and Q. M. stores condemned and turned in. Several orders and circulars came around. All bustle and commotion. Wrote home.

27th. Reveille at 3 A. M. Moved at 6. Moved through Winchester. Formed several times in crossing streams, etc. Seemed good to see Gen. Sheridan along on his black horse. Halted many times. Went into camp at 10 P. M. Very good rest. Woodstock.

28th. Reveille at 4 A. M. Brigade moved out in advance at 6. Waited at the Shenandoah for the pontoons to come up. Most of our brigade forded. One 3rd N. J. man drowned. Our regt. did nicely. Camped at Lacey's Springs.

MARCH, 1865

1st. Wednesday. By mistake up before daylight. Brigade in rear of column. Did not move out till 9 A. M. Advance captured the two bridges between Harrisburg and Staunton. Several prisoners captured. Camped six miles from Staunton. Wagons captured.

2nd. Thursday. Commenced to rain early. Our div. in advance. Massed just before reaching S. Reached our old camp at Waynesboro at 3 P. M. The Va. Brigade formed mounted. We formed dismounted. Went out where we could see the rebel line on a hill and in the woods, running almost around W. 2nd Ohio in advance as skirmishers. Forward was given and the 2nd went forward until it carried the woods and the hill, driving the Johnnies pell-mell. I was mounted and went in on the muscle, when the rebs gave way. Took a great many prisoners myself. Captured 1,300 prisoners, 10 guns and 150 wagons and 10 stands of colors. Advance charged through the gap and burned a heavy amount of supplies at Greenville. Gen. Early barely escaped capture. It is a wonder to me how the boys stood it so well. Gen. Custer gave us great credit. Camped just through the gap. Raining.

4th. Yesterday moved on to Charlottesville and burned three heavy bridges on Va. Central. Awful roads. Rainy still. Camped at C. Nice place. Burned bridges. Went out on Lynchburg road and tore up track. Clear and pleasant. Worked hard. Went back to old camp. Plenty of forage. Slept well.

5th. Sunday. Saddled up early but did not move out. One hundred men pulled down the burned bridges. More destruction of R. R. Went out with forage detail. Camped under the hill on which is the home of Thomas Jefferson. Rations and ammunition.

6th. Another clear, beautiful day. 1st Div. in yesterday. Saddled up at 4 A. M. Moved out to guard train at 6. Moved in rear of brigade at 9. Marched through a passage underneath the Virginia University. Rear guard. Marched all night. Halted every five minutes—burned many rails. Rather poor country.

7th. Went into camp for breakfast at about 8 A. M. 22 miles from Charlottesville—beautiful day. Moved on different roads—still in rear of train. Passed through Lovingston or Nelson C. H. after dark. Camped six miles on picket.

8th. In advance of train. Turned towards the river. Went by Arrington Station to New Market at the junction of the Tye and James rivers. Met the 1st Div. which went up the river from Charlottesville. Rainy night.

9th. Moved out in the morning at 6. My Batt. in the extreme advance. Passed Howardsville and Scottsville and camped at Hardware River bridge. Travelled down the tow path mostly. Rain at night.

10th. Moved on to Columbia at the junction of the Rivanna and James. Pleasant day—bad roads. Went into camp and sent out forage detail. Got plenty of forage and subsistence. Very wealthy plantation. Large number of negroes. Canal thoroughly destroyed.

11th. Saturday. Lay in camp all day. Cleaned up. Two inspections. Bathed and changed my clothes. Details went out for forage. Seemed good to get a day's rest. Improved it as well as possible with the work to do.

12th. Sunday. Reveille at 3 A. M. Marched at 5. A snail's pace all day. Clear and beautiful day. Moved north. 1st Div. moved off to the left. Have thought a good deal of home and friends today. God bless the dear ones at home. Camped at Frederick Hall Station.

13th. Monday. Reveille at 4 A. M. Out at 5:30. Went out on R. R. and destroyed a great distance of the R. R. The boys worked with a will. Burned several warehouses full of tobacco. Lay in camp from 1 A. M. 1st Div. up the R. R.

14th. Moved out at daylight. When 6 miles from the South Anna ground squirrel bridge, my battalion was ordered forward at a trot to support the 1st Conn. in a chase after Early with 300 men. Kept up the chase 12 miles. Crossed the Chickahominy—10 miles from Richmond—scattered the force. Custer offered 30 days' furlough to the captor of Early. Kept up the trot into Ashland, recrossing Chickahominy. No force. Very sore, chafed and tired. Moved back north of South Anna. Many horses played out. Ours did well. Lost but one. Held them at a square trot. Anniversary of an eventful day in my life. Have thought a great deal today of this day a year ago and the other days near them. It makes me sad to review them.

15th. Reveille at 1:30. Moved out on wrong road. Went to Ashland—stayed all day. Pickets rebel division came up and attacked us. 2nd drove back the advance. 2nd N. Y. lost several men. Camped north of the North Anna at 12 P. M. Heard firing from Richmond.

16th. Up at 4. No breakfast. Haversack empty for two days. Rained last night and this morning. Warm as in June. Our Div. in advance. Got into camp at 4 P. M. at Mangohick. Easton's Batt. and 50 men from 1st Batt. on a scout to Hanovertown Ferry. Boys had a hard time to get forage and rations. 30 or 40 miles from the White House.

17th. Reveille at 4. Moved out at 8, having been in line two hours. In rear of the train. Got into camp before dark. Plenty of rations. Passed through Aylett's Ware House and camped near King William Court House, 8 miles from White House.

18th. Reveille at 4. Out at 6. Arrived at White House at 11 A. M. Unsaddled and camped. Transports and gunboats. Forage and rations. Beautiful day. Took a bath. Saw a paper of the 16th. Pleased me much. Wrote home. Slaves gathered together.

19th. Crossed the river on R. R. bridge. 2nd went out on picket, to Baltimore Crossroads. My Batt. on outpost. Rode about the country to get a good idea of it. Scouts were prowling about all night. Changed position. Kept us on the alert all night. Several shots.

20th. Relieved by the 2nd N. Y. about noon. Returned to camp near W. House. Drew rations and forage. Inspection of horses. Estimates for clothing, C. and Garrison equipage. A very hot day. Seemed like Petersburg. Read old file of papers. Dreamed of Fannie.

21st. Clear and beautiful day. Warm. Cleaned up. Went to the landing. Could find nothing which I wanted. Rained. Papers of the 20th received. Everything seems to be moving off prosperously. God grant us an early peace. Dreamed of little Carrie.

22nd. Clear. Wind up. Soon after breakfast accompanied Col. Nettleton to the boat which he took for Washington and home on a five days' leave. Thede and I sent a letter. Would that we could go with him. How happy the home folks will be, especially Melissa and Minnie.

23rd. Sun shines out in its fullness. Dreamed of being at home last night. It was Sunday and I at church. Mail came. Glorious news. A child born, a nephew. (Albert Ellis.) Joy is in the household. Prosperity and happiness to the father and mother. Received Tennyson's "Enoch Arden." A sweet, sad story. Any number of old papers. Spent the day feasting upon good things. Splendid day.

24th. Tuesday. Wrote home and to several friends. Went to the landing and procured some little eatables and paper. Paymaster in camp. Saw him. Busy with the Michigan Brigade and 1st Vermont. Marching orders.

25th. Ready to march at 6. Took my pockets full of mail to the landing. Dismounted men went by boats. Our regt. in rear of Div. and train. Crossed the Chickahominy on pontoons and reached Harrison's Landing in evening. Fortifications.

26th. Had a very good view of McClellan's defensive works. Good. Moved up the river and crossed at Deep Bottom. An occasional shot. Heard of taking in 2,700 rebs in front of Petersburg. Camped at Bermuda Hundred.

27th. A beautiful day. Clear and warm and somewhat dusty. Crossed the Appomattox. Moved along the line to the Norfolk R. R. Seemed natural to hear the continuous firing once more. Few changes in appearance. Woods all gone.

28th. Rested in the morning. Charley Smith, Sergt., came over from the 60th Ohio. Went down to Hancock Station. Troops passing to the left. Orders to march tomorrow morning at 6. Work ahead. Broke up mess. In with Stearns.

29th. The whole night occupied in paying off the regt. Got very little money myself. Up early after a little nap. Boys sent their money home by Dr. Smith and Adj. Pike, who have mustered out of service. Went to Army Hdqrs. Moved out. Joined Div. near old picket line. Marched 4 miles beyond Reams and camped. Rained—awful roads.

30th. Rain continued. Lay in the mud till noon, then moved into the woods. Moved out just after getting fixed up comfortably. Moved 4 miles over awful roads and camped 5 miles from Dinwiddie C. H. Building a good deal of corduroy road. Put on picket. Barnitz uneasy all night. Allowed no rest.

31st. Cleared up soon after sunrise, but did not remain so long. Very heavy firing. Musketry and artillery to the right of and beyond Dinwiddie C. H. Very uneasy to know how the day is going. God grant us victory. Success now, the capture of the Southside and the Danville R. R. must bring peace soon. We can leave the cause in God's care. On to Dinwiddie—there at 6 P. M. 1st Div. all driven back. 3rd Div. engaged. 3rd N. J. ammunition exhausted. Go up at a trot, dismount and go in. Doublequicked half a mile—came upon infantry line which opened fire and charged. Had to fall back quickly. Horse wounded. Many good men lost. Fortified and lay on our arms.

APRIL, 1865

1st. Saturday. At daylight, without supper or breakfast, advanced. Rebels in front fell back. 5th corps up. Advanced dismounted 5 miles to the rebel breastworks. Built temporary breastworks. Held them under fire till 4 P. M. when the 5th corps came up and charged. Advanced through the pines till in sight of works and guns with a yell. Repulsed. Formed line again and in 15 minutes charged again. Got under the works and laid down. Here Brother Thede, noble and brave boy, was struck through with a piece of shell. Helped him from the field. Suffered awfully. In answer to my questions he said: "Luman, I think my wound is mortal. I can not live. I have tried to do my duty today. Tell mother I only wish I had been a better boy. I hope that God will accept me and take me to Heaven." He had his senses for 30 or 40 minutes when he sank away as we carried him along and died before we reached the hospital. I thought that he had fallen asleep. I spoke to him but received no answer. His pulse beat feebly. I knew then that he was going. The Doctor gave him some brandy, but no life appeared. I buried him in a rough box beneath a cedar tree in front of the house and across the road and cut the headboard with a knife. God sustain mother.

BROTHER THEODORE
Killed in the Last Great Battle at Five Forks, Va.

Monday, 3rd. Yesterday I wrote to mother and sisters. The fighting of Saturday was most severe. The 2nd Ohio lost 35 killed and wounded in the two days. 5 officers. Trees completely riddled where we were. How so few fell I can not see. Brilliant affair—but oh the cost. Petersburg ours, too. It seems hard to lose dear friends when peace seems so near. Picket's Div. captured nearly entire. Wrote the sad news home, also wrote Richard Bail's people. Moved out at 9 A. M. Crossed the south side R. R. between Fords and Sutherlands. 5th Corps across. Very little firing heard today. 1st Div. struck the rebs near the river road. Firing after dark.

LETTER FROM L. H. TENNEY TO HIS MOTHER AND SISTERS

Oak Grove, Alabama, Sunday P. M., April 1, 1866.

My Dear Mother and Friends:

I wonder if nearly the same thoughts are not in your mind this P. M. which are in mine.

The sun is just about as low now at 6 o'clock as it was a year ago, when our noble boy, Theodore, fell in the thickest of the fight, face towards the enemy, there in the pine woods at Five Forks. How vividly everything of that sad and yet memorable day comes up to me.

March 31st was a hard day for us. The enemy had driven our cavalry (save one division) from Five Forks nearly back to Dinwiddie Court House. Our Division was sent for (it was behind, hard at work, getting the train through the mud) and went forward at a trot. As we neared the Court House and heard the volleys of musketry, the cheers of the rebels, and saw our men falling back—many straggling—we knew that there was work ahead. How quiet our boys were during the few minutes while we were regaining our organizations. Soon we went forward at a gallop. A half mile at this pace and we came to Custer's and Sheridan's colors near an unsupported battery and in sight of the rebel line.

Advancing across a small valley before us, our regiment in advance, we dismounted, formed line by battalions and on double quick started forward in less time, I believe, than I have been in telling it.

The brave Custer, with staff and orderlies, colors flying, went forward with us.

We gave one Second Ohio yell, perhaps a little more faintly than at other times, for the prospect looked dark, and other regiments took it up. The rebel line faced about, but though stragglers left hurriedly, marched slowly. I was afraid. We were within range. It seemed the only thing to do, for we were too few to form a line and hold our position. Another charge was ordered. The Div. colors were not behind. We had hardly started again with a yell, than that rebel line, Pickett's Div. of Infantry in our front, faced about, fired a volley and came forward on the double quick.

My horse had been shot and I had taken position behind a tree. Thede was a short distance behind me. How well I remember how he exclaimed: "Oh what makes them run," and then: "Lume, Luman, come, our men are falling back, we'll get captured!"—and how closely he kept by me, always following me, as I went back slowly through the edge of the woods, my lungs troubling me. The sun had gone down and darkness came when we regained the ground where we had dismounted. We threw up rail breastworks and waited for the rebels. They were cautious, advanced skirmishers found our position and fell back to camp in sight of us. Volunteers were called for or rather "the best men" to a certain number were sent out as scouts to learn the whereabouts and whatabouts of the enemy. Thede was among the number. Without supper or sleep, we awaited the dawn of the day. Quite a number of our boys had fallen,

POPLAR GROVE, NATIONAL CEMETERY AT PETERSBURG, VA.

THE CEMETERY RECORDS BEAR THIS INSCRIPTION:

among then Capt. Newton. We talked about our casualties, and the narrow escape of many, and wondered what the morrow would bring. We felt that the fighting was to be decisive, but knew not whether one day would bring victory.

Occasional shots were fired by skirmishers. Morning came. The scouts reported that the enemy had commenced falling back just before day. Sheridan came out with his colors. Our horses were brought up and we marched forward. After going a mile firing commenced on our flank. We countermarched, dismounted, formed line and advanced again, driving cavalry before us. We had missed breakfast, and the boys were weighed down with ammunition, so they left their haversacks upon their horses.

Theodore looked pale and tired—said his bowels were troubling him. It was afternoon before we reached the enemy's position at Five Forks. We attacked and were repulsed. A gap between the Cavalry and Infantry was discovered, so that two hours were spent moving to the right and then to the left, in front of and in range of the enemy's works. Here, weak, faint and hungry, we threw up sufficient works of logs, etc., to cover our bodies when lying down. Thede and I were together. He got some crumbs of crackers from my saddle.

It was now four o'clock when the bugles sounded the charge, and the boys, forgetting their weariness, jumped up and vied with each other in advancing to within a few rods of the works, dark with clouds of smoke and belching guns. How grim, savage and hateful everything looked in our front!

You remember well the rest—the next charge—the bravery of the boy, his fall, his devotion to duty, certainty of death, remembrance of his sins, and faith for their forgiveness through Christ—the kind messages to Ma—and then his falling so peacefully to sleep. I never can forget the firm but pleasant look upon his countenance, as he lay among the groaning, dying and dead at the hospital. Then his burial. I thanked God that his brother could be with him in his last moments and lay his remains away to rest till the final trumpet call.

My thoughts were sad as I groped my way through the dark woods to our camp. I thought particularly of the mourning at home. I knew that you would be sad to feel that the boy should be taken in his youth, the hope of his mother and joy of his friends, and yet I felt that you would inwardly thank God that his death had brought glory to Him and freedom to men. The dearer he was to his friends, the brighter his hopes, the greater the sacrifice was in the eyes of God. We ought to feel—I do—that we have a living interest in this great good accomplished and sealed by the blood of our dearest friends. And we certainly have reason to trust that Theodore's inheritance is in Heaven, drawing us thither.

Luman H. Tenney.

Note—One year after the above letter, on April 16, 1867, Luman Harris Tenney and Frances Delia Andrews were married at Oberlin, Ohio.
. And about a year and a half later when the brother and mother went to Virginia to look up the burial place of "Brother Theodore" the following letters were written to me in our home in Sandusky, Ohio.

F. D. T., Feb. 5, 1914.

Petersburg, Va., Nov. 12, 1868.
Thursday morning.

My Sweet Child:

We arrived here safely a few minutes ago. One of Ma's first remarks after getting here was, "I wish Fannie, Minnie and Melissa could be here with us today." I have made the same wish in regard to my darling wife every day since I left her and the dear baby. (Bernard.)

We reached Washington Tuesday evening rather late. Yesterday spent the morning in looking up records. Found that Theodore was buried here in National Cemetery, "Poplar Grove," about two miles out.

Shall undoubtedly leave him.

Yesterday afternoon we drove over to Arlington Heights and the National Cemetery there, where some 13,000 soldiers rest—

"Sleep the sleep that knows not waking,
Dream of battlefields no more."
We shall go early to the cemetery and probably to Richmond for the night.
Much love, dear child, from

Your devoted husband,
Luman.

Washington, D. C., Nov. 14, 1868.

My Own Dear Fannie:

We reached here last evening after a very satisfactory visit at Petersburg and Richmond and pleasant trip back. * * * We found Theodore's grave very pleasantly situated in the National Cemetery near Petersburg. Everything seemed very satisfactory to Ma. We got flowers and put on the grave. * * *

Shall probably reach home Thursday.

Kiss our sweet "da-da" treasure many times for me. Accept much love, dear Fannie, from

Your Luman.

BERNARD FREDERICK AND HIS MOTHER

4th. Up at daylight. Sent telegram home. Moved up the Appomattox, our Div. in advance. Captured 300 or 400 prisoners, 5 guns and many wagons. Hill's Corps and cavalry on our front. Near Bevil's Bridge enemy made a stand at a crossroads to get a part of their column by. Artillery opened and rebs ran. Our regt. did not become engaged. Went out to pick up wounded. Quite a number of deserters. Camped on this ground. Richmond ours. God hasten peace. Clear and pleasant. Cavalry moved on up the Appomattox. 1st Div. in advance. Would that I could see mother now in her distress. Passed a part of the infantry. Made a feint towards Amelia C. H. Went into camp. 2nd on picket. Moved out again at 11 P. M. Returned to main road and marched all night.

5th. Wednesday. Reached Juttersville Station on Danville R. R. at 10. 5th Corps made a reconnoissance and captured a large number of prisoners, wagons, flags, cannon, etc. Suffered some. Rebs at Amelia C. H. Cox spied.

6th. Drew rations in the night. Moved at 7—whole army. Cavalry to the left of Burkeville. Charged the reb wagon train. Scattered the skirmish line and charged each way. Chester and myself charged nearly 4 miles, nearly to the head of train—no support. (Battle of Sailor's Creek.) Chester wounded in the head. Eggleston and Smith got several pieces of artillery. Got back to command by a circuitous route, the rebs having cut us off. Two divisions charged mounted and were repulsed. Reformed and charged again with success, the 6th Corps engaging the rear. Lt. Stearns killed. Several Co. "C" captured. Several thousand prisoners, many colors, Generals and cannon. 2nd credited 650 prisoners, 60 officers and 4 pieces of artillery. Lost good men.

In a letter from Capt. Chester dated March 23, 1914, regarding the fighting at Sailor's Creek he says:

"Our regiment and brigade was ordered to charge Lee's wagon train in sight, across a small stream with banks on the farther side. Our regiment was, as I remember it, the last one in the column so were the left of the line of battle or attack. We struck the wagon train and commenced taking prisoners. All formation of company or regiment was broken, every soldier acting independently. The driver of a mule team refused to stop when I ordered him to do so, and I was about to shoot him when it occurred to me that if I killed the driver the team would continue to go just the same. So I rode up to the "lead" mule (the one on the left hand side of head pair) and shot it. That stopped the entire team and blocked the narrow road. I then captured a rebel Major and turned him over to Sergt. Waters of Co. H to take to the rear. As soon as that was done Joe T. Haskell—now of Wellington—came to me. Capt. Tenney with his orderly, and Lieut. Stearns, came up, so there were five of us. We turned to the right and rode to the top of the bank or bluff and there the rebel train was in full sight again a mile or more from where we first charged it. The five men took position several rods apart so as to cover or show quite a line. As we showed ourselves the train guard fired on us. We each turned and called out loudly for the "pretended battalions" in the ravine to charge. We advanced on the gallop firing our revolvers and shooting as we went. The train guard was stampeded and ran. We followed along the train for a quarter of a mile to where the fence had been thrown down and the wagons were going into a piece of woods. I was a few rods from the fence when a rebel from behind a tree in the woods fired at me and missed hitting me. I fired my revolver at him, to no effect, however. He then reloaded his gun, stepping from behind the tree in doing so, then rested his gun beside the tree and took deliberate aim at me, and fired. The bullet knocked me from my horse. Capt. Tenney rode up, caught my horse and told me I was all right. I supposed I was mortally wounded. Haskell came to me and taking a suit case from a wagon found some white cloth and tied up my head. In the meantime other men came up and Capt. Tenney and Lt. Stearns led them to attack the train again going through the woods, some distance I think. Somewhere after leaving me Lieut. Stearns was killed by a train guard."

April 7th. Marched out, 32 reb colors behind Custer. Crossed S. S. R. R. at Rice's Depot. Passed through Prince Edward's C. H. and camped on a fork of the Appomattox. Lee's army off to the right on the Lynchburg road.

8th. Moved out early and met the 2nd Div., Crook's, at Prospect Station on R. R. A beautiful day. Troops all cheer for Cus-

ter. Captured at Appomattox Station 4 trains of cars, charged and
captured 24 pieces of artillery and heavy train of wagons after
fighting until 10 P. M. Did not stop till reached rebel camp at Appomattox C. H. Horse hit by a shell and I struck by a spent ball.

9th. Sunday. Fighting commenced early. 24 and 15 Corps
up. Infantry coming up double quick. Rebs attacked. Drove cavalry back. Infantry turned the tide. Grant summoned Lee to surrender. Lee asks for terms. Grant orders Sheridan to press him.
Whole thing moves up, Custer in advance. White flag meets him.
Silence reigns. The whole cavalry cheer. A rebel cavalry force
attack. Easily repulse it. Whole reb army before us. Glorious
day. Surrender.

On April 9, 1865, recognizing that the end of the war was at hand, and
that his relations with the Third Cavalry Division must soon be sundered, its
beloved commander promulgated to his troops that memorable address best
known as

CUSTER'S FAREWELL ORDER

Headquarters Third Cavalry Div.,
Appomattox Court House, Virginia, April 9, 1865.

With profound gratitude toward the God of Battles, by whose blessings
our enemies have been humbled and our arms triumphant, your Commanding
General avails himself of this, his first opportunity, to express to you his admiration of the heroic manner in which you have passed through the series of
battles which today resulted in the surrender of the enemy's entire army.

The record established by your indomitable courage is unparalleled in the
annals of war. Your prowess has won for you even-the respect and admiration
of your enemies. During the past six months, although in most instances con-
fronted by superior numbers, you have captured from the enemy, in open battle, one hundred and eleven pieces of field artillery, sixty-five battle flags, and
upwards of ten thousand prisoners of war, including seven general officers.
Within the past ten days, and included in the above, you have captured forty-
six field pieces of artillery, and thirty-seven battle flags. You have never lost
a gun, never lost a color and have never been defeated; and notwithstanding
the numerous engagements in which you have borne a prominent part, including those memorable battles of the Shenandoah, you have captured every piece
of artillery which the enemy has dared to open on you. The near approach of
peace renders it improbable that you will again be called upon to undergo the
fatigue of toilsome march, or the exposure of the battlefield; but should the
assistance of keen blades wielded by your sturdy arms, be required to hasten
the coming of that glorious peace for which we have been so long contending,
the General Commanding is firmly confident that, in the future as in the past,
every demand will meet with a hearty and willing response.

Let us hope that our work is done, and that, blest with the comforts of
peace, we may be permitted to enjoy the pleasure of home and friends. For
our comrades who have fallen let us ever cherish a grateful remembrance; to
the wounded and those who languish in Southern prisons let our heartfelt sympathy be tendered.

And now, speaking for myself alone, when the war is ended and the task
of the historian begins—when those deeds of daring, which have rendered the
name and fame of the Third Cavalry Division imperishable, are inscribed on
the bright pages of our country's history, I only ask that my name be written
as that of the Commander of the Third Cavalry Division.

G. A. Custer,
Brevet Major General Commanding.

Official:
L. W. Barnhart,
Captain and A. A. A. G.

CUSTER'S BADGE.

Extract from an account of the surrender given by J. T. Haskell, Co. H, at the Reunion of the 2nd Ohio Cav. held in Cleveland, Ohio, October 10, 1911.

"It seems fitting and proper as a final word of the 2nd Ohio Cavalry's part in this account of the surrender, Gen. Custer's Headquarters being almost in the immediate front of the Regiment, to give an account of his (Gen. Custer's) receiving the flag of truce from the Rebel officer carrying the same, and as that account is given by the Rebel General John B. Gordon better than any other account I have ever seen, I will give his words: He says, "I had received word from Gen. Lee informing me that there was a flag of truce between him and Gen. Grant, and that I should notify the Union Army in my front. I called for my Chief of Staff and said, 'take a flag of truce, bear this message to the Union commander, quick.' He said, 'I have no flag of truce.' 'O well,' I said, 'take your handkerchief and tie it on a stick and go.' He said, 'General, I have no handkerchief.' I said, 'Tear up your shirt, put that on a stick and go.' He said, 'I have no white shirt, and see you have none, there is not a white shirt in the whole Army.' I said, 'Get something, get something and go.' He got something and went. There soon returned with him one of the most superb horsemen that ever sat a saddle, and as I looked into his flashing blue eyes, with his long curls falling to his shoulders, I found myself in the presence of that afterwards great Indian fighter, that man who ought forever to hold a place in every American heart, the gallant Custer.

"With a wave of his sword, which embodied all the grace of the schools, he said to me, 'Gen. Gordon, I bring you the compliments of Gen. Sheridan. I also bring you, sir, Gen. Sheridan's demand for your immediate and unconditional surrender.' Just then a white flag was seen in my front, and with it rode Gen. Sheridan and his staff."

Note—Mrs. Elizabeth B. Custer, widow of General Custer, has recently presented me with a souvenir consisting of a part of this famous Flag of Truce (which flag was a crash towel), a fragment of the table on which Grant and Lee signed the Articles of Surrender at Appomatox, and a piece of the red necktie worn by Gen. Custer on this occasion. A. B. N., June 14, 1911.

LETTER FROM L. H. TENNEY TO HIS MOTHER AND SISTERS

"Oakland," Alabama, Sunday P. M., April 8, 1866.

My Dear Friends:

I am reminded every day of the campaign during those last days of the rebellion. On this day, one year ago—the sun far down in the west—our brigade with no noise save the clamping of horses' feet and the clanking of sabre scabbards, charged down upon the worried Johnnies at Appomattox Station. The surprise was complete. Three trains of cars, well loaded with provisions and munitions of war for Gen. Lee's mere skeleton of an army, with the force guarding them fell into our hands without the loss of a man. Three miles away to the east and rear was Appomattox Court House, where the flying and discomforted army was halting. Gen. Walker, Reb., had been sent ahead with the Artillery brigade to take the cars for Lynchburg, only twenty-three miles distant, where Lee was coming. The Artillery was just coming in from the east as we reached the station from the south. The Gen. wheeled his guns, 25, in the road where they were, hoping by a hard fight to get the station. Grape, canister and shell came thick and fast and infantry stood firmly by the guns as we made charge after charge. Night came. Other divisions were coming up. Gen. Custer became impatient. He rode along the line and shouted, "Boys, the 3rd Div. must have those guns. I'm going to charge if I go alone." The guns were belching forth red fire. The word was given. Gen. Custer did not charge alone. Guns, wagons and prisoners were ours and our boys did not stop until they had passed the Court House where the camp-fires marked the location of the rebel army along the hillsides. Several 2nd Ohio boys were there, Major Easton, Capt. Co. M and Lieut. Rand. The boys were full of enthusiasm and eager to "charge them." Mounted men were in our front. I ordered "cease firing" and asked who they were. "Gen. Geary and his staff," was the reply. Looking down to the left of the road, we noticed by the light of the camp-fires a line advancing. We were almost in rear of it. We expected a volley as we withdrew, but the confusion saved us.

At midnight our Div. was relieved. We camped at the station. We wondered what the morrow would bring forth. We knew that we were in front of Lee without Infantry support. And the continual skirmishing told us that Lee was not to be penned without a hard fight. The morning of the 9th came. The Cavalry was being pushed back rapidly towards the station. The boys were falling, scores of them—why was it with victory so near?—when over the hill a dark column was espied coming down the road in close column at quick time. What relief from the awful suspense! What cared we for the color or race of those men so they brought relief to us. We saw courage and determination in their coal-black faces. Give them the ballot, for they insured victory that day. The Cavalry, after being relieved, formed squadrons and at a trot, under flank fire, moved through the fields toward the Court House.

Lines of Infantry were in our rear, moving up from the south and west. Aids came down the line, shouting "Make no noise! Gen. Grant has ordered Lee to surrender and Sheridan to press him! We are going to do it!"

We reach the wooded hills, south of and in sight of the Court House. All at once the Artillery ceases firing. A white flag appears in front. The column halts. Gen. Custer meets it. Again Aids dash off and we see it in their faces, "Lee has surrendered!" Oh the wild and mad huzzas which followed! Pen can not picture the scene. The four years of suffering, death and horrid war were over. Thank God! thank God!! was upon every tongue. Peace, home and friends were ours. Yes, thank God! What wonder that we were crazy with joy? Right here some of Wheeler's Cavalry, not advised of the truce, came charging upon us. We held our fire, forbore till they meanly persisted, when our boys without orders drove them back. They learned of the truce just in time to save precious blood. Not eighty rods in front of us, when we halted in a hollow, was a brigade of rebel infantry with twelve pieces of artillery loaded to the muzzle with grape shot, waiting for us to come over the hill. Here Sergt. Weary of Co. A fell while demanding the colors of the brigade. He was a brave man and left a family of children to mourn him. How many loving friends were waiting then for the coming of their brave boys, who now mourn their noble dead, whose graves mark the bloody struggle during those eight days from Petersburg to Appomattox.

In the exultations of victory the fallen were well-nigh forgotten. Then on either side of Appomattox C. H. the two armies went into camp—all friends. Rations were issued to all—and the rank and file on each side happy and thankful, I ween, that no more bugle calls were to summon them to battle.

I have spun out this account, but I remember that Lu was absent at the time and the circumstances and incidents are so fresh in my mind that I have enjoyed reviewing them.

May the President and Congress so act as to secure the fruits of the dearly bought victory.

I don't know and cannot decide what is best in the way of imposing requirements upon the Southern people and establishing guaranties for the rights of freedmen.

The long and bitter discussion preparatory to action on the part of the government, I am confident, is working evil among Southerners. It tends to alienate them. They feel that the spirit of the majority of the Northern people is unfriendly towards them. The conduct of the people in this section has seemed consistent. We couldn't expect more.

Much more delay in giving them some kind of show will exasperate a great many, I think, and make them unfriendly to Northerners, unkind and unjust to freedmen and disloyal to the government, while now I think the reverse is true.

I enjoyed the letter from Uncle Albert.

With much love to all and two kisses to Carrie,

Your brother Luman.

10th. Camped last night side by side with Lee's army. A great jubilee among the boys. Soon after sunrise moved out. Sheridan passed us. Cheered him as he passed. Camped at Prospect Station.

11th. Marched out in advance of the Corps—Custer commanding. Grant passed us. Boys cheered him lustily. Went into camp 9 miles from Burke's Station. Little rain.

12th. Marched at usual hour in rear of Division train. Bad roads and very tedious marching. Col. Nettleton met us near the Junction. Had a good visit with him. Line from home. How anxious I am to see dear mother and sisters. I love them more dearly than ever. Camped at B. New colors arrived. Rained. All begin to talk of home and peace. I do desire to be a true exemplary Christian during my remaining days.

13th. Contrary to the general expectation, marched. A little rain. Went into camp near Nottoway Station. Put up picket poles and laid out camp in order. Letter of the 6th from home. Folks are all resigned and cheerful. I am so glad.

14th. Spent the day reading the papers and writing letters. Wrote to Mr. Porter and Bails' people. The whole north seems jubilant over the glorious successes, and becomingly ascribes the praise to God. All seem disposed to be lenient to the enemy, too, all but Davis. Salute fired. Four years today since the flag came down from Sumter.

15th. Wrote several letters and read the papers. Yesterday put in application for leave of absence. I am very anxious to see my dear mother. Would that Johnston would be wise and surrender. Think he will be. Thank God that peace is so near and a united country will live to advance religion, justice and liberty. Forage detail. Virginians thoroughly submissive.

16th. Reveille at 4 A. M. with orders to move at 6. Orders countermanded on account of no rations. Went to sutler's and got cheese, buttermilk and cakes. Beautiful day. Letter from Minnie. Papers. A report that Lincoln was killed a short time since by an assassin. God grant it may not be true, for the country's good. Am happy today, my mind peaceful. Saw F. last night and night before. Lincoln assassinated. How great the loss to the country. All boys but two took a verbal temperance pledge. Got my leave and took the cars in evening.

Note—After the surrender of Lee on April 9th, 1865, the Cavalry Corps, including the 2nd Ohio, marched southward to strike the remaining Confederate army commanded by Gen. Joseph E. Johnston, which was still confronting Sherman's army in North Carolina. Shortly after we had crossed the Roanoke River and entered North Carolina word came to us that Johnston had sensibly surrendered to Sherman and we marched northward to Richmond and Petersburg, and on to Washington, in time for the Grand Review. This episode in the Regiment's records is not mentioned in the diary because Major Tenney was at that time absent on leave at home.—A. B. N., June 10, 1911.

17th. Rode all night with paroled prisoners—Yankees. Cold. Reached City Point at 8 A. M. Got ready to leave on the mail boat at 10 A. M. Boat loaded mostly with Southern officers and a few Yankees, few citizens. Saw a telegraph operator with whom I was acquainted in Tenn. Read late papers. Accounts of the assassination. A little seasick. Most of the rebels seem submissive and willing to come under the old flag again.

Tuesday, 18th. Had a very good night's rest. Up early. Pleasant visit with an Indiana man. Several Southern ladies on board the boat. Great gloom in Washington. Excitement very high. Went to White House and viewed the President's remains in state. Everybody on the alert to discover the conspirators. Drew pay for January and February. Took the evening train via Harrisburg. Read papers and slept. The whole nation in mourning. All business places draped.

19th. Reached Pittsburg at 2 P. M. Left on Cleveland train at 3. Pittsburg in mourning. Rode in company with a Cleveland man, Briggs, I believe. Pleasant visit. Gave me a detail of the working of the carrier P. O. system. Passed through Cleveland at 10 P. M. Stayed over at Grafton. The funeral of the President took place today. Ceremonies throughout the Union. Johnson bound to deal roughly with traitors.

20th. Rainy. Reached home on the morning train. Met my good mother at the door. It seemed so good. She seemed perfectly resigned to the loss of Theodore. Never was more happy in my life. Ma and I went down to see Minnie and Melissa. Happy meeting. Beautiful little baby Bertie. Carrie a little angel, good and beautiful. Now could I only see Fannie and be reconciled as of old my happiness would be complete.

21st. Ate supper yesterday with Minnie. Spent the morning playing with Carrie and reading. Afternoon Minnie and John over to tea. Went up town with Melissa. Fannie in Bellevue teaching. Fortunate for me. Rode out with Charlie. Took Carrie along. Tea at Minnie's. Music from Joe and John. Fisher and Allie Norton there.

22nd. Went to town in the morning to market. Will Hudson came out. We boys got together and had a jolly time. Floy and George came out. Good visit. Chester came home. Walked with Will to the river, too late for train. A lame stiff neck. Spent a part of evening at Minnie's. Saw the Hudson family. F. Henderson and Will Keep. Hurrah!

23rd. Was unable to get out on account of my neck. Read Thede's diaries to Ma and Melissa, and talked about him. Minnie in a short time. Read *Atlantic*. Melissa went to church in P. M. Played with Carrie. Quite a wintry day. Prof. Peck very kind to the family.

24th. Spent the morning at home. In the P. M. went with the girls to Monthly Rhetoricals. Charley Fairchild had an exercise entitled, "One Year with Red Tape." Good. After his exercise we walked about town.

25th. Early in the morning started for Amherst with the children. Had a pleasant visit at Grandpa's. After dinner, Lissa, Mary, Floy and I went over to cousin Helen's. Tea there. Saw many old friends. Home at 8 P. M.

26th. Spent the day in O. Thought of going to Wellington with Chester but he was out of town. Read most of the day. "Cotta Family" and *Atlantic*. Some rain.

27th. Melissa and I went to Cleveland. F. D. Allen and C. G. Fairchild out, too. Spent a portion of the day with the boys. Dinner with Will. Called at Uncle Jones' in the evening. Cousin Minnie there. Spent the night with the boys.

28th. Saw the train come in. Commenced to rain early in the day. The procession was grand. Got wet through looking at it. The Bajida and other arrangements were splendid. Very unpleasant day.

29th. Saturday. Yesterday we came home instead of going to Madison, on account of rain. Spent a portion of the day with the boys at Charlie's—dinner. Went up to see Will off. Evening at Mrs. Holtslander's.

30th. Went to Sunday School in the morning with Delos and C. G. Mr. Fitch spoke splendidly. Went to church with Melissa. Mr. Finney preached on "Lasciviousness"—an excellent sermon—A. M. and P. M. Home in the evening.

MAY, 1865

1st. Monday. The day at home. Sat for a vignette at Platte's. In evening went with Melissa to Young People's Meeting. Seemed real good and like old times. Am trying to live a higher Christian life. Will try to make Ma and friends happy.

2nd. Cloudy in the morning. Went to depot for Minnie Newhall. Spent a part of the day at Minnie's with the girls. The rest of the time at home. Little time to read. Cleveland pictures came.

3rd. Cousin Minnie and I stood and sat for pictures. Had a jolly time. Minnie over at our house a portion of the day. Am enjoying my visit with Cousin first rate.

4th. In the morning, aided by the girls, I trimmed up the rose bushes and cleaned around the yard. P. M. we all went over to Minnie's. Uncle Dan telegraphed that he would be along on evening train. Went up to cars. Friends didn't come. Minnie disappointed. Played at chess a good deal.

5th. Uncle Dan, Aunts Roxena and Rhodilla, with the good Cousins Ella and Alonzo, came on morning train. Spent the P. M. at Minnie's. Went with the girls, Minnie and Ella, to Watson's and Platt's to see Carpenter's picture of Lincoln and his cabinet. Had a first rate time at home eating philopenas with the girls.

6th. Newhall friends went yesterday. Has been a very stormy, dreary day. Called at Dr. Steele's. Visited with Aunt Rhodilla and Alonzo. Read some. Got Mrs. Charles' writings.

"Cotta Family," "Early Dawn" and "Kitty Trevellyn's Diary." Also coarse Testament for mother.

7th. Went to Sunday School with Fred and C. G. in Prof. Penfield's class. A stranger from Natchez spoke. Went to church with Aunt Rhodilla, and Melissa. After service Charlie and I walked up R. R. Pleasant time. Have seen a good many friends today.

8th. Left on the 8 A. M. train. Reached Columbus at 2 P. M. Went up to Capitol and ascertained that Nettleton had been commissioned Col. and Seward's commission revoked. Wrote home and to Uncle Albert. Rained. Looked around the city a little.

9th. Went off on the 4:25 A. M. train on Ohio Central. Reached Bellaire at 10:30 A. M. Crossed the river and took the Baltimore & Ohio R. R. Very poor conveniences. Enjoyed the scenery along the Monongahela, Cheat river and Potomac. Slept considerably.

10th. Reached the Relay House at 9 A. M. Saw Rob and Okie McDowell. Reached Washington about noon. Got permission to remain in city till regiment came to Alexandria. Stopped at Markham's.

Thursday, 11th. Drew one month's pay on my order. Went through the Patent Office and to the Treasury. Went home with Mr. Mills to tea and remained over night. Rained. Had a very pleasant time with Flint, Lyra and Leof. Capitol yesterday.

12th. Cool morning. Saw Bigelow. Went to the hospital to see 2nd Ohio boys. Couldn't find Tuttle—will look again. Got some eatables from Ohio agent and took them to the boys. Went over in P. M. to Giesboro to see Major Welch. Went with him and Mr. Sloan's people to the theatre. Miss Milburn, and Johnson and Gaskill. Escorted Miss Milburn. Uncle Tom's Cabin. Very touching and good.

13th. After breakfast accompanied the Major on an inspecting tour to the various stables. Rode. A beautiful day. Seward gone home on leave and will muster as Lt. Col. Welch seems very popular at this depot, and very busy. Wrote to Charlie. Invited out in evening, but didn't accept.

14th. Went to church in morning with Welch. Kautz called. After dinner went on tug to Washington. Saw Chet at National. Letter from home. Told me a little about F. Chet and I went to Pres. Church. Services good.

15th. Was routed out this morning at 10 A. M. by Chester. Gave the P. M. General a call to learn about extra pay on resignation. Visited Navy Yard before dinner and Arsenal after dinner. Wrote to Mr. Wright.

16th. A cool morning. Up betimes. Dreamed till nervous about F. Would that I could reasonably get this subject out of my mind. God guide me. There would be satisfaction in a short look into the future. Chet and I called on Electa and Lorenzo. Went to a Catholic Fair.

17th. Chester and I walked about town. Cavalry arrived yesterday. At noon we got a carriage and drove over to Command. Seemed good to see the boys again. Beautiful camp, two miles from A. W. and A. with the Potomac, Giesboro and Heights in full view. Very romantic.

18th. Melissa came last night. Lu has gone over to see her. Talked of getting up a paper asking absent officers to leave the service. Dropped it. Rainy. Major Welch came over. Quite a time with Div. excitement.

19th. Rode a little distance with Major Welch. Told him of the plan talked of. Read in "Skirmishes and Sketches" by Gail Hamilton—much interested. Order for the Grand march in review. Good visit with Traver. Read me some of his leisure notes.

20th. Ordered to move. Went out beyond Fairfax Seminary to see 105th Ohio. Cumings and Wilcox away. Intended to stop to see Melissa as we passed through Washington, D. C., but found the marching order countermanded, so went back to camp.

21st. Up at 3 A. M. in the rain. Marched at 7. Moved through Washington with drawn sabres in platoon column. Passed by Willard's. Sheridan standing on the balcony. Stopped at Mr. Mills' over night. Nettleton rode to camp.

22nd. After breakfast M. and I called at Electa's and visited the capitol. Strawberries. Went to Patent Office, met the Holtslanders. When we got home found Stanton with horse. Waited at depot for Uncle till 10 P. M. then went to camp.

23rd. In camp near Bladensburg. Got ready early for the review. The whole Division in red neckties. Custer bade us farewell. 'Twas sad. Met Uncle and Aunt. Saw 2nd Corps and part of 5th pass in review.

Wednesday, 24th. Twelve of us officers went to town with orderlies. Ran guard. Saw Johnson, Stanton, Welles, Speed, Grant, Sherman, Howard, Slocum, Logan, Cadwallader, Sanford, Farragut and several other distinguished men. Grand affair.

THE GRAND REVIEW AT WASHINGTON, ON MAY 23 AND 24, 1865.

This historic event, briefly covered in the diary, under dates of May 23 and 24, 1865, had had no precedent in the past and is not likely to have a parallel in future. It marked officially the close of the great war, the restoration of peace, the preservation of the American Republic from destruction, and the gratitude of the American people for a result perpetual and inestimable in its value not only to them but to all mankind.

The troops participating in the Review numbered nearly Two Hundred Thousand Infantry, Cavalry and Artillery, being the veteran soldiers of (1) the Armies of the Potomac and James commanded by Generals Grant and Meade; (2) the Army of the Shenandoah, commanded by General Sheridan, including Sheridan's Cavalry Corps which in full ranks numbered 16,000 troopers; (3) Sherman's Army, which he had led victoriously from the Ohio River, through Kentucky, Tennessee and "through Georgia to the Sea," and thence through the Carolinas and Virginia to Washington. On the two successive days mentioned this combined host marched the length of Pennsylvania Avenue, and in front of the White House passed in review and saluted President Andrew Johnson and the distinguished group of men mentioned in Major Tenney's diary including Gen. U. S. Grant, Gen. W. T. Sherman, Generals Meade and Sheridan, Howard, Slocum, Logan, and Admirals Farragut and Porter. With these were also the members of the Cabinet including especially Secretary of War, E. M. Stanton and Secretary of the Navy, Gideon Welles.

This event was the signal for the disbandment and return to civil life of the nearly One Million volunteer soldiers and sailors then on the rolls of the Army and Navy of the United States. This was accomplished progressively and very rapidly, as fast as the troops could be paid off and transported to their homes.

Much to the dissatisfaction of the Second Ohio Cavalry that regiment was retained in service nearly six months after the close of hostilities, being sent to southwestern Missouri to look after some disorderly elements there, as mentioned under dates of May 27 to June 27, 1865, in the diary.—A. B. N.

25th. Nettleton returned to camp early. I went out at noon. Met M. and A. on Penn. Ave. Went up to Uncle's—discouraged. Started for Alexandria but was too late. M. and I went up to a restaurant for supper.

26th. Talked of going to camp today, but too rainy. Got a carriage and we six rode over to Arlington Heights, the forts, Arlington House and Freedmen's School. Wrote to Mother. Had a good time. Went to theatre.

27th. Still raining. Folks concluded to go to Richmond today. Went to camp on 8:30 train. Nettleton went down. Regiment ordered to Missouri. Too late for Richmond. Great feeling among the boys. Disappointed. Q. M. rations.

28th. In camp. Worked on my ordnance papers. Got them ready to send off. Nettleton went to town. Welch and Sloan in camp. Recruits not to go to Missouri. Paper circulating.

29th. Busy most of the day fixing up Company papers. Unable to find Company's desk. City Point boys up. Quite full company. Orders to move at 4 A. M tomorrow. Has been hard work to decide what to do.

30th. Reveille at 2 A. M. Turned in stores. Packed up. Went to town with Lu at 10. Got some strawberries at Mrs. Mills'. She has been very kind to me. Ice cream with Stanton. At 3 P. M. took the cars with Melissa for Cincinnati. Went as far as Frederick City and remained over night at U. S. Hotel. M. and I took a stroll up street. Had a very pleasant time. Talked about Fannie.

Her conduct seems very strange and yet I can not condemn her. I feel as of old. God will right things if it is best. I am very happy to be with my good sister.

31st. Arose late. Feeling well. A beautiful day. Visited hospital. Saw Sergt. Babcock and got him released. At 12 took cars. Got into Cumberland at 7:30. Stopped at St. Nicholas. Strolled up town. Some very pleasant residences. Crook and Kelley carried from here.

JUNE, 1865.

June 1st. Thursday. At breakfast met an old friend of the 2nd. Raised Co. F. Comfortably settled in the cars at 8. Melissa enjoyed the Cheat River and Cheat Mountain scenery first rate. Bellaire at dark. Some country lads and lassies on board. Met Birge on Central Ohio sleeping car.

2nd. Mr. Birge told us of Martin Fitch's death by drowning. God sustain the afflicted. After washing up at the Gibson House, Melissa went to see Ellie Bushnell. I attended to business and then went home with Albert. Pleasant visit. Like Mr. Morgan and family. Al and wife went back with us—ice cream.

3rd. Went to Court House and auction sales with Albert. Regt. came in early. Spent several hours with Watson. He is feeling badly. Am sorry for him. Many of the boys drunk. Two men drowned. Very sad. Co. E. Melissa received rather a rough initiation. Wheel broke, so had to lie by several hours near Cincinnati.

Sunday, 4th. Reached Louisville before noon. Overtook the Columbia. Our boat the Prima Donna. Slow time getting through the canal at Louisville. Columbia went over the falls. In evening had some music and rehearsal by Barnitz. Good.

5th. Another clear and beautiful day. Read "A New Atmosphere." Game of whist. Passed the Cumberland and Tennessee in the night. The riding in the evening was delightful. Gathered on bow and sung.

6th. Took on coal at Cairo. Rounded the point and entered the Father of Waters. Had a quiet and pleasant ride. Monotonous country along the levee. A great many wood yards.

7th. Some beautiful scenery today. High bluffs and a number of castle homes. Got into St. Louis a little before dusk. A. B. and M. got off at Carondelet and came up by cars. Took supper at Olive St. House. Wrote home. Letter from home.

8th. About 8 o'clock started for Benton Barracks. One lady ran out with flag and said "Welcome home." Learn that we are not to go to Texas. Went out on foot. Got a pleasant boarding place near camp. Chet and I near together.

9th. Field officer of the day. Went to the city for Melissa. Had a good visit as we rode out. Took her to J. R. Davies'. Spent the evening with the two families, Davies and Bostwicks. Enjoyed myself first rate.

10th. Relieved by Capt. Easton. Kept busy at my papers. Jones to be mustered out. Sent in Descriptive Rolls of Tiner and Barber. The paper signed by the officers was sent to Seward, Hillhouse and Wilcox. Think of resigning very soon.

11th. Attended service in the morning and evening at chapel. Saw Crumb—Chris. Com. delegate. Saw J. R. D. too. Chet and I had a cozy chat together. Talked of home and the happiness soon to be ours. Also talked of our Chris. experience.

12th. Went to city and got me a pair of boots, in the rain. Returned to camp for dinner. Chet sent in his papers. Called on Melissa with Chet. Miss Hamlin there.

13th. A. B.'s muster out came. He called the officers together and bade them goodbye, turning over the property. Attended prayer meeting at Christian Com. rooms—interesting.

14th. Spent the day in camp. Some rain. Sent in my resignation. The morale of the regiment is very low. A spirit of insubordination and independence prevails. Boys are very dissipated.

15th. Went to town and saw Sister M. and A. B. off at 4:20. Hated to see them go. Hope to see them at home soon. Very warm.

16th. Went to town to see about selling my horse. Chester left for Davenport, Iowa. I feel most homesick. I do dislike to leave the boys for many reasons. I love them all.

17th. Saturday. Took my mare to the city and sold her for $100. Very hot day. Began on my Q. M. papers. Sent Feb. returns in. Several resignations returned. Disappointed. Hope mine will go through.

18th. Letter from Cousin Minnie, also from home. Have made application for about a dozen furloughs and sent as many men to hospital for examination for discharge.

19th. Spent the day at my Q. M. Returns for March, April and May. In the evening spent a few minutes visiting with Chaplain Ives and Dailey's daughters. Had a cozy chat.

20th. A very hot day. Read some. Saw Hayes. Time hangs heavily while waiting. Played a good game of ball with Co. "H." Haven't been so much engaged for years.

21st. Got several papers from home. Report that we move tomorrow for Springfield, Mo. Dislike the thought of going myself. Will try to get my papers through. Read and slept. Wrote home.

22nd. Went to town with Billy Smith and Tuttle to see Birge about a horse transaction. Settled it easily.

23rd. Stayed at Lindell last night. This morning called at Dept. d rs. but got no satisfaction from Barnes. Regt. marched at 1:30 P. M. Some drunk and noisy. Some left. Went to city with Bosworth. Attended theatre. The Deans in "Stranger" and "Wonder."

24th. Didn't wake up till ten o'clock. Quite a joke. Lost our breakfast. Went to camp in time for dinner. Very hot day. June and other 2nd Ohio boys over to see me. Rained in the night. Thundershower.

25th. Did not go out to church in A. M. Wrote home and to George. Read in "Capt. Bonneville," by Irving. Several of the boys called. In evening attended service. Mr. Ives preached. Interesting meeting.

26th. A very cool, pleasant morning. Went to the city to see Ren Bosworth off on leave. Expect to be homesick now living alone. Got back to camp before supper. Got me some pants, vest, shirts and other necessaries for comfort.

27th. Passed the day in camp. Drew "Stumbling Blocks" and read. In evening went to prayer meeting at chapel. Mustering officer examined our returns. Boys moved down to Marine hospital.

28th. Saw Adams up from the regiment. They had an awful time going down to Rolla. Attended prayer meeting P. M. and evening. Also party at boarding place. Played chess with Miss Tripp from Wis., a Soldier's Aid lady.

29th. Ren back last night. Cloudy but hot. Wrote home and to Headly. Bosworth and I called on Miss Tripp and Mrs. Searle. Had a very sociable time. Saw Miss Lizzie Daily a few minutes, too. Read "Country Living and Country Thinking" and "Miles O'Reilly."

June 30th. Friday. Bosworth left for home. I read paper and books. Drew Longfellow's Poems and Carleton's "Days and Nights on the Battlefield." Enjoyed reading it. How near Gen. Grant came to losing everything at Fort Donaldson and Shiloh. Played five games of chess with Mrs. Forbes.

JULY, 1865

1st. Stayed at home and read most all day. Peck and a friend came down and stayed a few minutes. Ren left yesterday for his sister's in Ill. Hated to have him go. Am uneasy to get away myself.

2nd. Attended service at the chapel. Mr. Ives preached. A good sermon. I desire to get more religion, more of the love of Jesus. God give me grace to live an earnest, living, though humble Christian.

3rd. Peck came up in evening. Played chess and checkers. Have had several very pleasant visits with Mrs. Searle and Miss Tripp. Mrs. Forbes too, is very kind to me. No letter from home.

4th. After breakfast had a siege of chess with Mr. Barney. A very hot day. A great many friends around St. Louis. Remained in camp till evening when I went to city. Saw fire works and got ice cream. Met Albert Hinman.

5th. The little beggar girl, Emma, still comes around. Am sorry for her. Life has but few charms for her. Her father killed at Shiloh, her brother died at Sulphur Springs, a drummer boy, her mother had rheumatism, her little brother another little beggar. A very bad girl. God help the poor and afflicted.

6th. Yesterday Robert Brown came here to the Christian Commission. Went with him to see J. R. Davies and Bostwick. Made an engagement to go to tea today, but Brown did not get around in time. Had a pleasant evening chat with Cousin Sarah and Miss Tripp, Barney, Mrs. Forbes and Mrs. Daily also.

7th. Spent the day reading "Eliana" of Lamb's and "Oliver Twist." Much interested in both. In evening, Mr. McC. and Brown held a meeting near Post Hdqrs. Sang patriotic songs first, then a religious meeting. Several spoke. 1500 present. 800 rose for prayers. Very affecting. Mrs. Searle and other ladies out. Felt much benefited myself.

8th. Read in the morning. Went with Brown to Mrs. Kellogg's to dinner. Belong to Tenney family. Had a good visit. All act and look much like Tenney family. Another large meeting in evening. Great interest manifested. Several spoke.

9th. Inquiry meeting. About 50 men out. After breakfast, I went to the city. Took some notices to Mr. Parsons. Attended Sunday School and church at 1st Pres. Dr. Nelson. Good services but not much earnestness. Got back to camp for dinner. A silly sentimental poet on the cars. Chapel in evening. Rain.

10th. A cool delightful morning. Was disappointed in not getting my papers. Read in "Oliver Twist." In evening went to meeting (conference) in open air. Very interesting. God is at work here.

11th. In the morning read "Christian's Mistake" by Miss Muloch. A good story. In P. M. mail. Discharge came. Happy. Went to city. Saw Will Bushnell. Supped with him. Ice cream with 2nd Ohio boys. Like Cousin Sarah Searle so much.

12th. Immediately after breakfast packed up and went around to bid my friends goodbye. Felt sad as well as happy. God bless the friends at Benton Barracks. Got paid. Saw Will B. Off at 4 P. M. Made several acquaintances. Can hardly realize that I am going back home to stay.

13th. Got into Indianapolis at 5 A. M. Grafton at 2:30. Home 4:30. A very happy boy. Thank God for his mercies to us. I desire to live so as to show my gratitude.

Note—The diary closes with the following resumé. F. D. T.

In eight months fought

                    Eight Battles
                    Thirty Skirmishes

Receipts for   18 pieces Artillery
                      19 Caissons
                      12 Ambulances
                     200 Wagons
                     900 Small Arms
                    1700 Prisoners
                     400 Horses

During service passed through

                      12 States
                       1 Territory

Marched 22000 Miles

Watered horses in the rivers

Ohio	Cumberland	Rapidan
Mississippi	Tennessee	Rappahannock
Missouri	Holston	York
Osage	Potomac	Chickahominy
Kansas	Antietam	James
Marais des Gypres	Shenandoah	Appomattox
Arkansas	Bull Run	Nottaway
	Roanoke	

THE B. F. GROUP

Standing—Delos Haynes
Seated—Fred Allen, Will Hudson, Charley Fairchild, Luman Tenney

1860   B. F. MEMORANDUM   1877

The following extract from a letter written by Charles G. Fairchild explains the meaning of the term B. F.

"When we were boys of 13 or 14 we had a literary society. As my brother Henry and I came home one night he complained to my father that a few of the older boys—"big fry" he called them—got all the offices, though the small ones outnumbered them. From this date the terms "Big Fry" and "Little Fry" became catchwords and were bandied back and forth until finally the "Big Fry" were rounded up into an exclusive inner set of five members. Nothing was made of this in the literary society. But in the long summer afternoons we "B. F.'s" used to gather somewhere, get some lemons and sugar if they were in any way obtainable, take a long time in drinking a little lemonade, and listening perhaps to an improvised story or two from one of our members who was especially gifted in this line. At one time an illustrated paper in the interest of the "B. F." appeared. It was entitled "The Thunderbolt," laboriously written by hand and passed from member to member for perusal.

Not a boy of us realized that our club meant anything, but when marriage came and there followed a Bertha Frances, a Bernard Frederick and a Barbara Frances, all first born babies bearing the initials "B. F.", we first began to realize that "B. F." had struck tap roots deep in our hearts. From an unplanned beginning with no organization, nothing sober or specially rational, with no thought of the future, we had come, under cover of old jokes and an accidental name, to prefer each other, to like each other, to love each other.

What does "B. F." stand for? Perhaps for the greatest thing in the world. If we could only all love each other in a senseless, foolish way—simply love each other, with no questions asked and no special thought—what a changed world this would be."

This seal was adopted by the B. F.'s as their "coat of arms." The motto "Unus amore" was unearthed from the classics by one of the members; the introduction of periods between the first three letters opening the way for this unique translation:

"Unus amore," one in love; "more," in custom; "ore," in face; "re," in fact. The "unus" being read into each sentence amplifies the original motto as follows: "One in love, one in custom, one in face, one in fact."

It was at the last reunion of the B. F. boys held in March, 1877, at the home of Delos R. Haynes in St. Louis, Mo., that the idea was conceived of each one writing a brief account of his life since the year 1860. This meant recalling the history of eighteen years, but each "B. F." did this, and the five accounts were carefully put together in good form for preserving.   F. D. T.

Luman Tenney, N. Amherst, O. Born Oct. 1, 1841.

1 8 6 0

Very pleasant arrangement with F. (first). Went to Vermont in September. Taught school in Sudbury. Success. Visited Will at Williams. Stood by B. F.

1 8 6 1

Maple sugar in Spring; foot tramp to Canada; returned through Pennsylvania; arrived August in Oberlin. Enlisted in 2nd O. C. Sept. 9th.

1 8 6 2

With regiment in Missouri, Indian Territory, Fort Scott, and back to Ohio in December.   !

1 8 6 3

Promoted to 2nd Lieutenant. East Tennessee Campaign. Morgan raid. Summer furlough in Oberlin. More pleasant relations.

1 8 6 4

Furlough in March. Virginia Campaign. Promoted to Captain. B. F. shoulder-straps Christmas.

1 8 6 5

Five Forks and Appomattox. Brevetted Major. Mustered out in July, St. Louis. Was in Washington Review. Few enjoyments—enjoyments ceased. In Sept. came to St. Louis. Blind Asylum. In December to Alabama. Cotton at Demopolis.

1 8 6 6

Cotton crop and missionary works. Went Sandusky in May; local on Register. Oberlin excursion. Engagement July 11. Pleasant relations rest of year. First congregational Sunday-School.

1 8 6 7

Happily married Apr. 16. Trip to New York; entertained by C. G. Stave business in Sandusky with Dorsey. Everything went merry as a marriage bell.

1 8 6 8

Still happy and in every way prosperous. B. F. boy born May 4. The next important event was the B. F. reunion in Sandusky. Visited by Delos and Fred. B. F. cup presented; speech by W. N.

1 8 6 9

Organized Sandusky Tool Co.; dissolved partnership with Dorsey. Visit from Delos, Carlie and Fannie Hudson. Profanity and repentance.

1 8 7 0

Sought new worlds to conquer. Explored Lake Superior. Discovered the N. Pac. railroad enterprise and the foundations of a wondrous city at the head of the Lake. Invited Delos to come and drive a corner-stake with me. He came and I went east to sell N. Pac. bonds. Theodore Edward born Feb. 16.

1 8 7 1

Continued work at bonds much of time. Real estate business in Duluth not successful. Made trip to Salt Lake and did the Mormons. Delos took the public schools. Visited Charley in spring and fall. Fannie in Oberlin part of year.

1 8 7 2

Delos returned to St. Louis. Associated myself with H. Turner in Red River Colony scheme, which promised well, but turned out poorly. Mary Emeline born Aug. 27. Visited Ohio and Phila.

1 8 7 3

Continued colony enterprise with varying success till the panic in fall, when the enterprise was abandoned—failure. Will visited me in the summer. Visited mother and Melissa in Philadelphia.

1 8 7 4

Moved to Glyndon in the spring, combining wheat-farming, merchandizing and land-selling. Store profitable; lost crop of grain by grasshoppers. Superintendent of Clay County schools.

1 8 7 5

Business continued prosperous. Crops destroyed by grasshoppers. Organized Teachers' Institute for Northern Minnesota. Visited Fort Garry. Brother Arthur and Charley with us.

1 8 7 6

Aug. 1st removed to Minneapolis, continuing business at Glyndon. Fairly prosperous. Eddy Williams' Church. Young Ladies' Bible Class. More at home than for several years. Visit from father Andrews.

1 8 7 7

Business in safes and scales at Minneapolis, also old business at Glyndon. The event of the year was B. F. reunion at Delos'. Visited Ohio.

Note—Luman Harris Tenney was born in Minneapolis, Minn., May 18, 1877, after this last entry was written. Died in Sanford, Florida, Dec. 25, 1882.

THE TENNEY FAMILY
TAKEN IN MINNEAPOLIS, MINNESOTA IN 1879

FRONT VIEW OF THE ANDREWS-TENNEY HOME
TAKEN IN 1912
THE TENNEY FAMILY RESIDED HERE AFTER 1882

LUMAN HARRIS TENNEY
1879

IN MEMORIAM

From the Red River Valley News, Glyndon, Minn., Feb. 12, 1880.
Luther Osborn, Editor.

MAJOR TENNEY OF GLYNDON.

HIS DEATH TUESDAY MORNING AT THE AGE OF 38.

We have this week to write of the most impressive event in Glyndon's history which has transpired during the life of the News. Luman H. Tenney, who has been ill for a month, grew rapidly worse on the night of Saturday, was thought to be dying through Sunday, hovered between life and death all the following day, and on Tuesday at 10:30 A. M. quietly breathed out his life.

Although he died as many another man has died with admonition of the approach and progress of disease, after time enough had passed to give warning to friends and the community about him, and in the presence of full preparation on his part, yet a shock is felt among us almost as if he had been taken at a blow. Communities are never ready for the death of such men as Major Tenney! few communities have such men to lose.

The illness which has been apparent to his friends and neighbors has been but five weeks' duration, and confinement to the house was continuous for three weeks only. He was of the never-give-up type of men who have little tolerance for the idea of sickness in the ordinary sense. His latest planning and anticipating which have been arrested and put aside by his final sickness were of a visit to Florida for rest and health-getting during the re- maining weeks of winter; the starting of himself and Mrs. Tenney on this journey was set for the second week in January. February sees him laid to his last rest beside Northern oaks and elms and lindens that grow strong on winds and frosts, instead of breathing soft airs where oranges grow and magnolias bloom and cypress boughs wave. Yet we have his own word for it that it is well with him to take God's disposing in place of his own proposing.

A due estimate of Mr. Tenney's character this hand cannot pen on this day of his burial; and although the heart that moves the hand be wrung with the task, yet it would not for a world barter the privilege of laying an offering upon the tomb of one who was close as any brother and who has borne a brother's part without the impulse of natural kinship. The village children mourn him as one who seemed to be of them, young men learned of him and will venerate his memory and know why they do so, men of his own age will miss the fit object of their glad deference in daily counsel and action, and grayer and graver men will keenly know that their peer in ripe knowledge and a greater in wise doing has gone out from them forever.

The world knew Major Tenney for his character first, next for his talent, and third for his deeds. Those close to his friendship knew the Christian mainspring that moved him, saw the golden thread of conscience running through his days and years of sunshine and cloud, and were sure of the faith that kept him high-minded, that made him patient in labors whose end other good men sometimes could not see.

In mental characteristics he was obedient to heaven's first law of order, clear, simple, strong. In ways personal and social he was gentle, refined, unstudied, nobly human, and at large liberty as respects mere conventionalities. Sincerity marked his every going out and in before friend or stranger. In business he was a very engine of energy and precision, industrious we fear to rashness, conservative, enterprising, adhering to time-tested methods while teachable in the midst of the new events of a new country, of high integrity and faithfulness, requiring good faith in return from the party of the second part, be he lofty or lowly, employee or customer. For the community he had aspirations beyond the majority of his fellows. In holy fear of the calamities possible to follow the use of rum, he exercised the power he held in colony times to make legal stipulation that it should not be made or sold within the bounds of land conveyed. School and church and society all have felt his elevating influence. Ambitious to do excellent things, he was singularly free even from the willingness to have his excellences told. It would be like him, if he could, to restrain the hand that writes this much in his praise.

Men dying at life's meridian need not be counted lost. Though his mantle may not find a single pair of shoulders on which to fall, yet shall we not find among us here one and there another upon whom its several folds shall rest and who shall finish his work?

This word shall be "The News" memorial of him.

MILITARY ORDER

OF THE

LOYAL LEGION OF THE UNITED STATES.

MINNESOTA COMMANDERY.

BREVET MAJOR LUMAN HARRIS TENNEY, U. S. V.
(Deceased)

Brevet Major Luman Harris Tenney, of the Second Regiment Ohio Volunteer Cavalry, was born in North Amherst, Lorain County, Ohio, October 1, 1841. His father, Luman Tenney, M.D., formerly of Vermont, was a leading physician of the place. On the side of his mother, Emeline C. Harris, he was descended from a family of sturdy pioneers, who were among the earliest to remove from Massachusetts and settle on the Western Reserve, then almost an unbroken wilderness.

Removing to Oberlin, Ohio, at fourteen years of age, he prepared for college, and in 1859 entered the class of 1863. The disastrous battle of Bull Run was to him, as to many, an imperative call to duty, and in September of that year he left his classes and enlisted as a private soldier in the Second Ohio Cavalry, then organizing at Camp Wade, in Cleveland. He shortly went to the front with his regiment in the capacity of commissary sergeant of his battalion, and thereafter served in the field until two months after the surrender of the Confederate armies. He was successively promoted for merit to the grade of second lieutenant, first lieutenant, and captain in the line, and was subsequently brevetted major by the President, "for gallant service in the campaigns of the Shenandoah Valley in 1864." He was present in over fifty battles and lesser engagements with the enemy, including Grant's campaign of the Wilderness, Sheridan's battles of Winchester, Cedar Creek, and Waynesborough, the siege of Petersburg, and the closing campaign about Richmond, culminating with the surrender of Lee's army at Appomattox. At the bloody battle of Five Forks, April 1, 1865, Major Tenney especially distinguished himself for gallantry, coolness, and efficiency, winning the unstinted commendation of his superior officers. In this engagement, his brother, Theodore A. Tenney, fell at his side, fatally hurt by a shell from the enemy's artillery.

Returning to private life, he engaged in business pursuits. On April 16, 1867, he was married to Miss Frances D. Andrews, of Ohio. Later he removed to Minnesota. In 1871 and 1872 he was connected with the work of constructing the Northern Pacific Railroad. Settling at Glyndon, in the Red River Valley, he founded there an agricultural colony of European and American settlers. Here he made his home, engaged on a large scale in growing grain and handling the wheat crop of the Northern belt. Naturally a leader of men, he took a prominent and influential part in every movement that promised a betterment of existing conditions.

On February 10, 1880, Major Tenney died of heart-failure, meeting death as courageously as he had so often faced it on the field of battle.

MAJOR TENNEY'S COMRADES.

The surviving members of the 2nd regiment Ohio cavalry held their annual reunion at Chippewa Lake on Aug. 26th, 1880. A part of the exercises was an eulogistic address on the life and character of the late Luman H. Tenney of Glyndon, Minn., delivered by Capt. H. W. Chester, and a few extracts are here given.

On the morning of the 9th day of September, 1861, five young men, full of love of country and running over with patriotism, left Oberlin for Cleveland, and determined to "go to the war." They selected as their comrades the boys of the Second Ohio Cavalry— Wade and Hutchins' pet regiment—then being organized at Camp Wade. They cast in their lot with the determined men of Welling-

ton. As in the fall of 1858 Oberlin and Wellington joined hands
in their efforts to help the oppressed, so now her sons joined their
swords to drive the oppressor from the land, and compel him to
let the captive go free; although it would not have been admitted
at that time that such was the object, yet the issue was forced upon
us, and I am proud of the fact that it was accepted at last, and that
in consequence victory perched upon our banners.

Our departed comrade was one of the Oberlin boys. Upon the
organization of the Regiment he was appointed Battalion commissary sergeant. While in that position his executive ability was noticed, and promotion followed. It was while in the commissary department that his devotion to duty first appeared. Although he was
not expected to take a very active part on the skirmish line, yet
he never was known to shield himself behind his position and leave
the fighting to others, but where the greatest danger and the greatest need of help was, there he was sure to be found. All of you
who were in our first serious fight, at Steubenville, Ky., will remember it not so much for the numbers engaged as for the fierce-
ness of the attack, and the determined resistance made by our colonel, August V. Kautz. It was in this engagement, where Captain
Case was so severely wounded and several of our brave men killed,
that our comrade acted as aide to our colonel and displayed his
coolness and bravery under fire. This was only a faint indication
of the spirit that controlled him and became more conspicuous
during the following years.

During 1862 and 1863 he was to be found at his post of duty
doing faithfully and well whatever was assigned to him. In the
summer of 1863 our comrade was commissioned to second lieutenant, after passing a rigid examination before Colonel Kautz.
In November, 1864, he was promoted from second to first lieutenant, and in December commissioned captain, and assigned to duty
in command of company C. Under his command that company did
its full share of fighting, and I have no doubt but that the members
of that excellent company present with us today would testify that
in Captain Tenney they had a commander who would lead them
wherever their bravest would dare to go, and I know that he found
in that company men who would go wherever he would lead the
way. Many of you probably remember instances where our comrade displayed his unswerving devotion to duty and where he was
conspicuous for his bravery. I will give you one or two only:
I well remember his action at Five Forks on the first day of April,
1865. How in that terrible ordeal he appeared to be just as cool
and self-possessed as though his command was on dress parade;
how he passed along the line encouraging his men and instructing
them to take advantage of every opportunity to protect themselves,
at the same time unmindful of the danger to which he exposed himself. It was during this engagement that his brother Theodore
was mortally wounded by a piece of shell from the enemy's battery
in our front. Our comrade was standing near him at the time. I
shall not soon forget the evidence of a struggle between his sense

of duty as a soldier, and his love for his brother, as to whether he should carry him from the field or remain at his post. Just then the enemy's fire slackened so that he was enabled to accompany his brother to the rear, and receive his dying message to his mother, which was: "Tell mother I only wish I had been a better boy." He soon came back to his command, and was with them to the end. It was the 6th day of April, five days after the battle at Five Forks, at the battle of Sailor's Creek, that our comrade, in company with four others, formed a line of battle across a forty-acre field, and charged a wagon train guarded by five times their number. They deployed their line so as to present a long line of battle, and made a gallant charge, leading on their pretended battalions, driving the enemy from the field, and cutting their wagon train, which resulted in the capture of a train two miles long, with a loss of one-fifth of the charging party wounded. It was just after this charge that another fifth of this party was killed—Lieut. Stearns, whom you will remember as the gallant commander of company B.

At Appomattox Court House, Harper's Farm (Sailor's Creek), and High Bridge our comrade distinguished himself as a commander that could meet and overcome obstacles that would appal a less resolute spirit. He was in command of a battalion, I believe, at the surrender of Lee's army on the 9th day of April, and returned with his regiment to Washington, and participated with it in the grand review. Again at Cincinnati, when the regiment was en route for St. Louis, he displayed his control over men during great excitement, and succeeded in quieting a disturbance that might have resulted in a blot on the fair name of our regiment had it been managed with less skill. Soon after this he was commissioned major in recognition of his services to his country. It is well to remember the valorous deeds of the defenders of our country, and crown them with wreaths of laurel, and tell of their heroic acts to our children, and children's children. Still it is in civil life where most of us must fight the battles that make us heroes, or defeat us in all our efforts for the good of mankind; so with our comrade, although distinguished in war, it was in civil life that he found scope for his nobler traits of character.

It is quite remarkable how, in the ten short years that he was connected with the growth of northern Minnesota, he impressed his character upon that whole region. I cannot better describe his influence and the respect in which he was held than by quoting some of the many testimonials culled from the press of that State.

DULUTH NEWS.

"This news will bring sadness to the hearts of hundreds, who have recognized in the one who is so suddenly gone, a noble, Christian man, anxious to do what he believed to be right. We mourn for him as a brother, as those sad words, whose meaning is so hard to realize, force themselves upon us, "We shall see his face no more."

For ten years he has been a leading spirit in Minnesota, and the town of Glyndon is largely his creation.

He leaves his wife and four children in comfortable circumstances, and leaves them also the remembrance of a devoted husband and father, and the record of a useful life."

MINNEAPOLIS TRIBUNE.

"The news of the death of Major L. H. Tenney, formerly of Minneapolis, which occurred this morning at his home in Glyndon, will be received with general and undisguised regret. Major Tenney was an estimable man in every relation of life, an active, energetic business man, an excellent citizen.

He dies in the prime of vigorous manhood, and his loss will be deeply felt along the line of the Northern Pacific, where he transacted a large grain business, was widely known and highly esteemed."

Hon. A. McCrea, State Senator from this district, writes:

"It causes a feeling of sadness to hear of the death of Major Tenney.

Well can I remember the talk we had of our future prospects.

He has gone to realize the facts, while I still remain in a world of uncertainty.

I have no doubt his Christian fortitude held him up in his last moments. Although not intimately acquainted, I entertained great respect for him as a man, a very useful man of business, and one who will be missed not only in your village but all along the lines of railroad in this section of our state. His amiable wife and her family have my heartfelt sympathy. If I had been home in time I would have attended the funeral."

Then follow the few remaining lines of Capt. Chester's address.

We who are still on the battle-field of life would lay upon his grave our offering of love, our tribute of respect. Having done what we may for the dead, let us remember that devoted wife and the four fatherless children who must wait in vain for the return of the fallen soldier, and renew our expressions of sympathy, and invoke for them the tender care of our great Commander-in-Chief.

HEADQUARTERS

SECOND OHIO CAVALRY ASSOCIATION,

CLEVELAND, Feb. 21st, 1880.

Whereas, This Association has learned with deep regret of the death of our former comrade in arms

MAJOR LUMAN H. TENNEY,

which occurred at his home in Glyndon, Minn., on the tenth day of February, therefore.

Resolved, That while we bow in humble submission to the will of the Great Captain who has called him from among us, our grief is none the less poignant; our sorrow none the less deep; and we do and ever will cherish the memory of Comrade Tenney as that of one of the best, bravest and most patriotic soldiers of our old command; one who hesitated at no danger when duty called; and whose courage, devotion and Christian character was an example worthy to be imitated by us all. In his death the country has lost one of its noblest defenders, society an honored and useful member; each and all of us a generous friend; and his family has sustained a loss we find no words to express. To them in this hour of great sorrow we can only extend our warmest sympathies.

Resolved, That these resolutions be spread upon the records of the Association, and a copy be sent to the family of our dead comrade.

WALTER R. AUSTIN,   ALBERT BARNITZ,
    Acting Secretary.   *Brevet Col. U. S. Army,*
                                           Pres. of Association.

LETTER FROM COL. ALBERT BARNITZ TO MRS. LUMAN H. TENNEY.

Cleveland, Ohio, March 1, 1880.

Mrs. Luman H. Tenney,
    Glyndon, Minn.

Dear Madam:

Having just signed in the capacity of President of the Association, the engrossed copy of the resolutions passed at a recent meeting of surviving members of the old 2nd Ohio Cavalry, I have thought it not inappropriate, although personally a stranger to yourself, to add a few words, as testifying my personal regard and attachment for your late husband. I knew him scarcely other-

wise than as a soldier, and did not indeed, become well acquainted
with him until the vicissitudes of the service threw upon me the
command of the regiment, in the closing campaign of the war, and
then it was that I came to admire his unflinching courage and his
soldierly ability; at Five Forks, especially, he rendered distinguished service in command of his squadron—or battalion perhaps.
I was near him through a considerable portion of the engagement,
and well remember his valorous conduct upon that trying occasion.
It was there, too that his brother, a handsome and noble boy, was
shot down and instantly killed by a shell from the enemy's battery,
as he stood in the act of firing his carbine, and just as I was ad-
monishing him to shelter himself behind a tree near which he stood.
I am perhaps the only living eye-witness of the occurrence, and
unstrapped from my saddle the talma in which he was carried
from the field; and the circumstance is as vivid in my mind as if it
had occurred but yesterday and all the other marked events of the
engagement, and of the subsequent battles in which your husband
participated.

And so it is that although the war has been long ended, "And
our great deeds are half-forgotten things," yet I remember vividly
my intimate associates of the war, and think of them always as I
knew them in the field; and I think of your late husband only as
the faithful comrade, the prompt, energetic and ever-reliable soldier; and you—you who in your cruel bereavement will, more than
another, mourn his untimely death, will remember him only in
the peaceful and tender relations of domestic life, and may even
deem it strange that. by reason of the past, whereof you know not
except dimly, and as by tradition, a train of bronzed and weather-
beaten men should come across the intervening years, bearing
myrrh and incense, and ask to lay upon a soldier's bier some tribute from his comrades of the war.

Respectfully and sincerely yours,

ALBERT BARNITZ,

Brevet Col. U. S. Army.

THE TENNEY FAMILY IN AMERICA

IS DESCENDED FROM

Thomas Tenney, the first ancestor in America. He came over with the Rev. Ezekiel Roger's company from Yorkshire, England, arriving in Salem, Mass., Dec., 1638, and settling in Rowley, Mass., April, 1639. He was about twenty-four when he came over with his wife Ann. His English home was Rowley on the Yorkshire Wolds East Riding. Rev. Ezekiel Rogers was a man of learning, very devout, possessed of much zeal, and felt keenly the religious persecution of King Charles' order to the clergy to read in church the declaration of sports, in which the king directed that no hindrance should be thrown in the way of those who wished to dance or shoot at the butts (a target) on Sunday afternoon. Puritan Rogers, aggrieved at this and other persecutions, gathered to him in the parish of Rowley a company, Thomas Tenney and his wife Ann forming one family, for the purpose of emigrating to America.

Dea. John Tenney in 1682 was one of the eighteen who formed the first Cong. church under Rev. Zacharia Symmes in Bradford, Mass.

Dea. (Elder) Samuel Tenney was a Lieutenant in the Continental army and a member of the Colonial Assembly in 1725.

Jesse Tenney and Hannah were married in Norwich, Conn., 1773, moving to Bennington in 1774. When the war commenced Hannah took her son Isaac on horse back to the Connecticut home, Jesse entering the service. After the war they returned to Bennington to their fine farm near the "Battle Ground" which now has the highest battle monument from tidal point in the world. Jesse Tenney was very benevolent and kind-hearted, so much so that the Bennington neighbors, in referring to him, would say, "Take it, take it, says Tenney." In 1805 he moved to Sudbury, Vt.

Isaac Tenney settled in Orwell, Vt., on land which his father had purchased immediately after the Revolutionary War.

(These facts taken from "The Tenney Family" by M. J. Tenney.)

Ancestors of Luman Harris Tenney.

Dr. Luman Tenney
1809–1844, Orwell, Vt.

Isaac Tenney
1775–1828
Res. Orwell, Vt.
Mar. 1799, Nov. 28

Jesse Tenney
1741–1815
Res. Bennington, Vt.
Was Commissary in
Revolutionary War
Mar. Sept. 30, 1773

Hannah Griswold

Minerva Burke

Emeline Charity Harris
1809–1893. Mar. Aug. 21, 1836

Josiah Harris
Born Nov. 30, 1783
Mar. Mar. 30, 1807
Becket, Mass.

James Harris
Becket, Mass.

Martha Parks

Charity Messenger
Born Oct. 26, 1786

Hiram Messenger
Mar. Mar. 23, 1771
Becket, Mass.

Lydia Shapley

Dea. John Tenney, son of **Thomas**
1640–1722   and **Ann Tenn**
Rowley, Mass.

ea. Sam'l Tenney

l667–1748; Lieutenant
¹Bradford, Mass.

Mercy Parrot, daughter **Francis Parro**

Sarah Boynton

Born 1671, Died 1709
Mar. Dec. 18, 1690

John Wood, son of **Thos.** and **Ann Wood**

Mar. Jan. 16, 1680   of Boxford, Mass.
Boxford, Mass.

Edward Hazen

Isabel Hazen

Born July 21, 1662

Hannah Grant

Francis, son of

Capt. Sam'l Griswold

Samuel Griswold

Born Feb. 8, 1693
Mar. April 2, 1719

Born in Kenilworth, Eng.
Mar. Dec. 10, 1685

**Susannah
Huntington**

Dea. Wm. Rockw
of Windsor. Ct.

Dr. Sam'l Abell

Elizabeth Abell

Elizabeth Slurman

Ancestors of Luman Harris Tenney.

WAR OF THE REBELLION
OFFICIAL RECORD OF THE UNION AND CONFEDERATE ARMIES

Some of the Many References (over 200) Made to the 2nd Ohio Volunteer Cavalry

REPORTS.

	Vol.	Part	Page
Col. Doubleday, Round Grove, Cow Skin Prairie, Grand River	13		102
Col. Salomon, on Arresting Col. Wier	13		475
Col. Kautz, Captain West's or Rocky Gap	23	1	371
Col. Sanders, Sander's Raid	23	1	386
Gen. Shackelford, Morgan Raid	23	1	639
Col. Kautz, Morgan Raid	23	1	662
Gen. Wilson, 3rd Cav. Div., Apr. 7 to June 16, 1864	36	1	870
Gen. McIntosh, May 5 to June 22, 1864	36	1	886
Lt.-Col. Purington, May 5 to June 12, 1864	36	1	892
Gen. Ferrero, Piney Branch Church	36	1	986
Gen. Rosser, C. S. A., Piney Branch Church	36	1	1098
Gen. Ferrero, Harris Farm	36	1	987
Gen. Wilson, June 17-July 30, 1864	40	1	620
Gen. McIntosh, June 22-July 3, 1864	40	1	634
Lt.-Col. Purington, June 13-July 24, 1864	40	1	641
Col. Kautz, Wilson Raid	40	1	732
Gen. Sheridan, Abraham's Creek	43	1	24
Gen. Torbett, Aug. 8-Oct. 31, Nov. 12 and 21-23	43	1	421
Gen. Wilson, July 31 to Sept. 30, 1864	43	1	518
Gen. Custer, Oct. 9 and Oct. 19, 1864	43	1	520
Gen. McIntosh, Sept. 13 and 17, 1864	43	1	529
Lt.-Col. Purington, Oct. 9, 1864	43	1	539
Lt.-Col. Whittaker, Moorfield, Feb. 4-6, 1865	46	1	455
Gen. Sheridan, Feb. 27 to March 28, 1865	46	1	474
Gen. Merritt, Feb. 27 to March 28, 1865	46	1	484
Gen. Custer, Feb. 27 to March 28, 1865	46	1	501
Col. Pennington, Feb. 27 to March 28, 1865	46	1	504

CASUALTIES.

	Vol.	Part	Page
June 15 to 30, 1864	40	1	232
Sept. 19, 1864	43	1	117
Oct. 19, 1864	43	1	137
March 29 to April 9	46	1	591

ITINERARIES.

	Vol.	Part	Page
23rd Army Corps, Aug. 1 to Sept. 30, 1863	30	2	576
3rd Cav. Div., Aug. 1 to Dec. 22, 1864	43	1	98
1st Brig. 3rd Cav. Div., Aug. 4 to Dec. 31, 1864	43	1	101

REPORTS.

Index

KEY TO MAP

Battles, Actions, Engagements and Skirmishes of the
2nd Ohio Volunteer Cavalry

1862

NO.	PLACE.		DATE.
1	Independence, Mo.	Feb.	22
2	Horse Creek, Mo.	May	7

EXPEDITION INTO INDIAN TERRITORY.

3	Grand River, Cow Skin Prairie or Round Grove, Ind. Ter.	June	6

CAMPAIGN IN SOUTHWEST MO. AND N. W. ARKANSAS.

4	Lone Jack, Mo.	Aug.	18
5	Newtonia, Mo.	Sept.	30
6	Newtonia, Mo.	Oct.	4
7	Cane Hill, Ark.	Nov.	14
8	Cane Hill, Ark.	Nov.	28
9	Prairie Grove, Ark.	Dec.	7

1863

KENTUCKY CAMPAIGN.

10	Mount Sterling, Ky.	March	19
11	Monticello, Ky.	April	30
12	Monticello, Ky.	May	1
13	Monticello, Ky.	May	30
14	Monticello, Ky.	June	9
15	Rocky Gap, Ky.	June	9

SANDER'S RAID INTO EAST TENNESSEE.

16	Wartburg, Tenn.	June	17
17	Lenoirs, Tenn.	June	19
18	Knoxville, Tenn.	June	19
19	Knoxville, Tenn.	June	20
20	Strawberry Plains, Tenn.	June	20
21	New Market, Tenn.	June	21
22	Mossey Creek, Tenn.	June	21
23	Powder Springs Gap, Tenn.	June	21

NO.	PLACE.	DATE.
24	Powell's Valley, Tenn	June 22
25	Rogers Gap (Smiths), Tenn	June 22

MORGAN RAID.

26	Near Jamestown or Columbia, Ky	June 29
27	Columbia, Ky	July 3
28	Buffington Island, Ohio	July 19

SCOTT RAID.

29	Richmond, Ky	July 28
30	Blue Lick, Ky	July 30
31	Paint Lick Bridge, Ky	July 31
32	Lancaster, Ky	Aug. 1

BURNSIDE'S EXPEDITION INTO EAST TENNESSEE.

33	Winters Gap, Tenn	Aug. 31
34	Loudon Bridge or Lenoirs, Tenn	Sept. 2
35	Cumberland Gap, Tenn	Sept. 9
36	Carters Station, Tenn	Sept. 22
37	Zollicoffer, Tenn	Sept. 24
38	Jonesboro, Tenn	Sept. 28
39	Greenville, Tenn	Oct. 2
40	Greenville, Tenn	Oct. 3
41	Blue Springs, Tenn	Oct. 10
42	Rheatown, Tenn	Oct. 11
43	Blountville, Tenn	Oct. 14
44	Siege of Knoxville, Tenn	Nov. 17 to Dec. 4
45	Walkers Ford, Tenn	Dec. 2
46	Thorn Hill, Tenn	Dec. 7
47	Morristown, Tenn	Dec. 10
48	Cheeks Cross Roads, Tenn	Dec. 12
49	Bean Station, Tenn	Dec. 13
50	Bean Station, Tenn	Dec. 14
51	Rutledge, Tenn	Dec. 15
52	Rutledge, Tenn	Dec. 16
53	Blains Cross Roads, Tenn	Dec. 17
54	Blains Cross Roads, Tenn	Dec. 18
55	Dandridge, Tenn	Dec. 24

1863.—Continued.

NO.	PLACE.		DATE.
56	Dandridge, Tenn	Dec.	25
57	Mossey Creek, Tenn	Dec.	27

1864

WILDERNESS CAMPAIGN.

58	Wilderness, Va	May	6
59	Wilderness or Todd's Tavern, Va	May	7
60	Alsops Farm, Va	May	8
61	Spotsylvania C. H., Va	May	12
62	Piney Branch Church, Va	May	15
63	Harris Farm, Va	May	19
64	U. S. Ford, Va	May	21
65	Newtown, Va	May	27
66	Mechump's Creek, Va	May	31
67	Hanover C. H., Va	May	31
68	Ashland, Va	June	1
69	Haw's Shop, Va	June	3
70	Cold Harbor, Va	June	3
71	Old Salem Church, Va	June	4
72	Shady Grove Church, Va	June	11
73	White House Landing, Va	June	12
74	St. Mary's Church or Smith Store, Va	June	15

WILSON'S RAID ON SOUTH SIDE AND DANVILLE R. R.

75	Nottaway C. H., Va	June	23
76	Roanoke Station, Va	June	25
77	Stoney Creek, Va	June	28
78	Ream's Station, Va	June	29
79	Siege of Petersburg, Va	June to Oct.	
80	Mine Explosion, Petersburg, Va	July	30

SHENANDOAH VALLEY CAMPAIGN.

81	Winchester, Va	Aug.	17
82	Summit Point, W. Va	Aug.	21
83	Charlestown, W. Va	Aug.	22
84	Kearneyville, W. Va	Aug.	25
85	Berryville, Va	Aug.	31
86	White Post, Va	Sept.	3

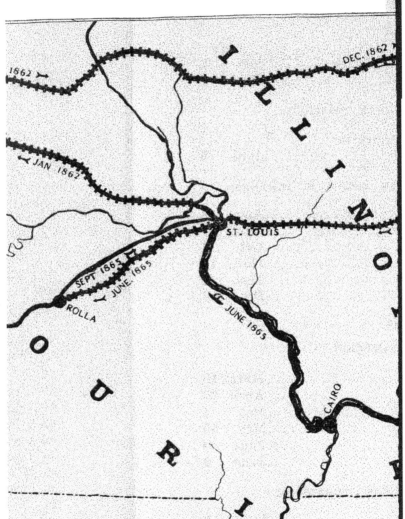

1863.—Continued.

NO.	PLACE.	DATE.
56	Dandridge, Tenn	Dec. 25
57	Mossey Creek, Tenn	Dec. 27

1864

WILDERNESS CAMPAIGN.

58	Wilderness, Va	May	6
59	Wilderness or Todd's Tavern, Va	May	7
60	Alsops Farm, Va	May	8
61	Spotsylvania C. H., Va	May	12
62	Piney Branch Church, Va	May	15
63	Harris Farm, Va	May	19
64	U. S. Ford, Va	May	21
65	Newtown, Va	May	27
66	Mechump's Creek, Va	May	31
67	Hanover C. H., Va	May	31
68	Ashland, Va	June	1
69	Haw's Shop, Va	June	3
70	Cold Harbor, Va	June	3
71	Old Salem Church, Va	June	4
72	Shady Grove Church, Va	June	11
73	White House Landing, Va	June	12
74	St. Mary's Church or Smith Store, Va	June	15

WILSON'S RAID ON SOUTH SIDE AND DANVILLE R. R.

75	Nottaway C. H., Va	June	23
76	Roanoke Station, Va	June	25
77	Stoney Creek, Va	June	28
78	Ream's Station, Va	June	29
79	Siege of Petersburg, Va	June to Oct.	
80	Mine Explosion, Petersburg, Va	July	30

SHENANDOAH VALLEY CAMPAIGN.

81	Winchester, Va	Aug.	17
82	Summit Point, W. Va	Aug.	21
83	Charlestown, W. Va	Aug.	22
84	Kearneyville, W. Va	Aug.	25
85	Berryville, Va	Aug.	31
86	White Post, Va	Sept.	3

KEY TO MAP

Battles, Actions, Engagements and Skirmishes of the
2nd Ohio Volunteer Cavalry

1862

NO.	PLACE.		DATE.
1	Independence, Mo	Feb.	22
2	Horse Creek, Mo	May	7

EXPEDITION INTO INDIAN TERRITORY.

| 3 | Grand River, Cow Skin Prairie or Round Grove, Ind. Ter | June | 6 |

CAMPAIGN IN SOUTHWEST MO. AND N. W. ARKANSAS.

	Lone Jack, Mo	Aug.	18
	Newtonia, Mo	Sept.	30
	Newtonia, Mo	Oct.	4
7	Cane Hill, Ark	Nov.	14
8	Cane Hill, Ark	Nov.	28
9	Prairie Grove, Ark	Dec.	7

1863

KENTUCKY CAMPAIGN.

10	Mount Sterling, Ky	March	19
11	Monticello, Ky	April	30
12	Monticello, Ky	May	1
13	Monticello, Ky	May	30
14	Monticello, Ky	June	9
15	Rocky Gap, Ky	June	9

SANDER'S RAID INTO EAST TENNESSEE.

16	Wartburg, Tenn	June	17
17	Lenoirs, Tenn	June	19
18	Knoxville, Tenn	June	19
19	Knoxville, Tenn	June	20
20	Strawberry Plains, Tenn	June	20
21	New Market, Tenn	June	21
22	Mossey Crek, Tenn	June	21
23	Powder Springs Gap, Tenn	June	21

1863.—Continued.

NO.	PLACE.	DATE.
24	Powell's Valley, Tenn.................June	22
25	Rogers Gap (Smiths), Tenn............June	22

MORGAN RAID.

26	Near Jamestown or Columbia, Ky........June	29
27	Columbia, Ky...........................July	3
28	Buffington Island, Ohio................July	19

SCOTT RAID.

29	Richmond, Ky..........................July	28
30	Blue Lick, Ky.........................July	30
31	Paint Lick Bridge, Ky.................July	31
32	Lancaster, Ky.........................Aug.	1

BURNSIDE'S EXPEDITION INTO EAST TENNESSEE.

33	Winters Gap, Tenn.....................Aug.	31
34	Loudon Bridge or Lenoirs, Tenn.........Sept.	2
35	Cumberland Gap, Tenn.................Sept.	9
36	Carters Station, Tenn..................Sept.	22
37	Zollicoffer, Tenn......................Sept.	24
38	Jonesboro, Tenn.......................Sept.	28
39	Greenville, Tenn.......................Oct.	2
40	Greenville, Tenn.......................Oct.	3
41	Blue Springs, Tenn....................Oct.	10
42	Rheatown, Tenn.......................Oct.	11
43	Blountville, Tenn......................Oct.	14
44	Siege of Knoxville, Tenn..........Nov. 17 to Dec.	4
45	Walkers Ford, Tenn....................Dec.	2
46	Thorn Hill, Tenn.......................Dec.	7
47	Morristown, Tenn......................Dec.	10
48	Cheeks Cross Roads, Tenn..............Dec.	12
49	Bean Station, Tenn....................Dec.	13
50	Bean Station, Tenn....................Dec.	14
51	Rutledge, Tenn........................Dec.	15
52	Rutledge, Tenn........................Dec.	16
53	Blains Cross Roads, Tenn..............Dec.	17
54	Blains Cross Roads, Tenn..............Dec.	18
55	Dandridge, Tenn.......................Dec.	24

NO.	PLACE.	DATE.
56	Dandridge, Tenn................................Dec.	25
57	Mossey Creek, Tenn.............................Dec.	27

1864

WILDERNESS CAMPAIGN.

58	Wilderness, Va...............................May	6
59	Wilderness or Todd's Tavern, Va............May	7
60	Alsops Farm, Va............................May	8
61	Spotsylvania C. H., Va.....................May	12
62	Piney Branch Church, Va...................May	15
63	Harris Farm, Va...........................May	19
64	U. S. Ford, Va............................May	21
65	Newtown, Va...............................May	27
66	Mechump's Creek, Va.......................May	31
67	Hanover C. H., Va.........................May	31
68	Ashland, Va...............................June	1
69	Haw's Shop, Va............................June	3
70	Cold Harbor, Va...........................June	3
71	Old Salem Church, Va......................June	4
72	Shady Grove Church, Va....................June	11
73	White House Landing, Va...................June	12
74	St. Mary's Church or Smith Store, Va......June	15

WILSON'S RAID ON SOUTH SIDE AND DANVILLE R. R.

75	Nottaway C. H., Va........................June	23
76	Roanoke Station, Va.......................June	25
77	Stoney Creek, Va..........................June	28
78	Ream's Station, Va........................June	29
79	Siege of Petersburg, Va..............June to Oct.	
80	Mine Explosion, Petersburg, Va...........July	30

SHENANDOAH VALLEY CAMPAIGN.

81	Winchester, Va...........................Aug.	17
82	Summit Point, W. Va......................Aug.	21
83	Charlestown, W. Va.......................Aug.	22
84	Kearneyville, W. Va......................Aug.	25
85	Berryville, Va...........................Aug.	31
86	White Post, Va...........................Sept.	3

1864.—Continued.

NO.	PLACE.		DATE.
87	Abrahams Creek, Va	Sept.	13
88	Winchester, Va	Sept.	19
89	Cedarville, Va	Sept.	20
90	Front Royal, Va	Sept.	21
91	Milford, Va	Sept.	22
92	Waynesborough, Va	Sept.	28
93	Bridgewater, Va	Oct.	2
94	Columbia Furnace, Va	Oct.	7
95	Tom's Brook, Va	Oct.	9
96	Cedar Creek, Va	Oct.	19
97	Mt. Zion Church or Newtown, Va	Nov.	12
98	Mt. Jackson, Va	Nov.	22
99	Moorefield, W. Va	Nov.	30
100	Lacey's Springs, Va	Dec.	21

1865

RICHMOND CAMPAIGN.

101	Waynesborough, Va	March 2
102	Goochland, Va	March 11
103	Ashland, Va	March 15

APPOMATTOX CAMPAIGN.

104	Dinwiddie C. H., Va	March 31
105	Five Forks, Va	April 1
106	Namozine Creek, Va	April 3
107	Sailor's Creek, Va	April 6
108	Appomattox Station, Va	April 8
109	Appomattox C. H., Va	April 9

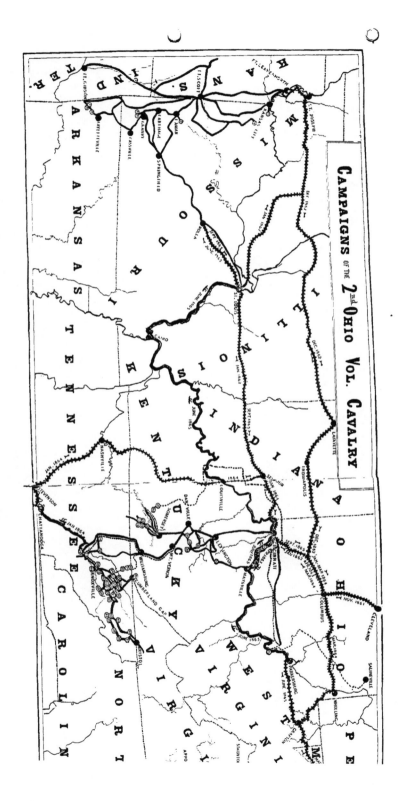

CAMPAIGNS OF THE 2ND OHIO VOL. CAVALRY

Lightning Source UK Ltd.
Milton Keynes UK
UKHW020626301118
333245UK00008B/210/P

9 781331 162063